# GRAPHIC DESIGN SCHOOL

**A foundation course for graphic designers working in print, moving image and digital media**

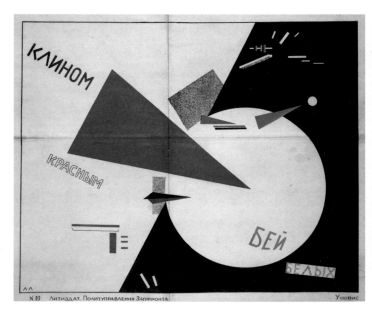

DAVID DABNER
SANDRA STEWART
ABBIE VICKRESS

eighth
edition

# GRAPHIC DESIGN SCHOOL

**A foundation course for graphic designers working in print, moving image and digital media**

First published in the United Kingdom in 2023 by
Thames & Hudson Ltd, 181A High Holborn,
London WC1V 7QX

British Library Cataloguing-in-Publication Data
A catalogue record for this book is available from the
British Library

ISBN: 978-0-500-29742-1

Printed and bound in China

# Contents

# Introduction

This book is written with the intent of providing an introduction to the underlying principles of good graphic design, whether it is print-based, digital or environmental. The content has been constructed to mirror, in part, how the subject is taught in college design programmes, and the visuals, which are a mixture of student projects and professional design work, have been carefully chosen to illuminate specific teaching points. Many of the sections contain step-by-step exercises and assignments, offer practical advice and point towards further resources.

The first part of the book, Principles, supports the idea that a thorough understanding of design principles should support the process of creating design works in response to specific briefs and problems, while allowing room for self-authored experimentation and visual freedom. As you are introduced to the basics of research, typography, colour, photography and composition, you will learn to become visually aware and able to articulate these design principles in your future works. You will also come to understand that these principles cross disciplines and are the vocabulary of visual literacy.

The second part of the book, Practice, introduces you to invaluable practical skills that are important support systems to the skill sets of research and creative process that you will have read about in Part One. They do not replace them, but serve as methods and practices for developing critical problem-solving skills and learning to manage complex projects. Designers need the whole range of skills to be truly successful, and expertise will

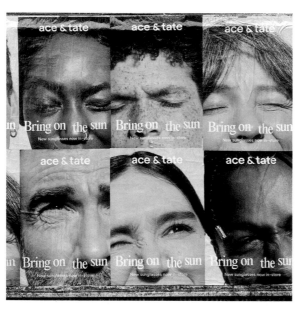

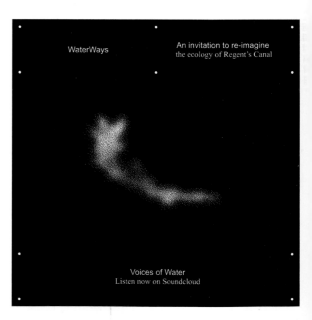

come with continued study and practice in both areas. Unless you learn the practical skills and technology of design production, including how to manage images, create digital files for specific media, and design, build and structure a website, you will be unable to bring your brilliant concepts to life.

None of these visual skills can be viewed in isolation from the context in which design happens and its larger role in society and the world. Designers are visual communicators, often giving visual voice to new and provocative ideas. They create images that can inform, persuade and entertain millions of people. This comes with great responsibility, and it is necessary to be aware of the role of design in shaping the world we live in, and changes in the discipline that transcend trends or the latest software.

While any kind of comprehensive account of these topics stands outside the scope of this book, becoming visually literate and technically skilled should go hand in hand with an understanding of such issues as global audiences, communication theories, systems theory, sustainable issues in design and the changing role of technology.

Finally, design education is a lifelong experience that can bring great personal satisfaction and reward. Technologies, styles and demands change rapidly in this industry and, as a result, graphic design is a subject to be taken on with independence and an expectation of lifelong learning and commitment. With this book as a gateway, a new way of seeing the world may lead you to a career path that will be a constant source of surprise and delight.

# Principles

The first part of this book is concerned with design principles, the building blocks that connect the basics of all good design. Every discipline has its own set of rules, methods, technical requirements and specialised technologies. Each one is rooted in the interactions of its histories, theories and practice, but unlike learning law or biology, the language of design is visual. It involves the need for a highly developed awareness of visual principles, and of the modern world and its complex practices. A good designer can filter this information and create relevant, engaging, visually eloquent design that responds to multiple problems, needs and contexts. While a design student needs to develop the research, concept-development, compositional and organisational skills associated with design, they also need to be engaged with the world, and interested, aware and sensitive to the changing contexts in which design plays a part.

Chapter 1 introduces the primary and secondary research skills needed by designers, followed by an introduction to theories of image, the importance of audience and of organising your work and time. In Chapter 2, the idea of form is spotlighted. Form involves composition of the fundamentals of design (text, image, proportion, space, colour, scale) and requires an understanding of the visual dynamics created by combining them with intent. Understanding form comes from the ability to see intrinsic and subtle qualities in the various design elements, and the observation of, and sensitivity to, the changing relationships between them. Chapter 3 introduces typography,

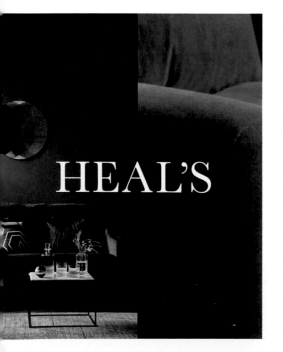

PART 1

a core skill for all designers that is layered with complexity, and cannot be understated for its beauty, versatility and ability to influence an audience. Developing an understanding of typography is of critical importance. Chapter 4 introduces colour as one of the primary tools in the language of design, including theory, terminology, associations, issues of legibility and emotional response. Managing colour and understanding its ability to communicate are skills that also evolve with greater understanding of its influences. Whatever design discipline you ultimately pursue, from editorial art direction to web and motion graphics, these basic principles will give you a solid foundation and serve as the groundwork for further exploration and understanding of design and the role of the designer.

# Research
# and Concepts

The first step towards becoming interesting is to be interested. The best creatives of all kinds – painters, designers, writers, musicians, sculptors, playwrights – make the world their inspiration, and draw ideas and content from both experience and research. They make it a priority to stay aware of what is happening, not only within the world of design, but in the world in general, and this level of engagement enriches their work.

## ➜ Documenting research

Research should be specific to each project, but the process of looking and recording your impressions should be ongoing and become a part of your daily routine. If something interests you, sketch it, write about it, photograph it, upload it, bookmark it or file it away. Everything you come into contact with can inform your work, so make sure you have an annotated collection you can refer back to time and time again.

Modern media demands an increasing amount of visual information to illustrate its content in print, packaging and motion graphics, in the built environment or online. Graphic designers are the conduits for all types of communications from multiple sources to specific audiences, and to be successful they must be well-informed, accomplished researchers with inquisitive natures.

### Broaden your outlook

Designers who seek information from the greatest range of references are those who successfully communicate with people of all ages, professions and lifestyles, and who properly contextualise their design work.

• Read about events from multiple sources. Compare stories, noting how information about the same events changes, how the language is used to target various audiences and what type of imagery is used to support the text. When researching facts, don't rely solely on editable web postings or crowd-sourced information.

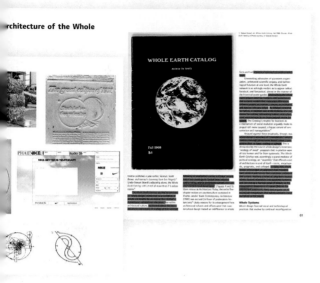

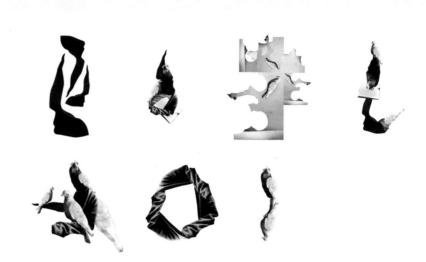

- You can never read enough books, but don't limit yourself to the kind you usually read. Reading only about graphic design can be particularly dangerous: although extremely useful for information and guidance, this may turn you into an armchair expert; you want to be an original practitioner. Expand your reading to include novels and plays, and books on sculpture, architecture, art history, cooking, sports, archaeology, travel and maths – it really doesn't matter, as long as they provide you with a broad spectrum of knowledge.
- Be open to new experiences. Visit galleries, clubs, retail environments, archives and museums you've never been to, listen to music you've not heard before, and eat food you've never tried before. Travel whenever you can, and learn about global issues and cultural treasures.
- Share ideas and listen to people. Create surveys, facilitate interviews and have conversations with real people. Whatever language they use, there is always a way to establish communication, if you try. Pay attention to what inspires them, and learn from others while also sharing your insights.
- Online research can be quick and provide extensive results, but also an un-unique solution. Try other forms of research to avoid duplicating the obvious ideas.

⬆ **Application of inspiration** This project started as a collection of visual imagery inspired by the content and narrative of *The Open Work* publication. Through experimentation, new creative forms have been designed and applied to the letterforms, providing a quick insight into the content.

## Research techniques

| Primary sources/ factual research | Secondary sources/factual research |
|---|---|
| • Previous knowledge/opinion/ memory<br>• Observation<br>• Conversation<br>• Analysis<br>• Role-play<br>• Interviews: in person or by email, online chat or phone<br>• Questionnaires<br>• Focus groups<br>• Commissioned video/written diaries (firsthand)<br>• Ethnographic research ('deep hanging out') | • Museums, archives, collections<br>• Newspapers, magazines, journal articles<br>• Published interviews<br>• Films, TV broadcasts, theatre<br>• Transcripts/recordings of film, TV, radio<br>• Books<br>• Music<br>• Internet: blogs, websites, forums, magazines<br>• Surveys<br>• Statistics<br>• Organisations, agencies, gatekeepers<br>• Lectures, public debates, conferences |

| Primary sources/ visual research | Secondary sources/ visual research |
|---|---|
| • Photography<br>• Drawing/sketching<br>• Media experimentation: 2D and 3D<br>• Rubbings/casts<br>• Typographic experimentation<br>• Compositional experimentation<br>• Image manipulation<br>• Photocopying<br>• Video recording<br>• Audio recording<br>• Writing | • Exhibitions<br>• Images/photographs from magazines, books, leaflets, Internet, billboards<br>• Work by other designers/artists<br>• Printed maps/diagrams<br>• Ephemera (e.g. tickets, receipts, packaging)<br>• Found or bought photographs, postcards, posters, drawings<br>• Imagery taken from films, video, performances<br>• Architecture |

### Other general work practices/approaches
• Put your own point of view into the subject
• Work in groups and respond to feedback from others
• Develop ideas by generating a number of visuals in response to one idea
• Explore the full capacity of your visual language

## Record it all

Constant, direct observation is one of the most important tools that a designer can use. Learning to look at anything as a designer requires attention to minute detail and the inclusion of all objects that surround the object of focus. Consider your way of seeing as a kind of inner zoom lens that draws you in and away from a point of observation. As you learn to see the world with a designer's eye, ordinary things can become amazing sources of inspiration. It may be as simple as a pattern of lace juxtaposed against flat, wide stripes, or as unexpected as the geometry revealed by light and shadow in an architectural setting. Textures, patterns, colours and visual relationships will begin to have a profound effect on the way you think about the design process.

With this in mind, every practising designer should carry some form of recording device, such as a sketchbook, camera or smartphone. Give yourself time for observation and research, taking this stage seriously as an integral part of your work. Designers, artists, writers and illustrators often keep scrapbooks/sketchbooks/collections of material that interest them. These pieces of inspiration need not necessarily have a clear purpose when they are collected, but the material can become an archive of ideas and inspiration that you can draw on at a later date.

If something commands your attention, sketch it, write about it, photograph it, upload it or file it away immediately. Collect ideas and build upon your initial thoughts by writing, drawing or sketching. Not only will your drawing and research skills improve if you do this consistently, but over time you'll also have a 'catalogue of inspiration' that can be drawn on at any point in your career and which will become especially useful when you are short of ideas. This kind of practised research will help you to begin defining your own outlook and to develop a distinctive visual voice.

Observing and recording your surroundings can also be a great way to overcome a creative block. The philosopher Guy Debord coined the term 'dérive', an unplanned journey through a landscape in which the walker disregards everyday perceptions, allowing them to be drawn into new sights, unfamiliar encounters and a new awareness of their surroundings. If you find yourself staring blankly at your work, go into the real world to observe things you might not have noticed before. How can these new interpretations inform your work?

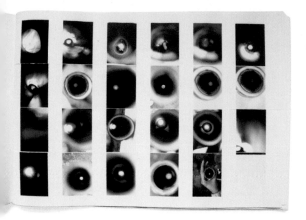

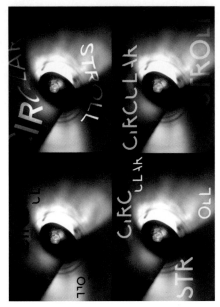

↑ → **Multiply the possibilities** Collect multiple images of every subject, and vary your techniques as you photograph. Each of these pictures captures a slightly different sensibility in light, colour, shadow and composition. When they are combined with deconstructed typography that echoes the abstract forms revealed in the photos, the results are striking.

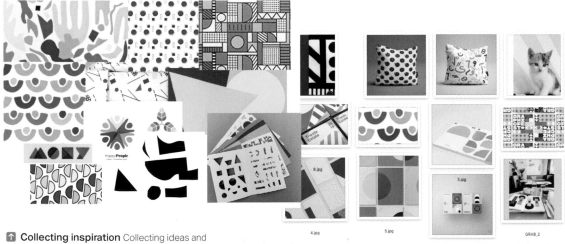

↑ **Collecting inspiration** Collecting ideas and inspiration together on a single moodboard or research board can help you make sense of a design brief and assist with design decisions. Build boards by hand or digitally on a computer. Shapes, a pre-school logo, is inspired by the bright colours and forms collected and pasted into the moodboards above.

| PART 1 | PRINCIPLES |
|---|---|
| CHAPTER 1 | RESEARCH AND CONCEPTS |
| MODULE 2 | **LINEAR REASONING/LATERAL THINKING** |

**In the initial stages of concept development, the two main ways to approach a design brief are to use linear reasoning and lateral thinking. These are virtually opposites – the first focused and methodical, the second diffuse and expansive – but both are equally useful as research and development tools.**

**GLOSSARY**

**Lateral thinking:** A form of research where the emphasis is on indirect, creative forms of inquiry and thinking.

**Linear reasoning:** A form of thinking that implies strategic thought process, one in which step-by-step logic is employed.

Linear reasoning implies a strategic thought process, using step-by-step logic, and follows a specific trajectory. This kind of reasoning frequently involves a predetermined idea or concept that is then worked towards in stages. Generally, this will involve splitting the idea up into manageable components, considering colour, type, composition and scale, and working each through to finalise the form to fit the concept.

Lateral thinking involves indirect exploration, generating ideas less readily available by linear reasoning (or hidden by the linear process, so that less obvious associations aren't readily seen or generated). The emphasis is on indirect, creative forms of research. Edward de Bono coined the term in 1967.

Brainstorming, or sketching in a non-linear diagrammatic way, approaches problems by exploring each component in as much depth and breadth as possible, finding connections and associations that work to strengthen the concept. This process aims to push achievable boundaries. Think of it as if it were a walk through a city. You may set out knowing exactly where you are going, focused on the end goal: reaching your destination. Alternatively, you could just stroll along the streets without any predetermined destination in mind. Each will provide very different experiences; in the non-predetermined form, you may notice things along the way that are not obvious if your sights are set only on reaching your destination.

You might consider beginning with a lateral thinking session – where you brainstorm as many ideas as possible – in order to generate your initial ideas, then move to a more linear process at a later stage. The two are not necessarily mutually exclusive, but often complementary ways of researching a design problem.

➕ **SEE ALSO:** BASICS OF RESEARCH, P10

⬇️ ↘️ **Lateral or linear?**
Whether your process unfolds in an orderly sequence or is a random scatter of thoughts, the practice of discovery and the sequential development of ideas are exciting parts of design. Relax, examine your recorded research and let the ideas flow. The more experience you have using these methods, the faster you will generate ideas.

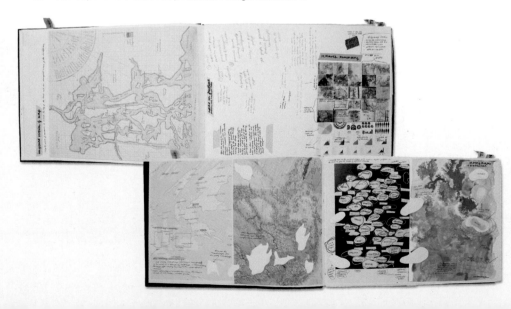

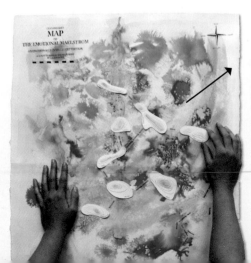

## Example – getting started

Your first brainstorming sessions may be intimidating, so it will help initially if you work with familiar tools and also combine linear and lateral thinking. Until you are able to think in pictures, begin with words. Make a list of absolutely everything that comes to mind when you consider your brief. Then, make a secondary list of things associated with each item on your first list. You can achieve this by hand or using a digital platform such as Miro.

### Monogram brief

Draw and design a monogram for someone you know. It should reflect their characteristics, their personal identity and any hobbies or interests they have. It should be creative, but must also be legible.

Consider what your letters might be used for (e.g. signage, a logo or brand identity, some packaging, a book cover or an illustration) and who it might be used/viewed by.

**1** Once you have determined the usage of the monogram and the type of audience you would like to reach, you can begin your descriptive list of ideas, drilling down to as many levels as you need to bring images to mind. Discard nothing at this stage; just allow your mind to make associations freely. There's no such thing as a bad idea in the brainstorming process; only ideas that communicate more successfully than others.

**2** When your first and secondary lists are long enough to allow you to visualise individual items, you can combine two or more thoughts from the different lists into one image. Now you can begin sketching. One idea will always lead to another, so never settle for just one, and save all your ideas as you work through the process. You may find the seed of something brilliant hidden in an idea you nearly discarded. Keep all of your sketches to refer back to. And don't forget to share the outcome with the person who inspired it!

⬆ **Brainstorming** This is a way to process thoughts and ideas you have about a project. Ideation, or coming up with ideas, is arguably the most difficult and rewarding part of the creative process. Give yourself enough time to reflect on who you are creating the product for and why, and what benefit you will gain from it as a designer. Remember, the first few ideas you note down are likely to have been done before.

➕ **SEE ALSO:** VISUALISING IDEAS, P18

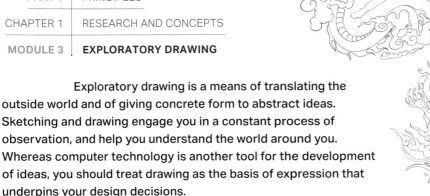

PART 1 | PRINCIPLES

CHAPTER 1 | RESEARCH AND CONCEPTS

MODULE 3 | **EXPLORATORY DRAWING**

Exploratory drawing is a means of translating the outside world and of giving concrete form to abstract ideas. Sketching and drawing engage you in a constant process of observation, and help you understand the world around you. Whereas computer technology is another tool for the development of ideas, you should treat drawing as the basis of expression that underpins your design decisions.

### Representational and non-representational

Representational, or observational, drawing is a form of documentation that is considered a core method for investigating the visual world. By studying your subject or surroundings in depth, from multiple perspectives, you begin to train your eye to see isolated elements. With practice, you will quickly be able to highlight the subtleties of a single subject in immense detail. Studies of still life and life drawing are great ways to practise and develop representational drawing.

Students often draw things the way they think they should look, rather than the way they actually do look. Educate yourself on what you see. Work quickly (impulsively) and slowly (with consideration), with your eyes continually moving between the paper and the subject and back again. Look at forms, shapes, colours, tones, depth, connectivity (how something exists in space and its relationship to other things around it), texture and density, and at how these all relate to one another. Transcribing a 3D subject to a 2D surface is difficult, much more so than drawing from a photograph, but results in drawings with depth and authenticity. Practice is key, and drawing should be a lifelong activity.

Non-representational drawing frees you from the need to represent what is seen and the results, gestural abstractions, can generate valuable, expressive drawn responses. Consider this approach as an exploration to find and embody an idea, as opposed to one that reaches an outcome. To escape preconceived ideas, let the drawing lead the way. Make crude marks and keep an open mind about what the marks mean. Look at the work as a whole and try not to be lured into details.

Even when you are documenting what you see, all exploratory drawing takes the form of translation, not replication. For example, a photograph represents the exact composition of the scene, whereas through drawing you can intentionally or subconsciously draw the focus to particular parts of your viewpoint. An example of this is reportage illustration, which is a type of visual journalism that relies on the illustrator being the translator of the scene in front of them. Drawing is both a thinking and physical process, allowing the illustrator to be selective and sympathetic to where the attention should be drawn and what will enhance the narrative of the image they have created.

### Understanding form

Whether creating representational or non-representational drawings, it is important to understand some of the fundamentals. The main one is form. An object consists of its own solid form, defined by the light and shadow that illuminate and surround it, as opposed to a solid line framing it. Creating black-and-white studies (representational drawing) is the best way to begin to understand form. As you render your study from real life, you are translating the language of colour into a tonal greyscale, substituting monochromatic values for the spectrum in the existing

**Thinking in pictures**
Tight-contour line drawings are used to explore the relationships between new and supplied elements in these studies for Nike packaging. Each study is carefully composed to fit within a particular space on the package before the colour is assigned.

## GLOSSARY

**Abstraction:** An aesthetic concept describing something that is drawn from the real, but which has been 'distilled' to its barest minimum form, colour or tone, often removed from its original context.

**Documentation:** The recording in written, visual or aural form of what is of interest.

**Representation:** Something that looks like, resembles or stands for something else. In drawing, this is also known as figurative, since it deliberately attempts to mimic the thing being drawn.

object. Be as direct and spontaneous as possible. For immediacy, do several studies in a short space of time. Use materials to describe form and mass, while using an outline only as a guide to subsequent layers. Concentrate not on an end product, but on the process of a rich description of forms. Figurative drawing from observation can produce beautiful studies, but it is also the tool that will sharpen your sketching abilities and eventually help you to generate ideas as you work through a design problem.

As you draw, you will notice that what you choose to include and what you choose to exclude are equally important. As an object exists in space, so your drawing lives within the finite boundary of a page, and the relationship of the study to the page is part of the image.

## Understanding tools

Experiment with a variety of media and methods to determine and influence your created image. Whether charcoal or pencil, crayon or brush, each tool you use requires some understanding of its specific effects and mark-making qualities. For example, pencils allow tonal control, detailed modelling and a strong line, whereas ink and brush will generate an entirely different, painterly mark. Try not to limit

yourself to conventional media; other implements, such as a toothbrush for a spatter effect, a piece of string or even a sewing machine, can create interesting images. Consider how you might manipulate the drawing tools you have at your disposal. Attach a pencil to a long stick or perhaps paintbrushes to each of your fingers and thumbs.

The aim is not merely to interpret objects pictorially (i.e. representing them as they look), but to interpret the image in your own way. Mark making, unconventional approaches to drawing and drawing the same subject with multiple materials are all great ways to investigate a subject and experiment with your techniques and approach to drawing and design.

When you complete a study, consider recreating the same subject using different media, eliminating all but the most necessary of descriptive marks. A gradual abstraction of the figurative image will help you to discover more about structure, form and spatial relationships as you work.

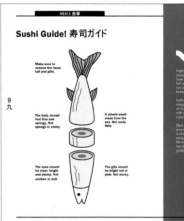

↑ **Exploratory sketches** At the beginning of this animation project a series of exploratory sketches is created to aid design thinking and to invent ways in which to develop the storyboard.

↗ **Sketch development** Development of these sketches and the introduction of colour allow the designer to create a sense of atmosphere. Consider ways in which colour, illustrative style, framing and facial expressions affect the final animation.

↑ **Sketching roughs** Multiple studies of the sliced fish are created as roughs for this sushi guide. Different angles and elements are explored and analysed before settling on the most successful composition for the final publication. Here, the illustration is coloured and created to a higher standard for production.

| PART 1 | PRINCIPLES |
|---|---|
| CHAPTER 1 | RESEARCH AND CONCEPTS |
| MODULE 4 | **VISUALISING IDEAS** |

All designers need to develop the skill of putting ideas down on paper. This involves preparing rough visuals/design sketches – thumbnails, scamps or roughs. Students often tend to bypass this process and set about producing ideas directly on screen. This practice can inhibit the development of ideas, because you may restrict yourself to only those images you are capable of producing with the available technology. It's better to think freely at first, and to produce as many ideas as you can sketch.

Initial ideas are generated more quickly and prolifically if you do a bit of brainstorming, recording your thoughts rapidly using various diagrammatic methods or other ways to structure information.

Start with your word lists, and as you begin to think in pictures, move on to sketching directly. In this process, co-ordination between brain, eye and hand can be amazingly fast, and by working quickly you can generate many diverse (and sometimes unexpected) ideas, concepts and associations. Your mind starts flowing and loosening up, and becomes open to the diverse aspects of the project, swiftly moving the thought process forwards. Literal and non-literal, lateral and non-lateral forms of thinking are used to maximum effect in these early sketches.

### Roughs and thumbnails

There is no predetermined size for rough drawings. Thumbnails are, as the term suggests, small. Designers usually begin with thumbnails, a series of rapidly drawn, stamp-sized compositions that block out the general structure and content of a design. Thumbnails should be spontaneous and prolific; they are the recorded thought process of developing ideas and should move as rapidly as you can think. Obviously, this can leave no time for the inclusion of any detail or refinement. These will be considered in the final stages of design development.

Thumbnails that have the most interesting potential are selected and a rough, larger, loose drawing, with more detail but as yet still unfinished, is created that further develops the composition and placement on the page.

### Drawing by hand

Although roughs require a certain degree of drawing skill, these will be learned easily for this kind of work, where the generation of ideas is the focus, not drawing as an end in itself. This is unlike observational drawing, or drawing as documentation, which needs to be precise. Hand-drawn ideas can be vague and leave a lot to the imagination, which can be a good thing. Excluding detail from the sketch will allow you to leave your options open for more deliberate decisions at a later point in concept development. Remember, the 'big idea' is the most important part of the process at this stage.

Once you have a number of ideas sketched out, you can step back and make judgments regarding their value, and potential for development, without having committed to any design in detail. This allows maximum flexibility and fluidity in the design process.

**⬆ Preliminary sketches**
Your first sketches can be loose and expressive. Try variations of each design before you begin to finalise the idea. Once you have selected your final idea – based on a solid rationale – mock it up in more detail, but continue to experiment with layout and form. In this instance, the experimentation was so successful it became the main feature of the posters and supporting animations.

**⊞ SEE ALSO:** LINEAR REASONING/LATERAL THINKING, P14

⬇ **Putting it all together** Looking spontaneous takes time. Finished artwork may be the result of experiments in various media and techniques, and it may be the sum of many successful combinations. Once you have the concept and the general proportions in mind, consider the best way to execute the style you want to communicate. Then, determine the right tool for the right job, and use as many as you need to get the right visual language for your message. For this poster promoting an exhibition of rock-'n'-roll music posters, the artist wanted an image that expressed the concept of 'art at 1000 decibels', a part of the copy line on the poster.

The bird was hand drawn with pen and ink, and the hands were drawn separately.

First, a sans-serif typeface was selected and type treatments were designed on computer in several variations, then printed in black and white. The result felt too static.

The printed type was placed on a copy machine and the paper copy was moved during the copying process to blur the image. Several versions were scanned back into the computer, and the best were combined then cropped. The balloon form was added.

The artist added a washy ink texture to the background, and a bit more to the top of the artwork by taping in place. All the elements were scanned into the computer and assembled electronically.

When all of the additional typography was complete, the artist explored several colour variations until they were pleased. Two different colour versions were printed: the magenta one (right) and a predominantly cyan version (not pictured).

An important advantage of developing the ability to produce quick, effective roughs is that when presenting ideas to clients, alternatives can be quickly sketched out, keeping your approach fresh and relatively unrestricted. This, in turn, gives clients confidence in your willingness to be flexible and open-minded, while also showing your design abilities.

## Computers and visualisation

Roughs are usually generated on a sketchpad. When generated on a computer, roughs tend to look too fixed and polished, and students can be reluctant to change or refine them. Wait until you have a sketch that excites you, then scan it and look at it on screen.

Once you have chosen an idea or shortlist of ideas that you feel may have potential, computers come into their own, because they enable you to produce as many alternate versions of your ideas as you wish, changing colours, typefaces, line weights and images. Typefaces and grid measurements become fluid decisions when you are working digitally, and you don't need to commit immediately. In fact, it may be better not to. It's fast and easy to change these on screen.

**Brainstorming:** A visual aid to thinking laterally and exploring a problem, usually by stating the problem in the centre of a page and radiating outward spokes for components of the problem. Each component can then be considered separately with its own spokes, so that each point, thought or comment is recorded.

**Roughs:** Loosely drawn compositions from thumbnail drawings.

**Thumbnail:** Small, rough visual representation of the bigger picture or final outcome of a design.

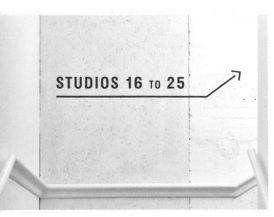

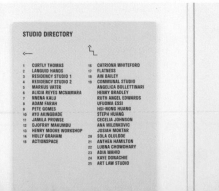

| PART 1 | PRINCIPLES |
|---|---|
| CHAPTER 1 | RESEARCH AND CONCEPTS |
| MODULE 5 | **THEORIES OF IMAGE AND TEXT** |

◀ **Dependable artwork**
International symbols transcend language and communicate instantly. The appearance of a symbol can vary greatly in style through line weights and positive/negative balance, as long as the symbol is easily understood. Symbols such as the universal symbol or signifier for disability (wheelchair) and healthcare (cross) are known worldwide and are instantly recognisable. However, this does not mean these symbols are not up for critque. The Accessible Icon Project is a great example of how dependable systems can and should be constantly re-evaluated.

The success of visual communication depends on the ability to reach a targeted audience and elicit a desired response. Sometimes the response is an immediate call to action and a clear, concise message with little open to interpretation. Most often, visual imagery is used to evoke an emotional state that will put the viewer in the appropriately receptive frame of mind to receive the message targeted at them.

Designers influence the message through the development of provocative imagery that may persuade, shock, entertain and provoke with purpose. In order for designers to speak clearly and say what they mean, they need to develop a clear and strong visual language.

### Rhetoric
With its origins attributed to ancient public speaking in Greece and Rome, rhetoric is a skill of persuasion most often associated with politics and public speaking. To construct a strong rhetorical speech, ancient philosophers used something kindred to contemporary design thinking to define and refine the categories of invention, arrangement, style, memory and delivery within a compelling dialogue. If we examine these subjects as design vocabulary, the same can be said for the construction of a successful and equally

↑ **Identity to icon** The first Apple Computer, Inc. logo was designed by Ron Wayne, a co-founder of Apple Computer. The original was illustrative and included a full image of Sir Isaac Newton sitting under an apple tree with type in a traditional banner arrangement as an integrated border. That logo was replaced in 1977 by graphic designer Rob Janoff, with an image of a rainbow-striped apple with a bite taken out of it. The bite was added for scale, so that the image would not be mistakenly identified as a cherry. This monochrome version was adapted in 1999 to be applied across multiple media and processes, while still being recognisable.

◤ **Messages and Information**
Environmental graphics should be beautiful in addition to delivering a body of information in a clear and immediate way. Economical use of space and direction and carefully considered typography, icons and imagery are essential for clear communication and wayfinding, such as this example by APFEL.

compelling visual. In visual communication, the concept of visual rhetoric usually describes the visual tone of voice chosen for a given communication task.

## Semiotics, signs and symbols

Ferdinand de Saussure is acknowledged as the father of semiotics. His theory divides signs, or all things that represent meaning, into two categories: the signifier and the signified. The signifier is the symbol that represents something from which meaning can be extracted; the signified is the actual object or meaning that it represents. For example, the universal symbol, or signifier, for healthcare (a cross) is instantly recognisable in a way that transcends language, while the signified is the actual hospital or healthcare centre. This type of non-verbal vocabulary of signs is increasingly relevant in the global reach of contemporary communications and, when designed well, can be recognised instantly.

## Didactics

The term 'didactics' refers to clear, pragmatically delivered information and instructions with unambiguous meaning. Airport signage, road signs and warnings are prime examples of didactic information. It is important to note that nuance can be added to most visuals, even in the strictest definition of category: didactic panels in museum exhibitions must deliver clear information, but can be associated with the subject matter in inventive visual ways.

## Symbol style

Signs can be simple or complex, depending on the accompanying message. A denotative sign denotes exactly what it pictures and should be visually direct, but can convey secondary information through the use of a particular style. A connotative sign will be single-minded and may convey a range of associated messages that are to be interpreted by the viewer. Symbols and signs can have rich layers of associated meaning.

The Olympic symbols are prime examples of design defining attitude. The symbol for swimming usually doesn't change much in content, but the designer may assign an element of playfulness, structure and discipline, or reference other time periods through the use of line weight, drawing style or colour. The five interlocking rings of the Olympic symbol itself represent the five continents or major geographical areas of the world that participate in the games. Exposure to the Olympic symbol, over time, has elevated it to iconic stature and it may now evoke an emotional response in some through its association with the actual events.

## Symbol families

Complex systems and extended families of symbols usually share common essential criteria. They have clarity and are easily recognisable with a simple message. All symbols in the system share a look, with similar treatment in line, style, weight and scale. They are also easy to reproduce in any size and will retain clarity, and they are flexible enough to be combined with other elements, and will still remain distinctive.

← **Make an impression**
Each of these approaches to package design has a distinct message. The chocolate packages are as rich in colour as they are in content. With luxurious metallics, deep saturated colour and intricate graphics, they invite elegant indulgence with every design decision. The clean simplicity of the die-cut labels on the bottles allows the actual ingredients to become the vibrant colour in the artwork, promising freshness and the visual implication that there is 'nothing added'.

↑ **Universal messages**
The pictograms used in the 1972 Munich Olympics set the standard for subsequent Olympic designs. Each sporting event is clearly represented through an economy of line and shape, yet each symbol is visually strong enough for signage and promotional use at any size.

⬆ **Abstract icon** The Nike 'Swoosh' was designed in 1971 by Carolyn Davidson. Originally, it appeared with the word NIKE above it. As the brand's recognition grew, the trademark was gradually streamlined.

## Metaphors

Signs and symbols are primary sources in the design and development of logos and trademarks, and are essential in the development of the visual metaphor, an image that will trigger associations to other meanings or signifiers, and is connotative in nature. A visual metaphor might be as obvious as a lightbulb to signify an idea, a heart to signify love or a book to represent learning. Logos become metaphors for the business, goods or service they represent through association, and some become so memorable that they need no words to explain them.

Carolyn Davidson designed the Nike 'Swoosh' in 1971. Originally, it appeared accompanied by the word 'NIKE'. As the brand grew, the trademark was streamlined to the positive, tick/wing of the current version.

## Poetics

Some of the most involving design work can deliberately engage the viewer for much longer periods of time. With current media, the attention span of a target audience is shortened by the number of competing stimuli encountered daily, and by the availability of viewing options, hand-held and environmental. They can pull your audience in too many directions to concentrate on your message. If you can engage your audience members, they are more likely to remember what you have told them or to associate your message with a visual style that can be revisited.

Poetic forms of work have much less immediately accessible meaning, and the message is deliberately left open to interpretation. Graphic designers make conscious decisions to leave the work open to provoke thoughtful

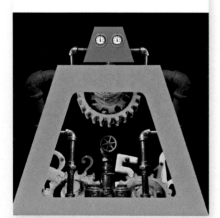

⬆ **Connotations** This book cover illustration uses visual connotations of industry to allude to inventiveness and power. The combination of these themes and the dark, unsettling colour palette hints at the violent and peculiar civilisations featured in the series of short stories.

⬆ **Colour** The use of striking shapes and the combination of textures in this bold illustration convey simultaneous messages of adventure, encounters and friendship. The colourful narrative is alluded to through the use of line, colour and composition.

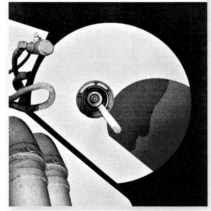

⬆ **Concept** Without resorting to clichés of space, robots and time travel, the illustrator has used composition and subtle photographic and block-colour collage to portray the book's themes of technology, theology, intelligence and human nature.

responses, to stir controversy or to tease. Ad campaigns, posters, and book and publication design are examples of media that can support more complex visual allegory, and the illustrative and graphic works that support them are often produced though a range of media and stand as works of art in their own right. Poetic work can be seen as the polar opposite of didactic, but all graphic design is visual communication, and the decision to use one or the other is part of the designer's problem-solving process.

## GLOSSARY

**Didactic:** A pragmatic and unambiguous method of giving clear information.

**Metaphor:** Word or image that sets up associations; for example, a 'piece of cake' is a metaphor for easy.

**Poetic:** A style that is less clear, but more artistic, more open to interpretation.

**Rhetoric:** A style of arguing, persuading or engaging in dialogue. For a designer, it is a way of engaging the targeted audience.

**Semiotics:** A system that links objects, words and images to meanings through signs and signifiers.

**Signifier:** An image, object, word or action that represents something that gives meaning. For example, a symbol of a figure in a wheelchair represents disability, even though not all disabilities need a wheelchair.

**Signified:** The concept behind the object being represented by a signifier. For example, the meaning represented by the wheelchair signifier (see left) is disabled access.

**Symbolism:** A way of representing an object or word through an image, sound or another word; for example, a crossed knife and fork on a road sign means a café is ahead.

⊕ **SEE ALSO:** AUDIENCES, MARKETS AND CONCEPTS, P24

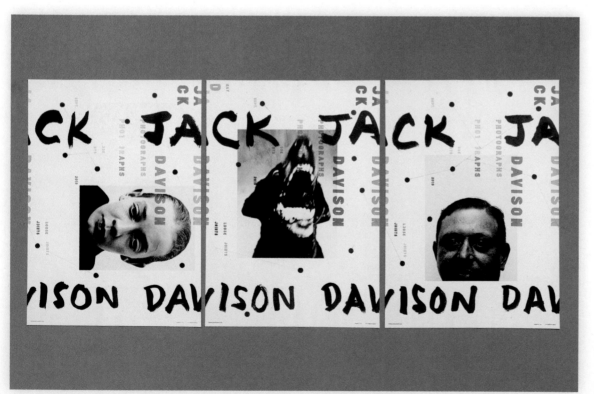

◄ **Combinations and collections**
Colour, forms and layering in this composition are used to imply and suggest an impression to the viewer, accomplished through a series of painterly, hand-rendered text, serif typography, black-and-white photographs and a range of layout orientations. A reduced palette and repetition of visual devices indicate that these posters belong to a set, and are intended to be read together. The elements of the set, when displayed correctly, connect together seamlessly, reinforcing the collection as a whole.

| PART 1 | PRINCIPLES |
|---|---|
| CHAPTER 1 | RESEARCH AND CONCEPTS |
| MODULE 6 | **AUDIENCES, MARKETS AND CONCEPTS** |

Good graphic design is not simply the result of brilliant execution or technique. It is the strong expression of clever, well formulated ideas, drawn from an ongoing engagement with research and an interest in the world at large. In professional practice, as in school, extensive exploratory research is invariably the key to the most successful projects, and research into audiences is a primary tool of effective design.

**⬆ Research and inspiration**
Researching similar aesthetic styles, designers that inspire you and other examples of what you are designing are all important steps in a design process. In this example, character design and storyboard frames are explored to develop the final set design and moving image.

It is vital to remember that everything you design will be seen by other people: designers are visual communicators and do not work in a vacuum. Therefore, it is part of your job to discover everything you can about the intended viewer. Before designing, think about the people who will be looking at your design work. What is the target market? What do you know about them? What can you/should you find out about them? Can you imagine how they might interpret a particular visual message? Think about the age of the viewer, their geographic and cultural influences, and the level of their education and experience. The more you discover about your audience, the better informed your work will be, increasing its potential effectiveness.

The Internet provides instant communication; what you post will be seen around the world with amazing speed. To complicate matters further, viewers have short attention spans and may split their concentration as they multitask with different electronic devices. Graphic designers have only a few seconds to grab the attention of any potential audience before they turn a page, click to the next website or jump to the broadcast or programme.

If your preliminary research is thorough, you will be able to speak a visual language that your target audience understands, relates to and responds to, thus increasing the odds that your visual communication will hit its mark by both communicating the message you intended and communicating it effectively.

## Think globally

It is the designer's job to deliver a message, and as we communicate globally, accurate information transfer becomes increasingly complex. Be aware that different cultures may react differently to colours, images and language. The colour red is used as a warning in some countries, yet is considered lucky in China. An image that appears delightfully contemporary in one culture can be offensive in another. Do your homework before you begin brainstorming, and pay attention to brands that advertise globally. Are there different versions of the same advertisement in different countries? What brands have instant recognition internationally, and how has the brand been developed? What type of image does it communicate?

## Market research

Large companies have whole departments devoted to what is formally called market research. They spend their time conducting surveys into their customers' needs and preferences. They do this by a variety of means, including questionnaires, surveys and focus groups where people carefully selected as representative of the target audience are brought together to discuss a product or campaign before it is launched into the public domain. If, however, you are the only team member on the project, you can still do some research. Modern communications make a large part of the world accessible. Use the Internet, libraries,

**GLOSSARY**

**Audience:** In its broadest sense, the consumers, voyeurs and occasionally participants of design work.

**Customer profile/profiling:** The process of creating a series of parameters or set of information that defines the desires, trends or interests of a demographic so that designs can be pitched or marketed to them.

**Market research:** The process of collecting and collating data from questionnaires, interviews and comments from the public regarding a concern, a problem or a possible solution.

**⊞ SEE ALSO:** BASICS OF RESEARCH, P10

LINEAR REASONING/ LATERAL THINKING, P14

museums and any other appropriate research venue at your disposal to do your market research, and find out as much as you can about your client and your audience.

Find out about your target and determine a reasonable approach to communications. Identify and research potential competitors, and see what type of brand image they are projecting. Define your target audience with your client, considering age, gender, ethnicity, level of education, income and location. If you are too far removed from your target audience, consider bringing someone on board as a collaborator. Having more perspectives on the same project will make your designs and approach to projects stronger. NRS social grades and Abraham Maslow's hierarchy of needs are both good templates to help determine who your audience could be. Develop a questionnaire, or have a series of questions ready to ask, and visit people in the target group firsthand. Use your developed powers of observation to note the various trends/habits/practices/attitudes of your target audience and record your impressions. Read as much information about the buying practices of consumers in your brand category as you can. When you have collected some information, imagine your target in as much rich detail as you can, and try to put yourself in their place. How would you respond to the ideas you are proposing? Bring your concepts right to the source and ask people what they think of them. You can create an informal focus group made up of friends, relatives and colleagues. Smart, informed design always begins with information.

## Make contact

Learning to articulate your concepts is the first stage in developing great presentation techniques, and explaining your ideas to others can help you understand what you're trying to achieve. Be prepared to listen to any opinions offered and try not to take criticism personally. Instead, use it constructively to uncover which aspects of your ideas aren't working and what you can do to improve them. You don't have to act on comments if you think they aren't helpful, but always remember your cultural and social bias may be different to that of the audience you're reaching out to. Good design is about perception and accurate information transfer to your audience, not necessarily yourself.

## Elimination process

Explore your ideas visually to see which have the most potential. Do not fret about detail; concentrate on expressing your ideas.

1 Make quick sketches to determine which ideas work well and have immediate impact. Use colour if it helps, but don't get involved in the subtleties.
2 Discard any sketches that are too complex or rely on tired visual clichés. Getting rid of the bad ideas quickly will help you focus on the good ones.
3 Select the strongest idea, then put together a presentation visual that demonstrates why your idea is so brilliant.
4 Now you can start working on the detail. The best ideas are often the simplest, but you need to show that careful thought and preparation have gone into your work. Consider how you will explain your idea to your client. You might need to 'sell' it to them, so think about what you would say to support your images.

⬇ **Make them curious** The use of experimental layering and three dimensions in this composition not only creates an intriguing visual, but also a sense of depth. Devices such as this encourage an image to be seen both from a distance and close up, pulling an audience in to learn more.

⬇◤ **Audience needs** Consider all of your audiences. In this example, it is beer buyers and beer sellers. The clever packaging concept functions as a box to store and transport the bottles. When opened, the box becomes a marketing display, showcasing the intricate illustrations on the labels.

⬇ **Macro** Look at the big picture. Preliminary ideas shown in a flatplan of a publication from start to finish will help you determine how the information is divided, and allow you to plan the rhythm and flow of images and text throughout the entire publication. If it becomes necessary to delete or rearrange content, a flatplan will help you to keep track of the changes.

| PART 1 | PRINCIPLES |
|---|---|
| CHAPTER 1 | RESEARCH AND CONCEPTS |
| MODULE 7 | **SCHEDULING, ORGANISING AND FINALISING** |

**Creativity, talent and originality are all expected, but if a design project can't be delivered on time, those first three attributes may not matter in the long run. Organised thinking is the key to understanding how to manage a big project. All design projects begin with the broadest of ideas and must be broken down into smaller, manageable parts.**

Read the design brief carefully, and ask questions if you need more information. Design briefs always involve interpretation by the designer. Some clients have little idea of what they need, and they look to the designer for clear analysis of, and a solution to, the problem. Other clients may have a clear idea of what they want, and these ideas need to be considered and respected – but also questioned if they are inappropriate. For example, green may be a favourite colour of one member of a group of clients, but it may be the wrong choice for the project. Similarly, it's important to recognise that clients have valuable insight into the workings of their organisation and its needs, and although they may not have the design skills, or the language, to implement their ideas, their input on these matters is crucial. Be open and flexible, but stand your ground when you know you are right.

**Check it**

There are as many different solutions to the same problem as there are designers. Your job is to choose the solution

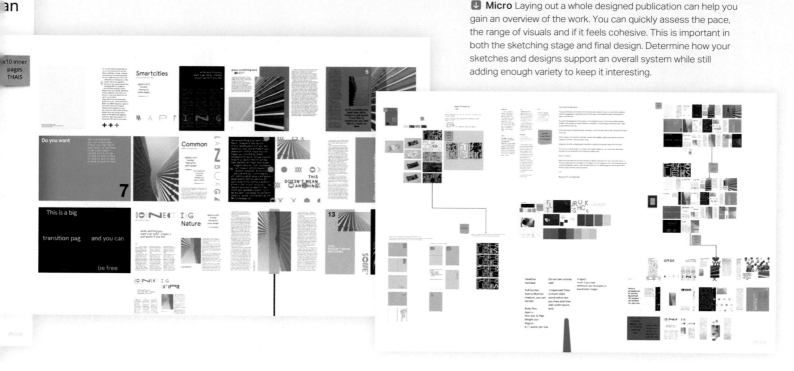

⬇ **Micro** Laying out a whole designed publication can help you gain an overview of the work. You can quickly assess the pace, the range of visuals and if it feels cohesive. This is important in both the sketching stage and final design. Determine how your sketches and designs support an overall system while still adding enough variety to keep it interesting.

that you think is the most appropriate. This decision-making isn't subjective; it comes from informed judgment. It's a good idea to set a series of checkpoint meetings/approvals with your client as you work through the design process. It's a better practice to have the client approve or reject an approach at the early stages, at which point you can adjust your design thinking accordingly.

## Think macro and micro

Good design works both at a macro scale (the large, overview structure, as though viewed from 'above'), and at a micro scale, where the tiniest details are important, down to letterspacing. Often you will have to give the information order and structure (hierarchy) as well as visual form. You will need to make micro decisions such as type size, individual page layouts and colour choices, and these will need to be balanced and related to the macro scale: the whole design needs to appear considered, as does every part of the project. In the case of a print or package design, every aspect of the project should be designed, including the

selection or creation of additional materials for closures, bindings and fastenings. If you can see it, your audience can, too. Rigorous testing is needed before launching digital designs to check for hidden errors and glitches you may not have noticed while designing.

## Scheduling and organisation

Time management and organisation are crucial aspects of a design practice, and their significance cannot be overstated. Organise your time, and plot out the progress of each project, from start to end, allocating time to each aspect of the design process. To help you do this, make a schematic diagram to identify how long certain aspects of the job will take to complete, paying particular attention to print and production time frames at the end of the schedule. If you are working on a project with numerous applications and different elements, it will help immeasurably. It's easy to be swept away on a wave of creative thinking, and aspects of your process can take longer than you think they will.

## Personal deadlines

Set intermediate deadlines for yourself. If you break down the process into manageable steps, you can set your calendar accordingly. A breakdown of the process might read:

**Research**
Sketches/concept development
Presentation sketches/roughs
**Client meeting**
Refined comprehensive concepts (comps)
Revisions
**Client meeting**
Finished files

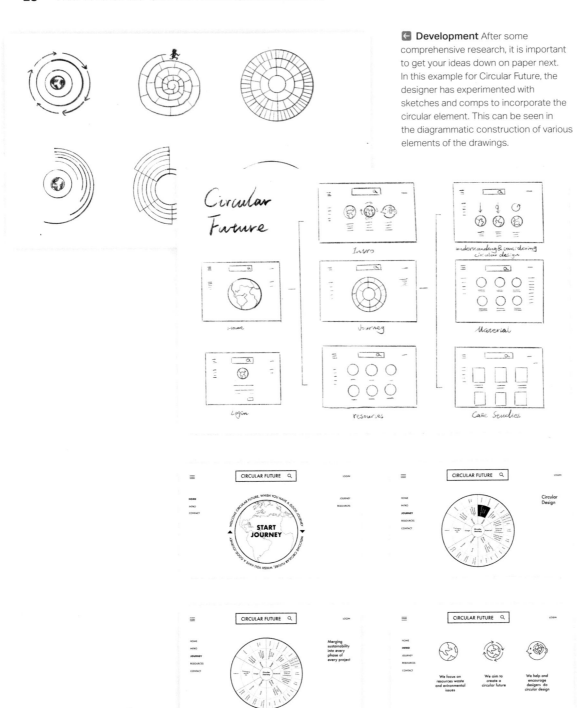

← **Development** After some comprehensive research, it is important to get your ideas down on paper next. In this example for Circular Future, the designer has experimented with sketches and comps to incorporate the circular element. This can be seen in the diagrammatic construction of various elements of the drawings.

🔴 **Remember**
- Write everything down. Don't rely on memory.
- Without a relevant concept, your visualisation has no meaning.
- Try creating a flowchart/ spider diagram with routes for different ideas.
- Look for professional criticism and use it constructively.
- Talk about your work. Learn to be articulate, and explain your intentions, influences and solutions.

🔴 **Timescale**
Research can be very time-consuming, so bear in mind that there has to be a cut-off point at which you have to start generating your visual concepts. 'Design' is a verb as much as it is a noun: it's about doing things, so jump right in. One idea will always lead to the next.

← **Presentation and production** When the concept is developed and sketches have advanced your ideas, start to digitise your strongest visuals to aid discussions with the client. Comprehensive designs that simulate the finished product are presented for approval before the artwork is sent into production. At this stage it is important to consider the output for your visuals. This presentation, for example, needs to clearly communicate on screen.

Over longer jobs there may be only one deadline per week (for example, interim presentations to the client); on shorter jobs this may be two deadlines per day (for example, multiple proof stages). One way to organise ideas into sequence is to write everything down on self-adhesive reminder notes and put them in a logical order. Job jackets, envelopes with deadline lists, approvals and everything else related to the job help keep track of multiple projects.

If you'd rather do it all electronically, software programs such as Excel and applications such as Evernote can be invaluable in plotting job progress and in maintaining an overview. Organise your digital files logically, making sure everyone working on the project knows the system, and back up your files regularly. You can create a timetable with each checkpoint assigned a date. Include all of the subcategories you need to cover until they become second nature.

Many good designers miss the importance of time management and organisation, and their work and client relationships suffer as a result. Get into the habit of good time management, now!

## Comps (comprehensive sketches)

Comps are the most finished approximation of an actual product and often look exactly like the real thing. They will evidence all design considerations, including final colours, tints and halftones, all typographic considerations, textures, and paper finishes and weights. If a project has many parts, comps for the extended system may be produced at different stages. After a client approves the comps, an artworker can take over the job, if needed, and match all aspects of the production to the designer's choices.

## Page plans/flatplans

There has to be a logical visual (and conceptual) sequence in any design project. Magazines and books are normally laid out in miniature on a page plan several times before full-size layouts are started. The page plan may consist of no more than the article title, but can be much more specific, including a list of all the page elements or a thumbnail drawing of the layout with text blocks and artwork sketched in. The page plan is intended to clarify logical sequence, distribution of colour, change of pace and so on.

## Storyboards

Storyboards give the client or production person enough information to allow them to begin to design their assigned spreads or pages of the final product. As well as in

⬆ **Storyboard development** Storyboards clarify the concept of a moving image sequence by showing the progression of the idea and the transitions from scene to scene. Moving image sequences, in any form, require consideration and planning. Spend time sketching possible ideas and intentions, then develop them by hand before moving on to a computer.

**GLOSSARY**

**Comps:** Comprehensive sketch, a close approximation of the printed product.

**Page plan/flatplan:** A document featuring a series of numbered thumbnails set out in an ordered grid that represents each page in a book.

**Storyboard:** A document that is similar to a flatplan, but with a sequence of thumbnails that specifically lays out the narrative for a comic strip or film.

multimedia design, storyboards are commonly employed in films, comic strips, animation and TV commercials. The storyboard contains a sketch of the visual aspect of the screen, information that will be present, descriptions of animations, interactions (for example, dialogue boxes), sounds and any other media. Although storyboards were originally linear (for film), non-linear elements are incorporated. Web design uses a similar approach through wireframes. Wireframes are used to plan individual pages or sequences before engaging a web designer.

These website flowcharts show how pages link up in a logical order (see page 160). The organisation of a website reflects the actual body for which the site is designed. It is important to get the structure right before designing the look of the pages.

# CHAPTER 1: ASSIGNMENTS

## ◘ Primary and secondary research

Primary and secondary research is vital before beginning any design project. By starting a project without a computer, you allow your ideas and design approaches to be influenced by unconventional references, making you a more unique and adaptable designer. Research for a particular project can take weeks, and the process has an important influence on the final outcome. The more you invest in the beginning of the project, the more successful the outcome will be.

Consider the tools you will need for primary research: a sketchbook, camera, smartphone, pens, pencils, charcoal, viewfinders, a container for collected ephemera, etc. Don't hold back – at the beginning of a project this is an exercise in quantity over quality.

**1** Visit a public building close to your home. This could be a shop, library, hair salon, etc. With permission, observe and record the activities within this context, filling an empty sketchbook. Concentrate on what is happening in front of you, while avoiding interfering with people's normal activities. Use your sketchbook to draw what you see and make notes of what you hear. Document the items that people interact with. Think about the time of day, and how that might impact what you see. Think about the type of area and what you might expect to see, as opposed to the reality of what is actually there. Take your time. What do you see when you really look?

**2** When you are satisfied with what you have collected and documented, create a brainstorm of what you saw and recorded. Note down the visuals (e.g. icons and signage, diagrams, drawings of people, sketches of the environment), but also moments when historical, social and political elements were found (e.g. discounted food items and what this means for the larger context of capitalism and food waste).

**3** Once you have had a substantial brainstorm, start to analyse your findings and observations, find connections and develop a concept. What was it about the experience that intrigued you most? What part of the experience do you want to share with others, and why? Continue to build up your research by adding secondary sources from the Internet, libraries and archives.

**4** When you feel you've researched in depth, begin to edit and curate the information to find the most interesting elements. Think about who might be most interested in your research or who is most likely to engage with it. Decide how you would best catch their attention and how the story should unfold.

**5** It is useful to see what people do within the context your designs are found. With this in mind, consider how your research can be presented back in the environment you began in. Start with ideation, coming up with ideas. Do this by creating a series of sketches using your edited research. Generate as many thumbnail drawings as you physically can, and use words, images and collage materials you may have collected. When you have a series of five thumbnails you are pleased with, enlarge them, either by drawing them again or by using a copier, and clarify your intentions by writing a short descriptive paragraph on each one.

**6** Choose one sketch and develop it into a format of your choice. Iterate this design until you are pleased with the outcome. The emphasis of this assignment is on the creative process, not on the final project, so use your skills in observation and research as expansively as possible, and consider all of the possible interpretations before you commit to a single idea or a particular form or media. It is always worth doing some research into the format you have chosen or the format written in your brief.

**7** Additional task
Once you are happy with your outcome, take it back to the environment in which you did your research. Present it to the people there for feedback. What do they think of your observations? Spend as much time as you can with these people, and aim to gain a firsthand understanding of habits, rituals and meanings around relevant activities and objects. Consider shadowing them to observe and understand their day-to-day routines, interactions and contexts. Collect this additional information and redesign your project with this in mind.

## ◘ Exploratory drawing and recording

Observational drawing and recording have become increasingly popular in recent years as a way for visual communicators not only to record their environment, but also to interrogate and investigate issues, locations and subjects in a journalistic way. The more you practise observing and recording what you see, the more your analytical and technical skills will improve, which will result in an increased confidence and awareness of visual language.

**1** Select a televised news programme that you can re-watch several times. Select one news story to concentrate on. A fundamental aspect of drawing is seeing. Spend some time sitting and observing, taking in the programme without drawing.

**2** Lay a large piece of paper (the biggest you can find) on the floor in front of the screen. Re-watch the news programme, concentrating on the information as it develops, and use drawing materials to draw what you see and hear. The following prompts will help you:

- Draw the story as a single sketch.
- Draw the story as a series of sketches.
- Make a blind drawing – don't look at the paper.
- Make a blind drawing – don't look at the screen.

**3** Watch the programme again and add notes and annotations to the same piece of paper. Highlight aspects that particularly interest you. The following prompts will help you:

- Make a note of all key words.
- Record snippets of conversation in writing.
- Summarise the story in one word, three words, and a sentence.

**4** Now focus in on a theme that you identified in the previous task. Is what you are observing and drawing appropriate to that theme? Does it explore/challenge/interrogate that theme?

Draw elements associated with this theme (people, objects, environments, etc.) for 5 minutes, 3 minutes, 1 minute, 30 seconds, 10 seconds and 1 second. Repeat for each element.

**5** Re-watch the article, this time concentrating on its composition as a designed programme. Select an object or person. Observe the subject that you're drawing as positive space – its boundaries, where it starts and finishes – and negative space – everything else. Observe the visual relationship this creates as shape and form to be drawn. Consider how movement affects what you are documenting and how your mark making can imply that movement is happening.

- Draw around a subject (person/object/etc.).
- Draw everything but the subject.
- Draw the movement of people/objects within the screen. Are they central? Do they appear and disappear throughout the programme?

**8** Additional task
Repeat this task in a physical environment. Compare this experience to your current sketches, annotating similarities and differences. Write a short paragraph about the difference between recording from screen and recording in person. Has it affected your drawings? Your experience?

## ◻ 100 ideas

There is always more than one way to solve a design problem or communicate a message visually. Your role as a graphic designer is not only to come up with the ideas, but also to decide which idea would be most appropriate and effective for your aims and objectives. Ideation can be difficult, but is an important stage in the design process to avoid an obvious solution.

Design a new banknote for your hometown. Research the area using primary and secondary sources. Spend some time in the area documenting its identity and character. Talk to the people who live there: what do they value?

**1** Start by brainstorming your ideas. From this brainstorm create 100 different sketched thumbnails of new banknotes without using a computer. Consider the shapes, metaphors, icons and symbols of the currency – think about what visual language for physical currency already exists, as well as more abstract forms such as cryptocurrency and NFTs.

**2** Select 50 ideas and compositions that you deem to be the most successful, and digitise them.

Consider the colours, contrast, form and hierarchy of each design element individually, and how they work together.

**3** From your digital banknotes, select the 25 you deem to be the most successful. Experiment with the variations of these notes. Consider size, materials and the method of creation (e.g. sketches, papercuts, painting).

**4** Select the note you think is the most successful and develop it into a finalised product. Present the note to your peers, explaining why you think it is more successful than your other 99 ideas.

## ◻ Symbols and icons

Symbols and icons are fundamentals of visual communication. We all look at an object and our mind interprets it into meaning. It is important to remember that our perceptions and bias will be different to those of others, which is why collaboration and comparison is a great asset in any graphic design project.

**1** This task requires a group of people to work together, ideally a class but it can also be done in pairs. Below is a list of 20 activities. Quickly sketch ten icons for each activity, and select your strongest to present to the others.

Astronomy; athletics; baking; camping; caving; cooking; climbing; cycling; drawing; fishing; gaming; gardening; music; painting; photography; reading; sailing; sewing; swimming; writing.

**2** Exchange and analyse your drawings. Find comparisons and differences between the interpretations of each icon. Extract interesting shapes and details. Add your notes from this conversation to your drawings in the form of annotation and sketches.

**3** Using these findings, collaboratively redesign the icons as a set. Each person should take one icon. If there are not enough for your group size, add your own.

**4** Additional task
Consider the audience of your icon set. Without changing the meaning of each icon, develop them to appeal to the following target groups:

- Specific customers: for example, people that work in the financial sector.
- Local marketing: for example, a new local community book club.
- Demographic: for example, women aged 18–25 in education.
- Customer needs: for example, hikers and outdoor enthusiasts.
- Customer preferences: for example, people who want to minimise their impact on the environment.
- Lifestyle: for example, jetsetters and luxury holidaymakers.
- Culture: for example, people who identify as punks and anarchists.
- Willingness to pay: for example, people with a high disposable income.
- Interests: for example, people interested in art and design.
- Values: for example, people who want more inclusivity and diversity in the workplace.
- Behaviour: for example, people who use social media as a status-seeking platform.

## ⊞ Further reading

Audrey Bennett, *Design Studies: Theory and Research in Graphic Design*, Princeton Architectural Press, 2006

Russell Bestley and Paul McNeil, *Visual Research: An Introduction to Research Methods in Graphic Design*, Bloomsbury, 2022

David Crow, *Visible Signs: An Introduction to Semiotics in the Visual Arts*, Bloomsbury, 2022

Daniel Chandler, *Semiotics: The Basics*, Routledge, 2022

Meredith Davis, *Graphic Design Theory,* Thames & Hudson, 2012

Steven Heller and Lita Talarico, *Graphic: Inside the Sketchbooks of the World's Great Graphic Designers,* Thames & Hudson, 2010

Ellen Lupton, *Graphic Design Thinking: Beyond Brainstorming*, Princeton Architectural Press, 2011

Norman Potter, *What is a Designer? Things, Places, Messages*, Hyphen Press, 2002

Ruben Pater, *The Politics of Design: A (Not So) Global Design Manual for Visual Communication*, BIS Publishers, 2016

Lucienne Roberts and Rebecca Wright, *Design Diaries: Creative Process in Graphic Design*, Laurence King Publishing, 2010

Jenn and Ken Visocky O'Grady, *A Designer's Research Manual*, Rockport Publishers, 2017

# 2 Fundamentals of Composition

Good composition is an essential element of all art forms, graphic or otherwise, and should be considered the foundation of visual communication. Successful graphic designers are masters of the fundamentals that underlie all aspects of design. Elements on a page or on the Web, in motion or in three dimensions, should always be led by concern for spacing, visual organisation, style, and the size and format of the finished work.

Graphic design projects use text and image in concert, with consideration for the relationships established between each of the elements. These compositions should also establish a visual hierarchy that directs the viewer's eye through a deliberate visual sequence.

**Composition refers to the visual structure and organisation of elements within a design. It concerns the process of combining distinct parts or elements to form a whole. Composition involves seeing the whole as greater than its parts, and is just as important as the individual elements that make up a design.**

Designers organise images and text – each with their own shapes, sizes, colours and textures – in many different media and in a wide range of formats: from two- and three-dimensional, black-and-white design through full-colour work to web-based and time-based (moving) imagery. A practical understanding and exploration of composition is crucial for effective visual communication: it is the most significant tool in guiding the viewer through the complexity of visuals to the intended message. To create effective design work, no matter which medium you are working in, you must understand the principles of good composition.

### → Building a composition
In this series, horizontal and vertical lines gradually translate into lines of typography to illustrate a concept. The same principles of placement and relationship apply to the placement of body text and headline, and the hierarchy should be examined carefully to ensure typography is read in the proper sequence.

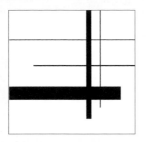

Carefully placed horizontal and vertical lines of varying weights show a gradually imposed order as they begin to form a grid.

The substitution of typography for lines, using the word 'structure', reinforces the concept and identifies the relationship between typographic point sizes and line weights.

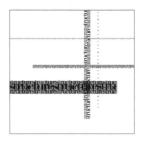

The structure of the series continues to build with layers of typographic lines working in concert to suggest heavier masses of line.

The final composition adds closely locked forms of typographic lines to create an architectural composition where each weighted area is visually supported.

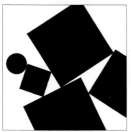
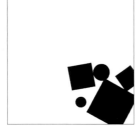

### ↑ Negative space
Placement on the page is critical. In the first composition, the shapes appear to be aggressively competing for space. When the objects are reduced in size and placed in the lower corner of the page, they appear to be racing to exit the image.

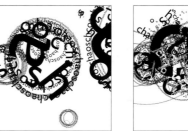

### ↑ Organised chaos
In the initial composition, the placement of the circles creates tension though asymmetry and cropped edges. As the second and third compositions develop, the same principles are in play, using texture to create mass, and repetition and variation in placement.

### ↖ Space and layers
By using type as image and transparent circular forms, this poster gives the illusion of layering. The relationship between positive and negative space, the strength of the horizontal letterforms and the variation in scale all work together to attract and direct the viewer's attention.

## Theories of composition

Throughout the history of the visual arts, different theories of composition have been advanced. Vitruvius, the Roman architect and engineer, devised a mathematical formula for the division of space within a picture. His solution, known as the golden section, golden mean or golden rectangle, was based on a set ratio between the longer and shorter sides of a rectangle. This principle profoundly affected theories in mathematics, architecture, painting, graphic design and industrial design regarding the use of spatial composition. The French painter Henri Matisse (1869–1954) put greater emphasis on inspiration, maintaining that composition is the art of arranging elements to express feelings.

Most contemporary theories have acknowledged the following elements as important considerations in composition: balance (the deliberate distribution of elements on a page); consistency or harmony (similarities in visual objects); contrast (obvious differences in visual elements); proximity (the relationships in the placement of the elements in play); repetition with variation; and white space (the deliberate open areas in a composition that give the viewer the ability to focus on everything else).

## Form and space

Positive space is a form or object that, to the eye, appears to exist. This can be a solid shape of any size, a line or simply a texture. Negative space is everything around or within an object, the 'empty' space that helps to define the borders of the positive image. It is important to learn to effectively control the relationship between positive and negative space, and to explore this in basic compositional studies, before moving on to more complex designs. In

The space around the rice-shaped white shape in the black box is repeated in the relationship of the typography in the square above it, and in the placement of the whole object on the page in the brochure.

**Expanded space** The perfect placement of a single white mark in a black square establishes the relationships for a greater extended system. Repetition with variation is demonstrated by the placement of the word treatment above the rice/box, reversing the angle of the rice by creating a triangle in the white space and enforcing the figure-ground reversal of the squares.

The packaging and display add texture in the choice of photography and in the use of the product itself.

The placement of the double box mark at the juncture of white space and image on the page echoes the packaging.

← **Layers of colour** This composition relies on colour contrasts and layering. The bright, translucent, red typography sits on top of black line drawings, allowing the shapes and illustrations to be seen through the written message. The impact of the black-and-white illustration is heightened with the addition of selective red colouring, tying the two layers of information together more intrinsically.

↑ **Make it new** Simple shapes, lines and circles suggest machines that defined an industrial society in this graphic illustration about the Modernist movement in arts and culture.

↓ **Creative composition** These three images show how the relationship of composition in photography can translate to graphic images and, in this case, to the development of a logo.

general, negative space works to support the positive 'image' in any given area (also called the picture plane). To create a more considered and effective composition, control the relationship between positive and negative elements, and recognise the effect each has on the other.

White space can create tension or contrast, or can add the welcome open space needed to reflect on complex, visually active and textural images. You can easily see the effects of open space on the overall feel of a composition by altering the ratio of positive to negative. If you place a single dot in the centre of a relatively large square of white, far from disappearing, the dot becomes more important.

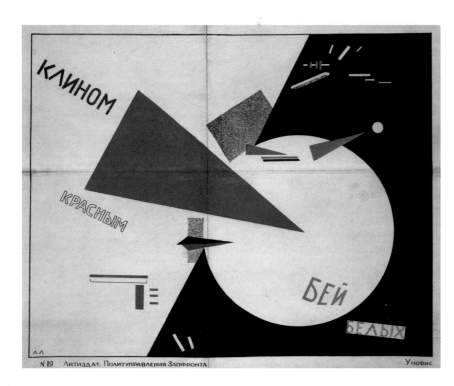

N 19  Литиздат. Политуправления Запфронта          Уновис

← **Symbolism** Dots, lines and shapes can be used as powerful symbols in the right context. Artist El Lissitzky combined geometric shapes and a bold red, white and black palette to create a strong political statement in *Beat the Whites with the Red Wedge*, 1919. The sharp red triangle of the Bolshevik army is invading and dividing the white circle in this graphic statement on the Russian Civil War.

**Balance:** The deliberate placement of objects on a page.

**Composition:** The arrangement of elements or parts of a design (text, images) on the page.

**Consistency:** The considered selection of design elements that have similar attributes.

**Contrast:** Obvious differences in elements in a composition: size, form, colour and weight.

**Element:** One small part of a composition, such as a point or line, an image, a letter or a word.

**Line:** A continuous form of connection between two points ('___').

**Negative space:** The white or coloured area around an element – for example, a margin of a page.

**Point:** A dot on a page, such as a full-stop (.).

**Positive space:** A form, image or word printed or formed on the page.

**Proximity:** The relationship of one object to another.

**Repetition:** The repeated use of select design elements within the same composition.

**Repetition with variation:** The alteration of selected aspects of a repeated element.

**White space:** The open space surrounding a positive image that defines shape and directs hierarchy.

---

This is because the expanse of white space highlights and focuses attention on the dot itself. You can also actively encourage ambiguity between picture elements and background. For example, a particular group of forms can come together to support each other and compete in such a way that the (normally negative) space is given form by the positive elements, as in figure-ground relationships (see page 36).

## Dots and lines

A dot exists as a mark, on its own, as a point in space, and it can also be the start of a line. Many points together start to set up a rhythm or pattern that, depending on uniformity, repetitiveness, scale or quantity, can suggest regularity or variation, and can express tense or relaxed sensibilities.

A line is a pathway between any two points. It can be straight, curved, thick, thin, horizontal, diagonal, jagged, solid, gestural or broken. Soft, sensuous lines imply tranquility and harmony, whereas sharp, zigzagged lines invoke discordance and tension. Two converging lines might imply a point disappearing in the distance, and can suggest the illusion of three dimensions in a two-dimensional space. Horizontal lines suggest open planes; vertical lines can suggest power and strength. Lines are elegant tools that imply motion, momentum, rhythm and upwards or downwards movement, and are primary aids in establishing visual hierarchies and closure. Simply put, closure is the ability of the human brain to observe an incomplete circle and to perceive it as complete in our imaginations.

Look at the expressive qualities of the artist Franz Kline's strong, emphatic painted line, or Cy Twombly's wandering, fragile drawn and painted lines. Examine Wolfgang Weingart's use of line in typography as a way to structure information or Russian Constructivist Alexander Rodchenko's powerful use of red and black line. El Lissitzky and Piet Zwart also used lines emphatically and expressively in their work.

⊕ **SEE ALSO:** FORM AND SPACE, P36

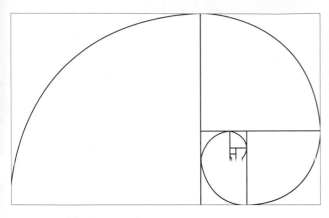

**⬆ Fibonacci spiral**
Each time a square is taken from the section, a smaller rectangle remains with the same proportions as the original. The spiral (also known as the golden ratio) can be used to create a proportional and harmonious composition.

**⬇ Tricks on the eye**
Figure-ground relationships produce different effects that confuse the eye. For example, the Rubin vase (top left) relies upon a visual confusion between figure and ground, so that the eye sees either faces or a vase.

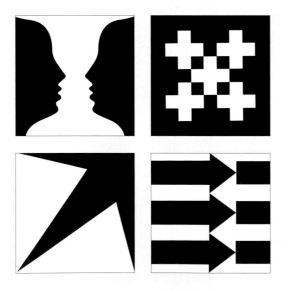

PART 1 | PRINCIPLES
CHAPTER 2 | FUNDAMENTALS OF COMPOSITION
MODULE 2 | **FORM AND SPACE**

**In learning to create meaningful compositions, it is important to understand the role of visual perception (the way our eyes and brains make sense of what we see) and its role in visual communication.**

Whether consciously or not, our eyes are constantly supplying information to our brain, which processes and makes sense of that visual input. Being able to control that process and understand how it works is crucial. Good design thinking requires an understanding of how the relationship between visual elements affects the way we perceive them, as well as an understanding of how to control and exploit them.

### Figure and ground

A form is always experienced in relation to the space it occupies and to other forms that may be present in the format. We call this the figure-ground relationship (where 'figure' refers to any object in a given space and 'ground' refers to the background, or space in which that object is seen). Another way to talk about this relationship is in terms of negative and positive space. Visual elements are always seen in relation to a visual field, background or frame. In other words, every form is seen in context and cannot be totally isolated.

Generally speaking, a form is considered to be positive and the space around it negative. The space within a format (the ground) is an important element of any design and not just something left over once a form is placed on it: it matters within the overall design, since the ground affects the form and vice versa. Usually, we tend to notice the form before we see the ground, or what is placed in a space before we see the space itself. However, a well-known example of where this relationship becomes confused is drawn from Gestalt psychology. 'Gestalt' is a German word meaning 'essence or shape of an entity's complete form'. Look at the Rubin vase (left), where the effect depends on whether we see the form as the white element, with the ground as the black, or see the black shapes as the form.

**Closure:** The ability of the human brain to observe an incomplete circle and to perceive it as complete.

**Gestalt psychology:** A theory that suggests that the mind perceives and organises holistically and finds patterns in that which appears to be unconnected.

**Ground:** The page, surface or area in which the design will be placed.

**Law of closure:** The mind creates a solid object on the page from suggestions of shapes and placement and proximity of elements.

**INTERSECTIONALITY**

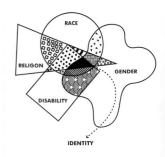

## The law of closure

Another phenomenon drawn from Gestalt psychology is the law of closure, which argues that we tend to 'close' or complete lines or objects that are not, in fact, closed. This can be a useful device in design, and is related to figure and ground, since it relies on our ability to collapse the space between foreground and background. It is also a primary tool in directing a viewer's eye through a composition in the designer's intended sequence.

## The rule of thirds

The rule of thirds says that most compositions become more dynamic when divided into thirds vertically and/or horizontally, with important elements placed within those thirds. Dividing a composition in half will halt the closure and keep the viewer's eye centred on the halfway point, especially if an object is placed at the exact centre point. The rule of thirds ensures movement on the page, and actively engages positive and negative space in the visual dialogue. The rule of thirds applies to graphic design for print, web and motion graphics and applies equally to framing for photography, film and video.

⬇ **Gestalt law of closure**
Examples of the law of closure demonstrate the ability of the brain to complete incomplete forms and, consequently, continue to move around the complete form. In page design, or any composition, it will keep the viewer's attention on the design at hand and move the eye around a page, package, poster or sign.

⬅ **Information graphics**
This example of abstract forms conveys the complex elements of intersectionality. It achieves this through an overlap of patterns to reveal different identity markers and how they intersect.

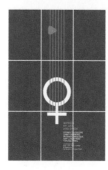

⬆ ⬅ **Thirds** Beautifully placed, simple geometrics and lines send a message of music in this dynamic example of the rule of thirds. The composition divides horizontally and vertically, with the placement of the most critical imagery right in the centre. Accent colour in the upper and lower thirds keeps the viewer moving between the two spots, lengthening the observation time.

| PART 1 | PRINCIPLES |
|---|---|
| CHAPTER 2 | FUNDAMENTALS OF COMPOSITION |
| MODULE 3 | **SYMMETRY/ASYMMETRY** |

Symmetry in design refers to a spatial relationship between elements, and specifically to a situation where the elements in a layout are centred, having equal space to the left and right or above and below them, a mirror image on either side. The second meaning of symmetry is more general, and refers to a sense of harmony, or balance, which in turn is seen to reflect beauty. Symmetry carries associations of perfection, tradition, order, and rationality and peace.

### Designing without symmetry

In asymmetrical design (without symmetry), elements are not centred, but utilise the whole format, creating dynamic compositions that play with scale, contrast, space and tension between elements. Negative space is usually less passive in asymmetrical design, and becomes easily evident as a part of the design. Asymmetry is generally associated with fewer rules and limits, and more expressive possibilities. However, each kind of composition has its place, and the important thing is to learn how to identify when it is appropriate to use one or the other. While asymmetrical design may seem less rigid, it is crucial to spend time learning how asymmetry activates elements in a given space, and to carefully control the effects you want to achieve rather than randomly placing the elements in the design.

### Choosing symmetry or asymmetry

Similar questions arise in any design you undertake. How should the space be divided? How should the subject matter occupy the space? Each decision you make on placement will affect the emotion of the design. A symmetrical composition makes for a calmer, more peaceful work, while something more dynamic can be achieved if the elements are arranged asymmetrically. Symmetry tends towards balance, and lack of movement, while asymmetry injects movement and spatial tension into a design.

⬆ **In harmony** The ancient Chinese duality symbol for 'yin' (black) and 'yang' (white) is perhaps the most famous example of perfect symmetry, each shape being a reversed mirror of the other.

⬆ **Typographic symmetry** Beautifully mirrored hand-drawn letterforms produce this symmetrical ambigram, which reveals the word 'excellence' in exactly the same way when turned upside down.

### Testing the theory

In these examples, various effects are achieved by simple variation of the position of the square within a stable frame.

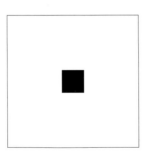

**1 Balance**
The centred square is stable or static, as the space around the square is equal on all sides.

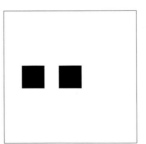

**2 Movement to the left**
When a second square is introduced, visual forces develop. There is a sense that the squares are moving left.

**3 Movement to the right**
Changing the position of the two squares suggests movement to the right.

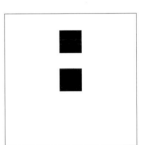

**4 Upwards movement**
The position of the two squares hints at movement upwards.

## GLOSSARY

**Asymmetry:** A composition where elements are juxtaposed and do not mirror the other forms on the page.

**Symmetry:** A composition where elements are balanced or mirrored on a page.

### ← Asymmetry

Placement of the image slightly to the right on the package is balanced nicely by the ghosted graphic on the lower left, providing balance and adding a bit of motion.

### ↙ Symmetry

Perfect symmetry is in place on the smaller packages, with a nod towards the motion associated with asymmetry addressed in the placement of spot colour in the photos.

### ↓ Different but equal

Equal weight is represented on opposite sides of this clean publication design composition. Both are aligned to the far edge of their respective sides, and the primary information on either side occupies about the same amount of space.

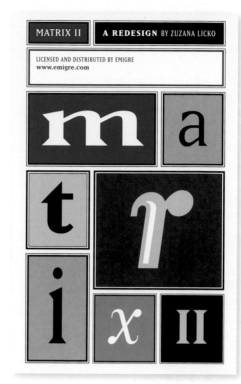

### ← Symmetry in asymmetry

Perfectly centred letterforms create symmetry within an active asymmetrical composition. The contrasts in placement and colour create visual rhythm in this dynamic composition.

### → Zang Tumb Tumb,

by F. T. Marinetti in 1919, uses creative asymmetrical typography to express the sounds of battle. In typography, 'onomatopoeia' refers to the use of type to express sounds in a literal way.

| PART | 1 | PRINCIPLES |
|---|---|---|
| CHAPTER | 2 | FUNDAMENTALS OF COMPOSITION |
| MODULE | 4 | **BASIC PRINCIPLES OF DESIGN LAYOUT** |

The term 'layout' refers to the organisation of disparate material that makes up the content of a design. Well-designed visual communications present information in a logical, coherent way, and make the important elements stand out. Basic principles of good composition are of the upmost importance in the process, and a thoughtful approach to the delivery of the material is, as always, the designer's first consideration.

The use of a grid system and consistently styled design elements helps the reader to absorb the information in a visually pleasing way, as well as enhancing the communication of the content. Good composition in layout design is dependent on the grid, and there are many configurations to choose from.

**Practical factors**

There are three basic stages in beginning any graphic design project. First, the designer receives a brief from the client, usually establishing what material should be included and the format for the project. This involves a combination of text or copy (main text, display copy [headings], boxes or sidebars, captions) and images (photographs, illustrations, maps, diagrams). The brief should also indicate the desired look or 'feel' of the work, which in turn will depend on the target audience. Should the layout look authoritative? Should it be densely packed with information? Does the message warrant a lean and structured design, with lots of white space? If the brief is vague, schedule time with your client to ask the right questions and help define the goals of the design.

Second, you will need to consider the format and budget. If there are many pictures and extensive copy for a small space, this will affect the look of the layout. Agreement should be reached on hierarchies within the copy; an editor may already have labelled their headings 'A', 'B', 'C', and so on, to indicate their relative importance. Such elements can be indicated typographically for emphasis, through differences in type size, weight, form and choice of colour. Determine how many colours will be used. Beautiful design work can be created with a limited palette or with a full range of inks and effects. The number of colours used will affect a print production budget, so find out before you begin to conceptualise a project for press. If the project is hosted online, your palette is free, but certain colours are easier to read on screen than others. For website design, see pages 144–187.

**Grids**

The third stage involves organisation. In print-based work and web design this means developing a grid system, in which various elements can be placed within a ready-made structure that underpins the entire design. The grid enables the layout of columns, margins, and areas for text and image. A well-designed grid allows for some flexibility of placement on individual pages while providing an underlying system that gives visual coherence across a series of pages. This is obviously crucial in any kind of editorial work, including books and magazines, but certainly applies to well-designed website pages, where some elements stay the same and others change.

A grid system should never restrict creativity; working within a structured format will offer many excellent opportunities to break the rules, but it's best to learn them first. If you are having issues, turn the grid off, play with the composition and, when happy, turn the grid back on and align your design to it.

**→ Divide and conquer**

Organising information on a page meaningfully is critical to the information transfer, especially when handling large amounts of text. There are many ways to divide the page and the choice should be a consideration of the type of design work, the format of the viewing platform, and the amount of information to be presented on each page or sub-division.

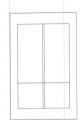

Individual units of equal size, separated by equal margins top and bottom, form a system perfect for compositions with many images. The units can be combined in any number for larger images or columns of text.

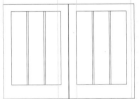

Three-column grids work well for mid-range amounts of text. The designer can use any given column in any system for added white space and can divide the page asymmetrically with text and image in this three-column system.

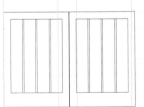

A four-column system begins to add more flexibility for variation in placement. The symmetrical division will add order, if desired, and added control in the overall system. A larger margin at the bottom of the page is particularly important in book and publication design as it makes the text more accessible/easier to read.

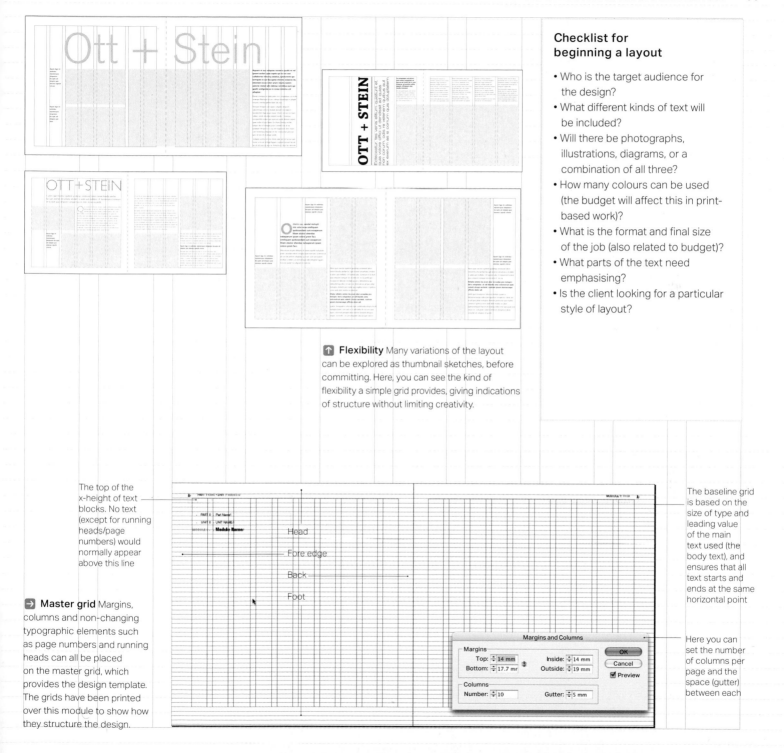

## Checklist for beginning a layout

- Who is the target audience for the design?
- What different kinds of text will be included?
- Will there be photographs, illustrations, diagrams, or a combination of all three?
- How many colours can be used (the budget will affect this in print-based work)?
- What is the format and final size of the job (also related to budget)?
- What parts of the text need emphasising?
- Is the client looking for a particular style of layout?

**↑ Flexibility** Many variations of the layout can be explored as thumbnail sketches, before committing. Here, you can see the kind of flexibility a simple grid provides, giving indications of structure without limiting creativity.

The top of the x-height of text blocks. No text (except for running heads/page numbers) would normally appear above this line

**→ Master grid** Margins, columns and non-changing typographic elements such as page numbers and running heads can all be placed on the master grid, which provides the design template. The grids have been printed over this module to show how they structure the design.

The baseline grid is based on the size of type and leading value of the main text used (the body text), and ensures that all text starts and ends at the same horizontal point

Here you can set the number of columns per page and the space (gutter) between each

Head

Fore edge

Back

Foot

**Margins and Columns**

Margins
Top: 14 mm     Inside: 14 mm
Bottom: 17.7 mr     Outside: 19 mm

Columns
Number: 10     Gutter: 5 mm

OK
Cancel
☑ Preview

## Margins, grids and structure

For any form of publication design you should begin by formatting a double-page spread that can then be applied to the entire publication. This is important because you need to see how the verso (left-hand page) relates to the recto (right-hand page) and judge how well they balance. Established practice in book design suggests that the back (inner margin) should be half the fore edge (outside margin), and the foot (bottom margin) greater than the head (top margin). These rules should ensure a balance, with the type area sitting comfortably in the format. Remember that the eye will need to move from one page to another, so the gap, or gutter (the two back edges combined), should not be too large.

When establishing page margins, consider the material, the client and the reader. For example, paperbacks tend to have tight margins to keep page numbers – and therefore costs – down, whereas heavily illustrated publications have generous margins and use white space effectively. Economic considerations play a part: brochures and promotional materials tend to have bigger budgets, so even more white space is possible.

The grid shows the layout of columns, margins and areas for main text, captions and images; it also shows the position of repeating heads (running heads) and page numbers. These elements normally stay the same over a series of pages.

**⬆ Modular variation**
This tight, four-column modular grid system shows the expressive freedom that comes with control. Grid systems should not limit a designer, but provide a structure to experiment with a range of shapes and sizes, images and text. This example shows spreads from the same publication that visually belong together but are playful in their pacing and structure.

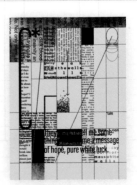

**⬅ A design tool**
The grid should be treated as a design tool in the sense that it is there to provide structure, and if you know the rules you can exaggerate or break them for aesthetic and conceptual purposes. These three examples all use grid systems for different effects, and therefore communicate very different messages.

After drawing your double-page spread, you can prepare some layout roughs: these can be small thumbnails or half-sized visuals in which your first ideas are sketched out. This preliminary thinking time is key in the page-design process; it's where you make important decisions about the composition of pages and the organisation of material. Preliminary sketches can then be transferred to the computer and several variations quickly produced, based on the main grid. It takes less time to sketch ideas than to create designs directly on screen. Remember, the computer is simply a tool; it cannot think for you, nor can it generate ideas. With initial sketches, the imaginative designer can fully explore ideas and options before moving to the production phase.

## Using a grid

The grid divides the available type area into proportioned units, providing an overall visual structure and helping to unite all visual elements. The most basic grid structure – used primarily for text-based material such as business reports or novels – is that of a single column. The width should relate to legibility, 8 to 10 words or 60 to 72 characters per line is usually considered optimum.

With complex layouts, in which text, images, diagrams and captions must be integrated, a more sophisticated horizontal and vertical grid is needed. Grid systems comprising between three and six columns enable you to use all kinds of elements. The more units used, the more flexibility you have to accommodate smaller pieces of copy such as captions, longer measures such as section openers, and displayed material. Never simply follow your computer's default settings for columns, but decide on your own.

Ideally, a grid should have some vertical controls, both for structure down the page and for order to the overall design. Give headings, subheadings, captions and page numbers set positions for continuity. Finally, be flexible. After two or three spreads the grid may seem too rigid, so adjust it. Grids should not be restrictive, but provide structure while giving rich compositional variations to spreads.

⬆ **Form and function**
Consider the format style and the user experience when you select a grid system. In this example, the use of accordion folds and French-folded pages means the content information can be neatly divided into components that aid navigation.

⊕ **SEE ALSO:** AUDIENCES, MARKETS AND CONCEPTS, P24

STYLES OF LAYOUT, P44

PACE AND CONTRAST, P46

SIZE AND FORMAT, P50

TYPOGRAPHIC EMPHASIS AND HIERARCHY, P78

| PART 1 | PRINCIPLES |
|---|---|
| CHAPTER 2 | FUNDAMENTALS OF COMPOSITION |
| MODULE 5 | **STYLES OF LAYOUT** |

In simple terms, page design, or layout, can be divided into two basic styles: symmetrical and asymmetrical. In broad terms, symmetrical style is a traditional approach in which design is structured around a central axis. This type of layout has its origins in the earliest printed books, which, in turn, borrowed their layout from handwritten manuscripts of the medieval era. Asymmetrical style is non-centred, dynamic and associated with 20th-century modernism and contemporary design.

⬆ **Asymmetrical page design** Asymmetrical page design is a great way to introduce variety across spreads. The overlap of images across the centrefold, or the use of text and image at different levels of hierarchy, keeps the reader engaged.

### Symmetrical style

Traditionally, symmetrical layouts are most commonly seen on title pages of books, where each line of type is centred above the others. Part of the tradition is also the use of serif typefaces, often set in letter-spaced capitals with, perhaps, the addition of an ornament or printer's flower.

Decorative borders and the addition of decorative elements became more popular in the 15th and 16th centuries, but until the 1920s most publications were designed with symmetrical formats. Achieving a composition that looks balanced within a symmetrical design is not as easy as it sounds. Type size must be carefully judged, and spacing between each line considered, since certain information belongs in the same typographic unit and should be grouped accordingly. Fine-tuning horizontal line space is critical. These judgments must be made while maintaining balance and beautiful composition. For some superb examples of symmetrical typography, see the work of Aldus Manutius, the Dolphin Press, and the Venetian printers from the late 15th century.

### The asymmetrical revolution

Asymmetrical layouts can be traced back to the 1920s and 1930s, in particular to the German school, the Bauhaus. Artists such as Kurt Schwitters and Theo van Doesburg experimented with layouts based on an off-centred axis, creating tension and dynamism. In this style, type is primarily ragged left; ragged-right setting is kept to a few lines, as Western cultures read left to right. Other predominant designers to note are Armin Hofmann, Herbert Bayer, Wim Crouwel and the work of Josef Müller-Brockmann.

The modernist movement also rejected ornament, and sans-serif typefaces, with their clean lines and modernity, were the popular faces of the school. The work of the Bauhaus and their stylistic descendents, such as the Swiss typographers of the 1950s and 1960s, favours sans-serif faces and often completely lowercase headlines. Rules, in a number of weights, are used as distinctive features in colour and in black and white, adding dynamic movement to the compositions.

⬅ **Balance** The symmetrical design system of these pages allows large display typography in different styles, both sans serif and serif, to divide the pages and play a central part as design elements in the compositions.

Another amazing typographer, whose work over a long career shows both styles well, is Jan Tschichold. Early on he was heavily influenced by the modernist philosophy of the Bauhaus, and is considered a pioneer of the asymmetric revolution. He later changed direction, rejecting the hardline approach advocated in his book *Asymmetric Typography.* Tschichold returned to the frequent use of centred, serif typography, but continued working in both styles.

## Integrating styles

Contemporary designers often integrate both theories of spatial arrangement and select the style to suit the project. Contemporary typographers, like Philippe Apeloig, also use both in their search for visual solutions. As a designer you need to understand both styles, and their historical precedents and contexts, so that your selections and design decisions are based on knowledge rather than guesswork. Read as much about graphic design history as you can, and follow the philosophy of Jan Tschichold: use both styles, but understand that mixing them needs to be undertaken with caution. Research and experimentation will be your best guides. Keep your options open, and be flexible and fearless in reaching appropriate solutions.

⊞ **SEE ALSO:** SYMMETRY/ ASYMMETRY, P38

BASIC PRINCIPLES OF DESIGN LAYOUT, P40

SIZE AND FORMAT, P50

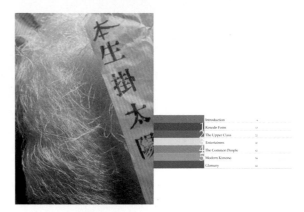

⬇ **Classically centred**
The *Hypnerotomachia Poliphili*, printed by Aldus Manutius's Dolphin Press, Venice, in 1499, is an example of the highest art of Renaissance printing. Its symmetrical typography harmonises with the wood-engraved illustrations.

⬆ **Combining styles**
Inserts, short pages and fold-outs create symmetrical and asymmetrical page designs and work in concert to evidence the decorative nature of pattern design in this book on the history of kimonos. The unusual combination is influenced by asymmetry in traditional Japanese art.

| PART 1 | PRINCIPLES |
|---|---|
| CHAPTER 2 | FUNDAMENTALS OF COMPOSITION |
| MODULE 6 | **PACE AND CONTRAST** |

Pace and contrast are vital qualities for catching and maintaining a reader's interest in graphic design: they provide variety and set the rhythm and the mood. This is particularly evident in magazines and image-heavy books, where it is critical to be able to direct the eye to different pieces of information in a particular sequence. Think in cinematic terms: the audience should be given different experiences, have different reactions, and enjoy the complete experience from beginning to end. The digital age has created a world of multi-tasking citizens, and holding their attention over time can be a challenge.

In continuous text, the reader takes more time to cover information and is primed to read every word. In a highly integrated design – with panels, pictures, captions, quotes, and so on – there is more competition for the reader's attention. An article may be skimmed over, some pages will be scanned for pictures or the reader might be seeking only a specific piece of information.

The pace of a publication will be dictated by the content and space available. Contrast is closely linked to pace and is an excellent tool for controlling the pace of an extended design system. You can create visual emphasis with large type and imagery, unusual cropping, sidebar information

**← Controlling the pace**
The same principles of design apply to any platform, whether it is web, print, motion or environmental. The website shown here maintains common elements in the positioning and hierarchy of typographic and photographic information, while varying the pace of the content with vivid colour combinations and imagery. The viewer has more options to zoom in and link to new pages online than in print, so these visuals should be planned out as a fully extended system.

**↓ ↘ Keep it varied** The publication *Works that Work* is comprised of a series of striking spreads. The strong full-bleed photography coupled with cropped and part-bleed imagery means that at the turn of each page the reader cannot predict the pace, and is therefore more engaged. This is also true of the typographic handling. While keeping to text systems, hierarchies and grids, these spreads provide a beautiful balance of consistency and variety.

graphics and full bleeds of image or colour. Alternatively, you can create a quiet interval by having text-only spreads and open areas of white space.

## Planning for pace

In order to achieve good pacing, with contrast and visual rhythm over a succession of pages, an overall plan is needed. Too much visual complexity can be counterproductive, but a succession of similar-looking spreads will become boring and you may lose your audience. One technique is to construct a flatplan showing the total number of pages in the publication. The flatplan can be drawn small (thumbnail size) in double-page spreads. It should contain page numbers, titles and content. A quick survey of this plan gives you a broad overview of how your material will unfold (see page 29).

When you begin your design process, don't become too dependent on the images you create on screen. If the final result is meant to be in print, print your document often during the process and view your pages at the actual size of the finished product. Type sizes and weights, image quality and scale, and the rhythm, pacing and transition from one spread to the next should be evaluated in the same format as the end user would see it. Check your pacing throughout the process and be flexible enough to initiate change where it is needed.

## Creating momentum and rhythm

At the beginning of an article, or section of a book, create momentum and rhythm and set the mood for a receptive reader using all the composition skills you have learned. You can use pictures as a frieze, in a narrow sequence of images running along the top of the spreads that moves the reader across the pages. You can create various mosaic arrangements on the grid, using one large picture and a series of smaller ones. You can break out of the grid at strategic points. Depending on picture content, you can create vertical movement with narrow vertical images. Conversely, with landscape-format pictures you can create a strong sense of horizontal movement.

You can control the pace by juxtaposing black-and-white images with bright spots of colour, or black-and-white with duotones, tritones and speciality inks. Variation between narrow and wide text measures will add pace to your pages, and using your grid system creatively is essential. Strong background colours or reversed-out type at specific points can also create a sense of movement to change the speed and vary the rhythm. Be deliberate in your decisions and interpret your subject matter thoughtfully. Keep it quiet if the material calls for introspection, or pick up the pace and build excitement if appropriate.

**➡ Pace and impact** The designer of the *Unforgettable* publication has treated each spread as a composition. A great deal of consideration needs to go into the visual impact after each turn of a page, as well as the overall flow through the publication. By varying the layout and the size and position of the images, while keeping to a structured grid system, the designer has provided enough variety to keep the pages interesting. Pace is varied through a contrast in scale, the use of white space, large bleed photography, bold display type and supporting text.

**➕ SEE ALSO:** BASIC PRINCIPLES OF DESIGN LAYOUT, P40

## Printed publications

In publication design, pace and contrast are fundamental. There are more types of magazines – print or electronic – than any other category of design. They range from high-brow, political, economic or philosophical journals to sporting, arts, satirical, and leisure and lifestyle titles. Each publication will require different solutions to the pacing, depending on content and readership. Magazine readers differ from book readers because they view the product in unpredictable ways and in differing environments. Some will be led by the cover images to the contents page, where they will select their articles in an ordered way; others will dip in and out of any part of the magazine; while others will always read certain sections in a peculiarly personal order. Magazine readers may view the publication at home, in a relaxed environment with no distractions, or they may pick up an issue in a waiting room or a public place. Engaged, entertained readers become loyal subscribers, so the visual should work with the content to transport the reader, like any good book. For a design to be memorable, visual interest should be present on every page and the editorial

**↑ Flexibility**
The layout of the Gloria Cortina Mexico brochure portrays the flexibility in composition available in one publication design. Through a series of dynamic spreads and interesting and unusual image placement and treatment, this flexibility adds rhythm and motion to the book and sophistication to each image.

personality of the magazine should be evident at every turn. Designers use every tool, including pagination and wayfinding marks, to reinforce the style and mood of a publication. A true master of magazine layout is the American designer Alexey Brodovich, who worked primarily in the 1940s and 1950s. Bradbury Thompson also understood the importance of pace and contrast.

In illustrated books, change of pace is also required. Generally, readers behave in a relatively logical way, moving through the publication from start to finish. They, too, will dive in and out, but not to the same extent as magazine readers. In book design, economic factors also play a part. If plenty of pages are available, then you can introduce section openers and use lots of white space to create drama with headings and placement. Each book design should have a strong visual identity. If the spreads are too diverse, it can have a hazardous effect on the book and become confusing to the reader.

**← Breaking the rules**
This alternative London guide takes inspiration from fanzines, where the traditional rules of graphic design are broken in return for a fast, rough and dramatic aesthetic. It is important that you understand the rules of layout and pace before deciding to break them.

### Digital publications

Digital magazines require different strategies; type and images interact much more immediately on screen. Imagery is much easier to manipulate and adapt to a variety of purposes and device formats. Some of the principles of print-based work may not apply directly to screen-based designs: one obvious difference is that, instead of turning pages, viewers scroll up and down for consecutive views of 'spreads'. Instead of using weight, style or position for emphasis, type might move or a static image may click through to a video presentation. Page structure and the placement of graphic elements must reflect the function of the site.

A new aesthetic continues to develop hand in hand with digital technology that ties form and function. Ultimately, though, basic issues of pace and contrast for print still apply, in part, for screen. The designer must still navigate the viewer through the maze of available information and present the appropriate markers for wayfinding. Due to the versatility and a different set of economic factors when designing digitally, it is important to challenge what can be done with digital publication design beyond what can be done in print. For example, most online newspapers are designed to the same space-saving specification and use flat information, which is rarely interactive, because their printed counterparts are used as templates. Digital publications offer a great opportunity to push what digital design could (and should) be.

Learning the basics of layout design from the model of print design is a stepping stone to the development of new ways of working in digital environments. The rules of good design should always be considered, regardless of format or media, and the designer should be able to apply them appropriately.

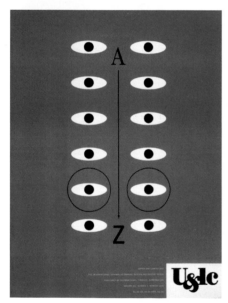

↑ **Sophisticated wit** With humour and a touch of surrealism, Carin Goldberg's beautiful, iconic magazine covers for the *New York Times* and the typography magazine *U&lc* reflect contemporary culture through the designer's playful eye.

→ **Complex systems** *Selvedge* is a printed and digital magazine that promotes textiles and textile makers from around the world. Both its online and offline platforms have complex systems that highlight multiple pieces of information and visuals. Well-designed digital publications should have all the excitement and visual narrative of the printed page. In *Selvedge* the visuals take centre stage. The bold colours and vivid detailing present expert editorial art direction at every swipe, scroll or zoom.

| PART 1 | PRINCIPLES |
|---|---|
| CHAPTER 2 | FUNDAMENTALS OF COMPOSITION |
| MODULE 7 | **SIZE AND FORMAT** |

**⬆ Purposeful shapes**
The inspiration for this project was an old-fashioned ice-cream van, and the die-cut cover conceals a traditionally shaped booklet inside.

Size and format are important considerations in any piece of design. They are affected by budget, practical restraints, the format in which they are to be produced, and by the needs of the job. The experience the end user has while interacting with the materials will affect the type of response the material evokes. Print is an intimate medium that's meant to be viewed close to the body. The tactile qualities of printed media are evidenced by weight, surface texture, binding, gloss, matt or metallic inks, foil stamps and die-cut surfaces, all of which play a part in the personality of the product. Digital, on the other hand, is evidenced by user experience and depth of interactive engagement.

### Primary considerations

In deciding on format, the designer is often limited by external factors. Certain elements of a corporate identity package, such as letterheads, envelopes, forms and websites, are usually a standard size; other factors, however, may also have to be considered. Cost issues loom large: can the size selected for printing be cut economically from a bigger sheet of paper or will there be unnecessary expensive waste? Carefully evaluate the sheet size with the number of copies required. Will the finished work have to be mailed out? If so, weigh a mock-up to estimate postage costs: a larger format may prove to be too expensive to send by post if you are printing thousands of impressions. Can the job be folded economically in relation to the grain of the paper? Work with your printer to find the most economical and environmentally sound solution, and determine your size and scale before starting the design process.

### Content determines format

In book design, print or digital, format should be determined by purpose or nature, with the user in mind. Text-only books pose fewer problems than books with a heavy concentration of photographic or illustrative subjects. For continuous reading, a good point size in a readable, attractive font with adequate margins in play can help to determine the format as either portrait or landscape, and in paperbacks, which need to be both cheap and portable, point size is typically small. In illustrated books, the images should resonate the mood of the subject and a larger

**⬆ Book art** Unusual formats can transform a simple design into conceptual art. An alternative binding, as well as unusual printing techniques or paper stocks, can be used to enhance the tactile user experience and reinforce the content in subtle ways.

| 09.00/ | 10.00/ | 10.45/ | 11.00/ | 11.30/ | 12.45/ | 13.15/ | 15.45/ | 16.30/ | 17.30/ |

**⬅ Dramatic landscapes**
The horizon line in the two-page bleed photographic image determined the typographic sight line on the preceding page, and adds drama to the page design.

↑ **Nostalgic** This clever accordion fold was produced to celebrate and commemorate a community arts project run by artist Mark Storor in the seaside town of Jaywick. The concept design and format mimicked a vintage-style folded postcard.

format book is appropriate – but check your size in a mock-up version before you begin, to ensure the book won't become unwieldy. Illustrations and photographs do not necessarily lose information value if they are smaller than first anticipated, and there are benefits in making a product easier for the reader to handle. The largest formats are generally reserved for art and design subjects and museum catalogues, in which excellent-quality illustrations are central to the book's success. Digital publications are less of a concern as a user can zoom and navigate information slightly differently.

Whenever possible, content should determine format. Think about your subject matter and examine all available materials for inclusion before you determine the final format. If there are beautiful panoramic landscape views to be featured in the book, a horizontal or full-screen format may be your obvious choice.

Experiment in your initial layout sketches and determine the best way to showcase your materials to the greatest effect. If the subject matter calls for white space to be part of the design, be sure to anticipate the additional dimensions for your margins and gutters. Multilingual publications pose their own set of problems. It is probably best to try to accommodate two or three languages side by side to achieve a consistent flow of text and, if illustrated, to ensure that text references are on the same page or screen as pictures.

Although international standardisation in paper sizes helps keep prices down, the same old formats can become boring. There are some inventive solutions, but be sure they fit the design concept of the publication.

## Folds and binding

With smaller publications and brochures, folds can play a big part in enticing the reader into the subject matter. The aesthetically pleasing square format is simply achieved by folding the sheet in a different way. Organising copy to follow folds – whether rolling folds or concertina folds – creates a sense of fun and is an excellent way to entice the reader into the publication.

Simple binding ideas can also enhance the appeal of smaller publications and can be used inventively to add to the wayfinding of the content. You might consider trimming each spread a little shorter than the preceding one, giving the area at the end of the page a space for information graphics or subheads. An untrimmed fore edge makes for an attractively handcrafted feel, as does visible coloured thread for the stitching. These ideas are easy to implement; they don't necessarily cost a lot and can make your designs different and memorable. Be sure to consider all aspects of the project as part of your design process from the very beginning: changing one or two elements will affect your other decisions as well, and may cause you to back up the process and redesign certain elements. Part of the fun of design work is in the discovery of inventive solutions, new materials, new mediums and new combinations of tried-and-tested techniques.

Take the time to consider the importance of your choices and remember that if you can see something, your client can, too. Every aspect of the project should be evaluated with a designer's eye, right down to the smallest detail.

## GLOSSARY

**Concertina folds:** Folds in alternate directions.

**French folds:** Sheets of paper are folded in half, so that they are double thickness. The two folds are at right angles to each other and then bound on the edge.

**Gatefold:** A way of folding paper so that the outer quarters of a page are folded to meet in the centre. The result works like symmetrical doors that open onto an inner page.

**Paper grain:** The direction of wood fibres that make up a piece of paper.

**Perfect binding:** Method similar to paperback binding, where loose sheets are encased in a heavier paper cover, then glued to the book spine. Edges are trimmed to be flush with each other.

**Rollover folds:** A way of folding a page so that successive folds turn in on themselves and the page is folded into a roll.

**Saddle stitching:** Binding method where sheets of paper are folded in the centre, stitched together along the fold, then glued into the cover spine.

⊕ **SEE ALSO:** BASIC PRINCIPLES OF DESIGN LAYOUT, P40

STYLES OF LAYOUT, P44

PHOTOGRAPHY AND ILLUSTRATION, P56

Few things are designed to work as stand-alone pieces. Look at a successful branding: the logos and corporate identity, advertising campaigns, direct-mail campaigns, annual reports, websites and social-media presence all have common design elements, binding them together and identifying them as part of the same brand. Look at the total content of any magazine or newspaper: the information changes, yet the publication looks consistent, issue after issue, and at a glance, we can easily and immediately identify our favourites on the shelf.

This brand identity is achieved through a co-ordinated design and effective design strategy that is fluid enough to allow for variation and change, but is consistent throughout. With newspapers and magazines, this can be achieved with strict rules. For example, major headlines will be set in one font and ranged left; secondary headlines in another font and centred; body text in yet another font with fixed point size, leading and justification; feature articles in a bolder font with looser leading and alternate justification. These rules are never broken, but they should be comprehensive enough to allow for any situation while maintaining a consistent 'look'.

Authors may write more than one book, and publishers almost always use co-ordinated designs for their book covers. If a publisher is repackaging the back catalogue of a bestselling author, they will use a co-ordinated strategy for the covers that allows for changes of colour, image and titling, but enables book buyers to identify the titles as part of a set, or brand. Perhaps the unchanging element is the type, set in the same face, at the same size and in the same position throughout. Or it could be the style of the photograph used – black and white, full colour, abstract – or the illustration: pen and ink, painting, digital, collage. A good designer ties together all of the

◄ ◣ **Design cohesion** The cohesion of colour, typography and styles across the range of packaging materials for Bakerie expresses an obvious brand unity. This unity helps the customer to trust the company, perceiving it as a well-managed and organised food retailer.

◣ **Web cohesion** Design cohesion needs to extend to all digital platforms and not just be confined to packaging. On this mobile site, high-quality images have been used as a substitute for the actual product (the loaves), thereby successfully maintaining the colour palette and brand.

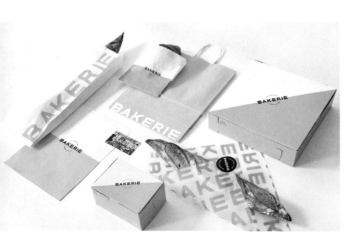

elements, creating a formula that not only makes each individual piece striking in its own right, but also ensures easy identification with its counterparts.

## Creating identifying characteristics

Well thought-out extended systems are the building blocks for all complex design projects. Corporate identity systems will partner clean, easy-to-decode logo designs with supportive graphics or photography that become an extension of the brand and can be used interchangeably on multiple applications. Most will also include a distinct colour palette and a particular typographic sensibility that support the content without diluting the brand's original message. These design assets keep the brand fresh and exciting, and enhance the presence of a product, something that motivates all manufacturers and organisations competing for attention in the marketplace, whether the product is books, chocolate, a gallery or an online music

service. The next time you go shopping, or attend a cultural event, look for this principle and you will notice that many of the products with the most eye-catching and co-ordinated identity schemes are those of the most successful businesses and organisations. This is not a coincidence, and designers who can successfully co-ordinate a brand or a company will always find their services in demand.

## Know the content

Getting to know your brand and your target audience is part of your preliminary research. To speak to your audience accurately, you must also understand the content. In package design the product is usually easy to recognise, sometimes visible through the packaging material, and positioned for attention in the marketplace. The architecture of the package and the details in the design system work together to create an image-aware brand that proclaims itself as expensive, healthy, fashionable or traditional

↖ ↓ **Understated elegance** Simple shapes and large fields of colour define these elegant design systems by Carin Goldberg. The boxed set of books for New York's School of Visual Arts uses the rectangular form of the books and carefully placed dots to mark volumes one through four in the series, and extends the system of colour blocks and simplified and gestural shapes to the inside page designs. The system for the works of Kurt Vonnegut uses bars of colour that are reflected in the collective spines of the books.

by the very nature of the design system the artist creates and the materials used in the packaging. It should also lead consumers through the functions of opening, dispensing and reclosing without making them work too hard to get to the product. In complex packaging, there may be enclosures, hang-tags and labels to design. The extended design system can enhance the product but should always remain true to the brand. In addition to housing and protecting the product, package design is advertising at the place where the consumer actually makes their purchase, sometimes in large displays that become part of the retail experience. To be really successful, it must communicate the correct message at a glance if singular, or work together in big displays of multiples, if it is to compete with other goods.

## Interpretation and detail

In editorial design, the content must be carefully considered for its message and the author's point of view. A book jacket is, in effect, a piece of packaging that advertises both product and publisher. It should be approached in the same way as an advertising campaign, but the imagery can sometimes deliver its message in a more thought-provoking, poetic way. Any book must compete with all the

**↙ Cohesion and variety**
The clever use of smartphone dimensions within the advertising for the Shine app puts focus on the purpose of this platform. The bright, yet changing, colour scheme shows cohesion but also variety, making this seemingly simple design concept quite complex.

**↓ Form and colour** The use of a simple colour scheme ties together all the elements of the WayUp platform. The identity has been used subtly to anchor the online platform, but also as an aesthetic element on the tote bag, created by enlarging and cropping the smaller details that make this brand what it is.

⬇️ ➡️ **Spine-out** The book's front cover should indicate the contents as well as grab the attention, drawing in potential readers or buyers. With this in mind, consider the role of the book's spine: what information would your audience need about the publication if they could see only its spine on a bookcase?

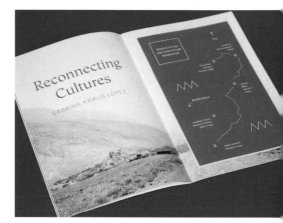

others on display, leaping out from the shelf before informing potential buyers as to what the book might be about. In some book displays only the spines will be visible, so how these detailed areas work as small-space designs is important. The same principle of multiples in package display is in effect here, but on a much more economical scale. A series of covers with spines in bold black text on acid colours will create an impressive patch when a dozen or so are stacked along a shelf. The spine should be part of the overall cover image and work as a stand-alone design element when seen in multiples.

Book jackets begin telling the story to the consumer. A concept for a book-jacket design will be influenced by a number of factors, but the concept development should begin by considering the content. Consider whether the book is fiction or non-fiction; consider the genre the book belongs to; the subject matter – is it fun, grave, romantic or scary; and, most importantly, who the book is targeting for readership. When designing book jackets, good designers make it their business to ask the publisher lots of questions – and to read the book! After all, your jacket design should inspire people to buy the book. Think about how your design might stand out enough to entice curiosity, or be provocative enough to convey information in an intriguing way, and try to create visuals that represent your author and the subject matter of the book.

↖️ ⬆️ **Design details**
There are a number of clever ways that the cover design or the format of your publication can hint at its purpose and contents. For example, the small publication *Common Thread* is bound together using looped staples, which are usually used for hanging publications in an exhibition context. In addition, the front cover is slightly smaller in width, giving you a glimpse of the physical publication inserts and the themes and contents inside.

**⬅ ⬇ Lightly whimsical** Choosing the right visual style to tell your story can be difficult. Sometimes a single technique is inadequate to communicate the nuances, so custom combinations are invented. Delicate line art evokes the look of old etchings, but combines offbeat images in unusual pairings and colours to make a contemporary statement on these lighthearted wine labels.

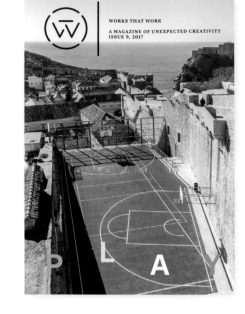

| PART 1 | PRINCIPLES |
|---|---|
| CHAPTER 2 | FUNDAMENTALS OF COMPOSITION |
| MODULE 9 | **PHOTOGRAPHY AND ILLUSTRATION** |

**Whether to use photographs, illustrations or even type as images – or all three together – are important design considerations. A look that is well co-ordinated is a hallmark of good design, and the way you plan, edit and incorporate images significantly affects the outcome.**

**⬆ Type with image** The combination of playful type and photography on this magazine cover evokes a sense of fun. The header and identity remain consistent, allowing for a more imaginative approach to the visuals underneath. The striking photography contains natural, muted colours, allowing the bright colour schemes of the letterforms to stand out.

Boundaries between photography and illustration are blurred by digital art; a straightforward choice between a realistic photograph and an illustrator's interpretation is still possible, and digital techniques allow for a merging of the two. Within the three categories are both relatively direct and obscure approaches, so you need to think about how you want your message to be understood and interpreted.

Much will depend on the category in which you are working. Advertising can be obvious or subtle, but it can also be crucial to show the brand your client is endeavouring to sell. Food packaging or car ads often feature beautifully photographed and highly realistic images showing the product in a flattering situation. If you are working on corporate design, the company's ethos is as important as its products or services. In this circumstance, a more abstract or evocative set of images could work. In magazines and books, the look of the images will have been considered at the initial styling stage, when all the questions about the target audience will have been discussed. A mix of diverse styles – illustrations and photographs – can be used to differentiate between various editorial sections while maintaining the defining image of the publication.

**Creative constraints**

Some clients will have definite ideas about the types of images selected to represent them. They might send you the pictures they want you to use along with the initial brief, so sometimes the decision has already been made for you. Photography might not always be possible for logistical reasons – distance, budget or difficulty in gaining permission – in which case creating or commissioning an illustration is the only route.

Technical manuals, company reports, educational books, or anything that aims to explain how things work, benefit

**➡ Layering and contrast** The pastel tones used in this dog photoshoot create a soft set of visuals that have been offset by the layering of typography in a dark and contrasting colour. This allows an interesting composition to be created while still keeping the poster legible.

from visualisation. This might be a specialised form of technical illustration, in which designer, illustrator and author/originator must liaise closely. Information graphics, charts and data representation can be beautiful, inventive and entertaining. Try to turn every constraint into a creative opportunity. Limitations set you free from certain decisions so you can concentrate more fully on others.

## Budget and schedule

Commissioning an intricate illustration, such as a big design of a busy street scene, might not be appropriate if you do not have a large budget, in which case it might be more cost-effective to work with photography or photomontage. Conversely, asking a photographer to set up a full-day shoot involving several models, a make-up artist, a stylist, as well as complicated sets and props, may be outside your project budget, in which case it might be more cost-effective to commission an illustration.

Occasionally you may have to produce something for which there is an impossibly small budget. Don't let this stop your creative energy or curb your enthusiasm for the project – there are always creative possibilities. Contemporary designers should be able to generate imagery, even if there's no budget for a specialist. Inventive, evocative typography can function as illustration, and copyright-free pictures can always be found if you know where to look. Creating a fresh approach using stock images is an exercise in reinvention. Use your newly developed ability to see things differently, and transform the ordinary into something fresh and inventive. Try duotones, tritones or spots of brilliant colour on neutral fields. Think about layers of texture or open space, and fresh typography to pull it all together.

## Photographers, illustrators and libraries

You may be working on a self-initiated project or to a brief; either way, the illustrative approach may be immediately clear, or you may have to work harder to decide on the right style of image. First, ask yourself what would be suitable for the market and the message you are trying to communicate, then consider the scope of your budget and your time frame as you research your potential sources.

Begin this phase as you begin all others, with research. You may need to create images yourself, or commission a freelance illustrator or photographer. There are many ways of looking at people's work beyond flipping through a portfolio. For example, you can see work on the Internet, social-media outlets (Flickr, Instagram, Facebook, Pinterest, etc.), at exhibitions, graduate degree shows and agencies, and in other graphic works and design publications. Professional associations have active websites where members often post work and you can view those that win awards for excellence.

⬇ **Photography and illustration**
Combining photography and illustration can sometimes feel overcrowded. In this example, Winkbeds has created a set of minimal photographs with a limited colour scheme, supported by delicate product illustrations. By stripping back both types of imagery and leaving some white space, the spreads and applications are allowed breathing space, and are therefore easy to understand and follow.

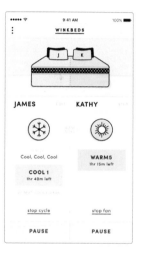

There are also several online photographic resources that represent photographers and illustrators: type 'picture library' or 'illustration agency' into a search engine and you will find plenty. Generally, such companies allow you to use a low-resolution version for rough concepts, either for free or for a small fee. Then, when you have finalised your idea, you can buy the rights to use that picture. Always check what the final fee will be before committing yourself. These sources also now supply downloads, scans or CDs of royalty-free images (you can use them without paying further fees) – so if you intend to cover a certain subject or style repeatedly, it might make sense to buy one of these. Another source is archival, copyright-free images, which can be useful in a number of ways.

## Collect and store

The best way to ensure you have imagery to hand as you need it is to keep an image bank of your own. Most designers keep files of photographers' and illustrators' work. Sometimes you'll receive promotional work that has been sent in speculatively. If you like it, or think it might prove useful in the future, file it away carefully for potential future use. If you have a need for speciality photography, perhaps architectural interiors, food styling or fashion photography, look for experts with strength in that area.

**Image making** You will often find, or be given, suitable images for your concept that aesthetically do not work, or are too low resolution to use. In these instances you can use experimental design methods to make your images work. This is a great example of how, through a simple, reduced colour scheme, multiple visual languages can become one unified design.

**SEE ALSO:** THEORIES OF IMAGE AND TEXT, P20

**Diagrams and illustrations** Diagrams and illustrations should be presented clearly so they can be read, viewed and understood. In this example, the collection of diagrams and illustrations is placed and framed individually, yet come together to form a cohesive set when bound together.

← **Type as image**
Typography is a system of simple shapes that can be used to make complex patterns when they are combined in a dynamic composition. These fluid and playful vector letterforms create an innovative and visual language for Queer Vision.

→ **Context** It's important to capture your work in context. In this example, we are not seeing the digital poster file, but a series of produced outcomes in the context in which they are intended. This highlights the material quality of the work, as well as an element of reality – as opposed to a mock-up or overly controlled representation of the work.

## Tips and checklist for selecting images

- **Image, style and theme** Determine the look before you commit. It's fine to be inspired by images you see in your research, but be sure to resolve the concept before you make a purchase or hire a freelancer.
- **Be contrary** Consider the opposite of what is expected: this will either give you a new angle or help to consolidate your original thoughts.
- **Budget and schedule** Check that your solution is affordable and feasible in the time you have available.
- **Age/gender/socioeconomics of the target audience** Who will

see it? The visuals for the horoscope page of a teenage magazine, for example, could certainly be more quirky and abstract than the imagery for a financial company report and accounts.
- **Shelf life** The images in a weekly magazine can be transient, whereas those in an expensive book with a selling potential of ten years or more need to have more lasting resonance.
- **Clarity of information** The images for an editorial design might be deliberately obscure, whereas those for a technical manual must be clear and didactic.

- **Perceived value** This is tricky to pinpoint, since often something that is inexpensive is marketed as valuable through its image, and something that is really expensive can seek to appeal to a mass market through a casual, trendy approach.
- **Design criteria and usage** Do you want a dynamic cut-out shape or a square image bled off the page? Will you use it in black and white or colour?
- **DIY** Can you create this image yourself? Graphic designers with image generation skills are more likely to be hired than those without.

# CHAPTER 2: ASSIGNMENTS

## ◘ Poster series

This task can be done electronically or by hand; however, it is highly recommended that you develop your craft skills and work with traditional media. You can use cut paper, a copier or draw each of the elements with pencil and fill them with black paint, but be precise.

Choose an existing music festival and make a note of the title of the festival, the dates, location, price of tickets, list of the acts and the website or social-media handle. Design a series of posters for this festival. You must use the same content each time, but follow the compositional rules that follow:

**1** Positive/negative
• Using only black squares, create a layout that suggests something positive, looking at positive space or 'positive placement'. Once complete, add your music festival text.
• Using only black squares, create a layout that suggests something negative, looking at negative space or 'negative placement'. Once complete, add your music festival text.
• Using what you've learned from this exercise, create a poster that explains the history and benefits of negative and postive in composition.

**2** Hierarchy
• Using only photographic images, create a layout that has hierarchy in the top half of the page. Once complete, add your music festival text.
• Using only illustrations or diagrams, create a layout that has hierarchy in the bottom half of the page. Once complete, add your music festival text.
• Using only typography (music festival text), create a layout that has hierarchy in the centre of the page.
• Repeat the typography exercise above with a different typeface. (Do this several times.)
• Using what you've learned from this exercise, create a poster that explains the history and benefits of hierarchy in composition.

**3** Minimalism/maximalism
• Using any form of black square/type/image, create a layout that uses as few squares/type/

images as possible (minimalism). Once complete, add your music festival text.
• On page 2, using any form of black square/type/image, create a layout that uses as many squares/type/images as possible (maximalism). Once complete, add your music festival text.
• Using what you've learned from this exercise, create a poster that explains the history and benefits of minimalist and maximalist composition.

**4** Symmetry/asymmetry
• Using typography (music festival text) and a single image, create a symmetrical composition.
• Using typography (music festival text) and a single image, create an asymmetrical composition.
• Using what you've learned from this exercise, create a poster that explains the history and benefits of symmetrical and asymmetrical composition.

## ◘ Typographic structures

For these exercises you will need three full spreads (two opposite pages) from a printed newspaper. These should include feature editorial spreads and spreads that contain a mixture of multiple images and text.

**1** Using a black pen, colour each section (e.g. header, subheading, quote, body text, caption, image, etc.) so you are left with a series of black squares and rectangles.

**2** Write a brief summary reflecting on the typographic and editorial structures. How valuable is the information provided by typographic structures beyond the visual message?

## ◘ Grid systems and layouts

Begin by selecting two books. These can be from a public library or your own, but they must have different design styles.

**1** Using sheets of tracing paper, identify and draw the different grid systems being used in each book. Trace the grid lines on each piece of tracing paper.

Look for the column widths and where possible rows could sit. Consider the margins at the top, sides and bottom, and to the left and right of each column (gutters). Look carefully for the edges of all the elements placed on the page, some of which may reach over two or three columns, so your lines may cross right through an element on the page.
• When you have finished, identify the system on each page. Is your selection based on a two-column, six-column or a modular system?
• Write a brief summary of your findings, explaining why you were attracted to the pages you selected and how you think the grid system supports the design work.

**2** Translate what you have discovered onto paper, sketching out the most interesting spreads you have discovered. You don't need a lot of detail at this stage; simply create a series of boxes with labels of image, body text, header, etc. If you were designing your own publication, this is how you would begin.

**3** Once you are happy that you understand the systems being used in the design of each book, apply the content of one book (the text and imagery) to the layout of the other. This can be done digitally, or by hand using a copier. What do you notice about changing the form of the content? How does it impact the meaning and messages being conveyed?

## ◘ 32pp zine

Publication design requires attention to detail and a keen eye for organisation and the hierarchy of information. The following tasks require you to think carefully about how layout, typography and imagery can be structured to lend variety, anticipation and drama, whether the publication is printed or appears online.

The following exercises require a basic understanding of InDesign (see pages 106–109).

**1** Carry out some research into zines. Find some examples and identify the design strategies used to vary the pace. How is the white space used? Are there variations in the grid system? Is there a grid system? Does the placement of type and image vary in size and scale? Is there a smart use of contrast and scale? Are certain pages making you pause for a lengthier examination?

**2** When you are satisfied with your research, plan your own zine on a theme of your choice. It's important to gather lots of content from a variety of sources. Remember to consider copyright issues within this process. When you select your text or imagery, consider the grid system and typographic structures that would be most appropriate. Think about the hierarchy of the layouts – what is the most important feature on each page – and the pace of each page as you navigate your way through the text. A dramatic story, for example, might need to be dynamic and full of information, but equally could be slower and more paced for suspense. Consider the tone of voice when choosing your typefaces. Think about scale, tension and visual drama, and about telling the story.

Begin by sketching out ideas for layouts. Using InDesign, set up the most appropriate grid from your sketches, for your information. Consider margins, columns and gutters. Select a typeface that best represents the tone of voice for the information. Experiment with serif, sans serif, point size, weight and leading.

**3** Repeat the exercises, altering the grid systems each time. Experiment with different typefaces and type systems. Remember how symmetry and asymmetry affect composition. Think about placement on the page, and test the flexibility of the grid systems you have chosen.

**4** Additional task
Consider how you would translate your print publication into an online equivalent. What needs to change and what must be kept the same? Consider the use of the scroll, the click and the reveal of hidden information.

## ◘ Extended systems

**1** Create an new identity for your favourite museum. It can include any type of logo – pictorial, letterform or abstract. Consider the character of the institution, their services and professionalism.

Start with sketches and develop the identity by digitising your logo into a vector using Adobe Illustrator (see pages 114–117), making sure your designs can be reduced and enlarged without losing legibility.

**2** Identify three characteristics that make your system constant on all three designs (e.g. colour scheme, positioning, scale, etc.).

**3** Using what you've discovered about extended system patterns in Chapter 2, apply your logo across multiple printed formats (e.g. posters advertising upcoming exhibitions, an exhibition catalogue, exhibition graphics within the show, etc.).

**4** Add a fourth digital element and extend your system. It could be the design of a website, social-media profile, or you might imagine your museum has its own app or animation. To do this, look carefully at the work you have just completed on the logo and supporting material. What needs to be added or amended for it to work on a screen?

## ➕ Further reading

Jess Baines, Susan Mackie, Anne Robinson, Prue Stevenson, *See Red Women's Workshop: Feminist Posters 1974–1990*, Four Corners, 2016

Jan-Frederik Bandel, Annette Gilbert, Tania Prill, *Under the Radar: Underground Zines and Self-Publications 1965–1975*, Spector Books, 2016

Amaranth Borsuk, *The Book*, The MIT Press, 2018

Alessandro Ludovico, *Post-Digital Print: The Mutation of Publishing Since 1894*, Onomatopee Projects, 2013

Jens Müller and Julius Wiedemann, *The History of Graphic Design Vol. 1. 1890–1959*, Taschen, 2022

Jens Müller and Julius Wiedemann, *The History of Graphic Design Vol. 2. 1960–Today*, Taschen, 2022

Josef Müller-Brockmann, *Grid Systems in Graphic Design: A Handbook for Graphic Artists, Typographers, and Exhibition Designers*, Verlag Niggli, 2008

John Phillips, *Posters from Paddington Printshop*, Four Corners, 2019

Timothy Samara, *Making and Breaking the Grid*, Rockport Publishers, 2017

David Reinfurt, *A \*New\* Program for Graphic Design*, Inventory Press, 2019

Beth Tondreau, *Layout Essentials: 100 Design Principles for Using Grids*, Rockport Publishers, 2011

# 3 Fundamentals of Typography

Typography is the process of arranging letters, words and text for almost any context imaginable, and it is among the most important tools a designer masters for effective visual communication. Graphic designers learn the nuances of typography in order to use it creatively, with imagination and a sense of exploration, while maintaining respect for its rules and traditions.

Typography is the visual manifestation of language, utilising all its expressive and practical qualities, and occupies a unique place where art, science and communications connect. You need only look to art movements such as Futurism and Dada to see typography's significance as an aesthetic medium. It also involves the design and selection of type for both legibility and communication of information, and, in some instances, aesthetic experimentation takes a backseat to pragmatic concerns.

Expressive typography and hand-drawn letterforms are a calligraphic art form in their own right. With so many interpretative typographic choices, sketching and experimenting with layouts will help you learn to evaluate the readability and nuance of the message before working on screen, essential stages that help in learning about the subtleties of type.

**New vintage**
Hand-drawn letterforms evoke the decorative typography of another century in this beautiful logotype by Tom Lane. The configuration of the letterforms, the overall shape created by the type design and the selective use of ruled lines for depth and underscoring keep the composition unified. The overall effect is one of tradition and craftsmanship.

| PART 1 | PRINCIPLES |
|---|---|
| CHAPTER 3 | FUNDAMENTALS OF TYPOGRAPHY |
| MODULE 1 | **TYPOGRAPHY AND MEANING** |

**By definition, a typographic message, aside from an intrinsic beauty, must convey a meaning. Meaning, and its expression, is at the core of typographic activity, at the level of both individual words and entire passages of text. This is called linguistic meaning, since it resides in language.**

Letters and words have an abstract beauty, seen and appreciated through experiments in type anatomy, which isolate the forms and separate elements of individual letters, and frequently reveal them as shapes, rather than meaningful linguistic objects. However, the instant words materialise on page or on screen, they begin to express ideas and possess this elusive quality we call meaning. Linguistic meaning, an essential element of typography, can be expressed, controlled and amplified through such typographic variables as size, weight, typeface (or font), placement on the page and letterspacing.

Sometimes, as in the pages of a book, the visual aspects of typography must take a backseat to the process of understanding. However, designers use such visual techniques all the time, to communicate messages effectively;

building confidence in working with text in this way is important, so that linking typographic form to linguistic meaning becomes second nature.

## Meaning

But what is 'meaning'? An alternative term is 'semantics', an important subtopic within all aspects of design, which is worth exploring in more detail. Semantics is the study of meaning and applies to both images and language. 'Syntax' (or grammar) refers to the rules that govern the organisation of elements of a sentence or paragraph, so that meaning is conveyed. If the syntax is wrong, then language becomes nonsense, or meaningless. In a general sense, to say that something has a meaning (a semantic value) relies upon its ability to present its idea in a form that can be communicated and shared. In linguistic meaning (the language-based meaning that typography participates in), this communicability is based on sets of symbols in the given language, which include letters and words, and also on the space between words, punctuation and placement of the characters.

Typographers such as Wolfgang Weingart, Willem Sandberg and H. N. Werkmann pushed the expression of meaning in typography to its very limit and, in so doing, expanded its visual vocabulary and expressive potential by working at the boundary between language and meaning.

Dada and Futurist artists such as Kurt Schwitters and Tristan Tzara, Marinetti and Wyndham Lewis experimented with the relationship between language and meaning. These historical practitioners are worth studying closely, as are their inspirational typographic experiments. Look at the works of the concrete poets e.e. cummings and Apollinaire, and contemporary designers such as Robert Massin, Johanna Drucker and Erik Spiekermann. Look at the experimental work of David Carson, who used type as texture in *Ray Gun* magazine, and at Paula Scher's graphic type solutions in poster design and environmental graphics.

### ➡ Word as object, object as word

Expressive typography can be used as an image, and the meaning of the words can be linked to the image for impact. Here, the term 'equal pay' is physically stitched onto the seat of a public transport vehicle, alluding to many political themes surrounding feminism and equal rights.

### ⬇ Constructed letterforms
Dimensional letterforms die-cut with lacy patterns are illuminated to create graphic shadows in the composition. The positive and negative shapes are defined by light and shadow in the delicately half-toned photographic image used in the final poster.

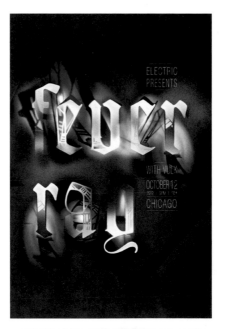

### ⬋ Expressive typography
These dynamic, abstract letterforms create a playful composition for this brand, conveying a friendly and approachable character. The bold colour and use of illustration complement the type and add to the strong personality.

## GLOSSARY

**Font:** One size, weight and width of a typeface: Garamond Roman 12pt is a font.

**Linguistic:** Of, or relating to, language.

**Semantics:** The study of meaning in language and elsewhere.

**Syntax:** The study of the rules for the formation of grammatically correct sentences.

**Typeface:** The set of visual attributes (design or style) of a particular group of letters: Garamond is a typeface.

| PART 1 | PRINCIPLES |
|---|---|
| CHAPTER 3 | FUNDAMENTALS OF TYPOGRAPHY |
| MODULE 2 | **THE ANATOMY OF TYPE** |

Familiarity with the basic structure of letterforms, the anatomy of type, is essential to understanding how typefaces differ and what characteristics they share, and allows the designer to make decisions about selecting and using the multitude of typefaces now available. The most basic element of typography is the letterform, and each typeface has its own unique characteristics, while sharing a basic language that describes its parts.

**Typeface** A block of letterpress type, showing the face of the letter, whose surface is inked and printed, giving us the term 'typeface'. **a** face, **b** body or shank, **c** point size, **d** shoulder, **e** nick, **f** groove, **g** foot.

Oblique, angled stress, associated with old-style typefaces

Semi-oblique stress, associated with transitional typefaces

Vertical stress, associated with modern and sans-serif typefaces

**Identifying characteristics** The different stresses of typefaces are essential information in identifying their place within the classification systems, and to locating them within an historical timeline.

**Language of letterforms** Each distinct part of a letter has its own name, forming a 'language of letterforms'.

Common terminology of typefaces includes the size of the x-height, counterform, serif (or sans-) style and stress of the letter (vertical/oblique). The ability to compare these characteristics between typefaces gives essential knowledge about the suitability of a particular typeface. By providing valuable information, or 'earmarks', about how typefaces relate to classification systems, such as old-style, transitional, humanist, modern and serif/sans serif, knowledge of type anatomy helps graphic designers to identify and select appropriate typefaces for different purposes.

Technology has accelerated the creation of new faces and produced digital versions of classics. There are so many choices available that selecting an appropriate typeface can be daunting. There are some digital fonts on the market that are of limited use, often downloadable for free. Many don't have much to offer in terms of versatility and lack a timeless quality. An argument can be made that they do appear different or somewhat experimental, and novelty has its uses in certain circumstances. For general use, especially where readability is a key concern, however, it is better to select classical fonts. Criteria for selection should normally be based on a careful evaluation of the media, the readership and the design objective.

**Key terms**

There are over 25 anatomical terms applicable to letterforms. For general typography it's not necessary to know all of them, but some are essential to making visual judgments that aid typeface selection for different situations, and you should be able to describe those differences in a technically correct way. For example, you may want to argue for the use of the beautiful 18th-century typeface

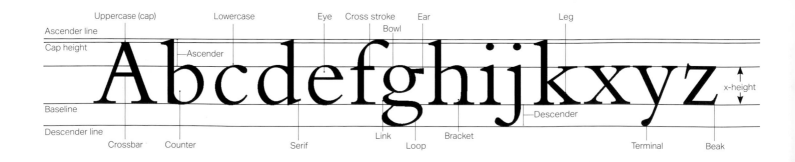

Bodoni in a particular design. You should be able to state that its characteristics include a vertical stress and a high degree of contrast between thick and thin strokes, and that the humanist quality of the font is appropriate to the readership and message.

Information about the difference between x-heights of typefaces is very helpful, since this allows the designer to choose typefaces that are more or less readable at smaller sizes. The x-height is the size of a lowercase 'x' in a given typeface, and the ratio between x-height and the ascenders and descenders of the lowercase letters, such as 'g' and 'h', define the overall appearance of a font. As with all design decisions, the space around the design elements, type or image is part of the picture and should be considered. Typefaces that have a large x-height may need more space between the lines (leading), so that they don't appear visually heavy on the page.

Typefaces of the same point size can appear larger or smaller. Futura has a small x-height, and long ascenders/descenders, whereas most sans-serif typefaces, such as Helvetica, typically have large x-heights. Although a general understanding of the terminology of typefaces is adequate for most designers, if you become interested in designing typefaces you will need to develop an intimate knowledge of type anatomy, in all its nuances, and have an excellent understanding of typeface history and development.

Times New Roman    Bodoni Book    Times New Roman    Bodoni Book

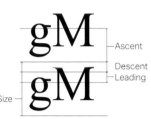

**← Measuring** The point size of type is measured from the baseline of one line of type to the baseline of another. Leading is the vertical space between lines of type, which affects the readability of text.

**↑ Impact of x-height** The x-height is the height of a lowercase x and determines the visual size of type. The x-height size varies from typeface to typeface: some, like Bodoni, have a small x-height, whereas Times New Roman has a large x-height. However, each type has the same body size. Type with large x-heights tend to have small ascenders and descenders, whereas type with small x-heights have large ones.

**❗ Small x-heights**
In typefaces with small x-heights, such as Caslon and Futura, there is more white space above and below the lowercase letters. Such type is easier to read, because the eye can travel back and forth along lines without difficulty. Use less leading in these typefaces, or even set them without any additional leading ('solid'), and set them in a larger point size.

**❗ Large x-heights**
In typefaces with large x-heights, such as Bookman or Helvetica, the lack of white space above and below the lowercase letters, and the larger white spaces within the letters, requires more space between lines. Increase the leading so that text is easier to read, and the overall 'colour' (another term for type density or texture) on the page is less heavy.

**Baseline:** The line on which the lowercase letters sit and below which the descenders fall.

**Earmark:** Identifying or distinguishing marks or characteristics of a typeface.

**Point size/pica:** The relative size of a font. There are 72 points in an inch.

**Stress/axis:** The angle of the curved stroke weight change in a typeface. Seen clearly in letters such as 'o'.

**Type anatomy:** The language used to describe the various parts of letterforms.

**x-height:** The height of a lowercase 'x' in any typeface.

**➕ SEE ALSO:** UNDERSTANDING AND SELECTING TYPEFACES, P66

1234567890
1234567890

**← Numerals** Aligning (above, set in Palatino) and non-aligning (or old-style) numbers (below, set in Bembo Expert).

Helvetica    Futura    Bembo

# Typefaces of | the same size | look different

## sizes | because they | have varying | x-heights |

Bodoni    Bernhard Modern    Times New Roman

| PART 1 | PRINCIPLES |
|---|---|
| CHAPTER 3 | FUNDAMENTALS OF TYPOGRAPHY |
| MODULE 3 | **UNDERSTANDING AND SELECTING TYPEFACES** |

Since the introduction of digital typefaces, the number of fonts available has increased exponentially; it is virtually impossible to know them all, or be able to reference all of their attributes. However, it is always advantageous to know a typeface's historical background since this can help in relating its characteristics to the content of the text. Selecting and understanding typefaces is a complicated business, one that becomes easier with practice.

For example, a sans-serif typeface such as Univers references modernity in a way that a serif font such as Garamond does not. Bodoni, designed in the late 1700s, has certain formal characteristics that, in their own era, were considered modern, including its use of perfectly vertical stress and sharp contrast between thick and thin lines, departing from 'old-style' typefaces based on pen-drawn forms. In a modern setting this font is associated with classicism and history. Although it can be used in a contemporary way, it's important to understand Bodoni's history and associations, and to take these into account when considering its use. Understanding a typeface's

historical origins and references, and its associated formal (visual) characteristics, is crucial when it comes to matters of selection. Broadly, contemporary typefaces such as Futura and Univers tend to work in modern contexts, whereas traditional type such as Garamond might be more apt for a literary classic. Of course, all these conventions are there to be played with and broken, but only when you have a full understanding of their significance. Research and read books on graphic design history, since our design past is always influencing the present.

⬆ **Newspaper fonts**
Sans-serif fonts were first seen in 1786. Shown above is an early use of a sans serif working with serif fonts, in a French newspaper, from 1898. Until this time, newspaper text and headings were set in serif fonts, and to this day, text setting is usually in serif.

## SERIF

### oAad
Bembo regular

**Humanist Old-Style**

Typefaces of the 15th and 16th centuries are based on hand-drawn calligraphic letterforms. They are characterised by having slanted (oblique or diagonal) stress, bracketed serifs and low contrast between thick and thin strokes. Sabon, designed by Jan Tschichold in 1966, is a contemporary example, based on the 16th-century typeface Garamond.

### oAad
Baskerville regular

**Transitional**

A more vertical axis is visible in these 18th-century typefaces. The sharp contrast between thick and thin strokes was considered controversial at the time. Serifs are still bracketed, but they are moving away from the calligraphic influence. Baskerville is an example of a transitional typeface.

### oAad
Bodoni Book

**Modern**

In the late 18th and early 19th centuries, typefaces became significantly more abstract. Bodoni shows a highly exaggerated contrast between thick and thin strokes, a perfectly vertical stress and serifs that are no longer bracketed, but straight lines.

### oAad
Rockwell regular

**Egyptian and Slab Serif**

In the early 19th century, in response to the Industrial Revolution, many new typefaces were designed for use in advertising. Their bold, robust, decorative forms grew from this context. Egyptian typefaces are typical of this period, with their heavy, slab serifs and 'industrial' quality.

## SANS SERIF

### oAad
Gill Sans Book

**Humanist Sans Serif**

Sans-serif typefaces originated in the early 19th century but became dominant in the 20th century. Gill Sans, designed in 1928, combined the characteristics of both old-style serif and sans-serif fonts, with its calligraphic qualities but lack of serifs.

### oAad
Helvetica regular

**Anonymous Sans Serif**

Sans-serif fonts were first produced by Caslon in 1816 (in capitals only), and William Thorowgood in 1832 (with lowercase), and they were known as Grotesques, since they were thought to be ugly. Helvetica was designed in 1957 by Max Miedinger, and is one of the best known sans serifs.

### oAad
Futura Book

**Geometric Sans Serif**

Typefaces such as Futura (designed by Paul Renner in 1927) are extensions of earlier sans serifs, but have a more geometric design, based on monolines (lines of one thickness, with no variation of thick and thin as in old-styles), perfect circles and triangular shapes. Such typefaces are associated with Modernism in the early part of the 20th century, but continue to be popular.

## Type classification

Before you examine the various factors involved in selecting type, it is worth considering the broad categories into which typefaces can be placed: type classification systems. Categorising type is never an exact process, and there are many layers to the classification process, but a rough guide can help in distinguishing the characteristics of typefaces and learning the appropriate uses for the various type families. A clear initial division is sometimes made between text and display type, each of which has its own criteria for selection, but there are also faces that function well in both roles.

## Text type: old style, transitional and modern

Primarily, text types are meant to be read in continuous form or at least with few interruptions.

- **Old-style serif typefaces,** such as Bembo, Garamond and Caslon, are ideal for this purpose. They are regarded as 'classic' fonts because they have stood the test of time and still command respect. These Roman fonts have been in use since the origins of printing in the 15th century, and are considered humanist, because the original designs referenced the hand-drawn characteristics of manuscripts. Much later, during the 1930s, a number of new 'Romans' were introduced to coincide with the new monotype hot-metal typesetting system and many of the classics were also re-cut for the same purpose. Times New Roman and Imprint are good examples of this group, known as 20th-century Romans. Later the German type designers Hermann Zapf and Jan Tschichold added, respectively, Palatino and Sabon to this group. Contemporary Romans, such as Minion, have now been designed using digital tools.

- **Transitional Roman fonts** have a vertical stress, sharp and bracketed serifs, and in most cases a medium to high contrast between thick and thin letterstrokes. Baskerville and Century Schoolbook are prime examples. The term captures a movement away from the old-style group, influenced by pen-drawn forms, towards modern faces rooted in geometry rather than the traditional pen stroke.

- **Modern serif faces** also have a vertical stress, but an abrupt contrast between the thick and thin letterstrokes, fine horizontal serifs and a narrow set width (in most cases). Bodoni is one of the earliest and best-known examples; Walbaum is a slightly more contemporary version of a 'modern' typeface.

There are many fonts in these three groups, which cover pretty much all kinds of book work. They can also be found in brochures and magazines, but other groups are more often used for this kind of publication.

◀ **Classifying differences** Type classification charts are useful guides to the various characteristics (sometimes known as 'earmarks') of different typefaces. They allow you to place typefaces within their historical contexts and to see how their basic visual attributes are shared across different, but related, fonts. For example, Romans always have serifs, while sans-serif humanist typefaces such as Gill Sans share properties associated with both old-style Roman and sans-serif typefaces.

Correct fonts

*Italic*    **Bold**    Small Caps    Condensed    Expanded

Pseudo fonts

*Italic*    **Bold**    Small Caps    Condensed    Expanded

Unless you choose a real italic from the font menu, a computer will only slant Roman letterforms

Pseudo bold is simply thickened digitally rather than being the true, carefully crafted font

Small caps are used within lowercase text when smaller, non-dominant capital letters are required. In traditional typesetting they are used for emphasis

Artificially condensed or expanded letterforms should be avoided, since the computer distorts them by applying a percentage reduction or expansion. Always use a 'true' condensed or expanded typeface

**Old-style serif faces**

ABCabc
Bembo

ABCabc
Garamond

ABCabc
Caslon

ABCabc
Times New Roman

ABCabc
Imprint

ABCabc
Palatino

ABCabc
Sabon

ABCabc
Minion

**Traditional Roman fonts**

ABCabc
Baskerville

ABCabc
Century Schoolbook

**Modern serif faces**

ABCabc
Walbaum

ABCabc
Bodoni

## Display type

Major social changes in the 19th century brought about the need for display type. The Industrial Revolution brought the masses into the cities, increasing production and consumption of goods and services, which led to the need to communicate to a wider audience. Existing fonts were used primarily for books, then limited to an elite sector. Printers found the available typefaces inadequate for the new billboards, posters and pamphlets produced, especially since there were many more messages being displayed in public spaces, all vying for attention. Bolder, stronger faces were needed to suit this new context, and to meet demand.

The sans-serif typeface was bolder and more 'industrial' in its look, along with slab serifs and thickened modern letters known as fat faces. The Victorians were innovative; their typefaces are full of vigour and still fascinate today. John Lewis' book *Printed Ephemera* has excellent examples of Victorian display fonts used on posters and playbills.

## Sans-serif and script typefaces

The 20th century saw the extensive development of the sans serif, notably by the Bauhaus school in the 1920s and 1930s. Their philosophy was to sweep away the traditional forms characterised by excessive ornament, employing the principle of 'form equals function'. Simple typographic structures called for clean, functional typefaces, hence the interest in the sans serif with its mono weight and functional forms. Futura was introduced in 1927, and two years later Gill Sans was unveiled. In the decades that followed, well-known fonts such as Helvetica and Optima in Europe, and Franklin Gothic and Avant Garde in the USA, kept the sans serif among the most popular of type styles.

A significant advantage of the sans serif is the large number of potential variants within one typeface. In 1957 Adrian Frutiger introduced a complete family of different weights and forms when he conceived the design of Univers, which comprises 21 variants ranging from light condensed to bold expanded.

# Stone Sans Semibold
## Stone Sans Medium

**This intro type is set in Stone Serif Semibold, this intro type is set in Stone Serif Semibold**

This body type is set in Stone Serif Medium. Designed in 1987, the Stone family consists of three types of font – a serif, a sans serif and an informal style – all designed to work together. The styles are legible, modern and dynamic, combining the old with the new. The Stone fonts integrate perfectly with each other, giving the typeface a wide range of design applications.

**← Perfect harmony**
Type designers have recently produced serif and sans-serif versions of the same typeface – for example, Officina and Stone. The advantage is that you can use a serif for the text setting and a sans for the display, and they will harmonise perfectly because they have been specifically designed to work together.

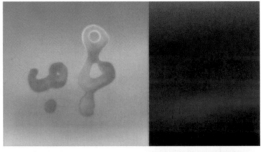

Launching 30 June 2021        #CSM2021 #CSMbloom

**← Computer-generated letterforms** In this example, AI has been trained to create beautifully formed letters in multiple scripts. Even though this is a digital technology, the letterforms are powerfully organic in appearance.

 ⬅ ⬆ **Experimental type** *Emigre* magazine was published between 1984 and 2005. Only 69 issues were produced, but the experimental design and the innovative use of typography are still influencing contemporary design today. *Emigre* was among the first publications to champion digital typography and to recognise the impact of the personal computer on the discipline of graphic design.

⬆ **Inspiration before and after** Iconic graphic designer Paula Scher's Best of Jazz poster for CBS Records in 1979 shows the influence of constructivism and the beginnings of her own influence on the contemporary use of type as image. Recommended reading: *Make it Bigger* by Paula Scher (2002).

⬅ **Custom typography** Master typographer John Langdon styled this custom lettering for a heavy-metal band. The designer cited the influence of Century for its classic formality. Designing custom letterforms requires excellent knowledge of typefaces and letterform construction. Work your way up to it, and reference existing fonts when you begin.

⬅ **Handmade** In this example, a logotype – logo made from typography – has been handcrafted. Sketches and experiments have been developed to convey a sophisticated decorative emblem for the Walnut Street Theatre.

## Selecting fonts

The content of the material and the purpose of the design are the main factors in deciding your choice of font. Design clarity is essential in information dissemination, and it is telling that sans-serif types such as Interstate, with their simple mono-weight structures, are designed to maximise readability for highway signage. Sans serif is also ideal for small notation in diagrams, captions and maps. The font Futura is one of the most widely used for onscreen and web, and arrives pre-installed in most computers.

- Font choice can be influenced by subject matter, and knowledge of the font origins might help in the final decision; for example, Caslon and Baskerville are classical English, Garamond is French, Goudy American, Bodoni Italian, and so on.
- Publication design can be more adventurous, because magazine readers tend to jump in and out of the text rather than reading from cover to cover. With small segments of copy, unusual fonts can sometimes bring freshness to the overall feeling of the design. However, it's wise not to mix too many fonts together in one design.
- Display types offer much more variety than text types because their purpose is expression rather than readability, so you can engage in playful experimentation in your headline design.
- Sans-serif and slab-serif faces are seen as more authoritative and bolder than typefaces that are designed for reading over long periods. If you are reversing out type or printing tints in small sizes, sans serifs are a good bet. For elegance, serifs have the advantage of tradition.
- Not all fonts are web-friendly. When designing an outcome that runs across online and offline mediums it is important that you research compatibility before you start.

⊞ **SEE ALSO:** THE ANATOMY OF TYPE, P64

→ **Opposites attract** The use of multiple typefaces is sometimes overwhelming. In this example, however, the delicate balance of serif and sans-serif typefaces conveys multiple voices and a modern take on a traditional institution.

← **Simplicity rules**
The development of the logo for New York's Public Theater, and the sophisticated simplicity of the sans-serif type on the theatre's promotional materials, show the influence of old wood type in different weights. Designer Paula Scher developed a typographic style that defined the theatre for years to come. For Sam Shepard's play *Simpatico*, 1994, a staircase of condensed letterforms easily brings the eye up and down through the composition.

**Sans serif:** Without serif. Typefaces such as Univers, Helvetica, Aksidenz Grotesque and Futura, characterised by their lack of serifs. Predominantly associated with the 19th/20th centuries.

**Serif:** Structural details at the ends of some strokes in old-style capital and lowercase letters.

| 45 Light | 45 Light italic | 47 Condensed light | 47 Condensed light italic | 55 Regular | 55 Regular italic |

| 57 Condensed | 57 Condensed italic | 65 Bold | 65 Bold italic | 67 Condensed bold | 67 Condensed bold italic |

| 75 Black | 75 Black italic | Extended | Extended italic | Ultra condensed | Bold extended |

| Bold extended italic | Extra black | Extra black extended | Extra black extended italic |

**Univers** Designed by Adrian Frutiger in 1957, Univers is a modular system, with 21 numbered typefaces in various weights, widths and oblique versions. This flexibility makes the font ideal for incorporating many differing levels of information within a design. It's interesting to compare the slight but important differences with other sans-serif typefaces such as Helvetica. You should learn to observe the fine distinctions when choosing between one sans serif and another.

A symphony of growls erupted.

**Bold communication**
Well-chosen fonts can support the message they deliver. In this example, angular and disfigured letterforms evoke the noise of a growl.

**Delicate communication**
Gentle fonts with softer edges can evoke an atmosphere. In this instance, the subtle use of type in combination with the bright colour sets the more assertive yet friendly tone in which the publication is to be read.

SMALL PRACTICES: In Conversation with Malaysian & Japanese Architects

| PART 1 | PRINCIPLES |
|---|---|
| CHAPTER 3 | FUNDAMENTALS OF TYPOGRAPHY |
| MODULE 4 | **SPACING** |

Understanding how to deal with space in typography is essential. Proper spacing affects legibility, and space is also an integral and powerful part of any composition, whether symmetrical or asymmetrical. Develop an eye for detail, and consider the role of space in both legibility and meaning as you progress through every stage of the design development.

In most cases, the designs you produce will consist of a mixture of images and copy in the form of either headings (display type) or body copy (text). Display type ranges in size from 14pt and upwards, whereas the main text (also referred to as body copy or body text) generally falls between 8 and 14pt. It is advisable to avoid the default setting of 12pt where you can, because it is industry default and suggests you have not made a design decision to change it. As you design, important choices will need to be made regarding typefaces, sizes and measure (width of line). You will also need to decide about spacing (letter, word and line) and, later, adjustments will need to be made by eye, even if the tool is a computer. There is no automated function on any computer that can replace the keen eye of an experienced designer.

### Letterspacing

When you keystroke or import text from a file, a computer sets the type at default space settings, both between individual letters (letterspace) and between lines of type (leading). The computer doesn't make the fine-tuning decisions that a designer must. If your type is too close together, with the letters almost touching, the letterspacing needs to be adjusted (called kerning). If they are too far apart, individual word shapes break down and legibility is compromised. One of the most common mistakes that new designers make is to set their text either too closely or

➡ **Kern your caps** Kerning is the process of optically adjusting the space between (mostly capital) letters, so that they appear evenly spaced.

too widely, or to accept the computer's spacing decisions. Designers need to learn as much as possible about the ways in which leading affects readability and impacts on the overall texture, sometimes called 'tone', of the text on the page. There are many programs to help you understand readability, and the website type.method.ac is a particularly useful reference.

Extra or negative letterspace can be inserted to customise and reinforce a particular idea, but these are the exceptions and need to be carefully considered. Hyphenation is often used to allow for more text on a page, but it is notorious for disrupting reading flow. Bear these factors in mind when deciding how to lay out your text. Type designers for software programs are careful to produce settings for good visual spacing between letters at different sizes. However, never take this for granted.

⬆ **Delicate balance** The variation in type hierarchy within this leaflet means consideration needs to be given to spacing. The title, subheadings and body copy are all different typographic devices used for different reasons, so it is vital that the typography keeps the correct visual balance in letterspacing, even when there are dramatic changes in scale.

IEFKHN

These upright letters appear much tighter visually than the rounded letters below

OQ

Rounded shapes give the illusion of more space between each letterform

AVID

The word 'AVID' has been set with InDesign metrics auto kerning; the same word below has been adjusted by eye to visually even out the letterspacing

Reduce space  Add Space

AVID

For instance, condensed typefaces should always be treated cautiously, as should those set in justified measures: in these cases, small additions or subtractions can improve the evenness of spacing, or allow a word to be taken into a line to avoid widows or orphans (single words from the end of a paragraph left at the end or beginning of a column of text).

## Design objectives

The main aim in display and text type is to try to achieve visual evenness throughout a series of characters. Consistency is important, because readers interpret shapes of words rather than individual letters. If there is unevenness in letterspacing, the eye can be distracted by the space rather than seeing the words.

You can test the importance of even letterspacing by setting text with different spacing, including altering it within the same line. As type size increases the unevenness can worsen, requiring the designer to make optical adjustments. This problem is prevalent with capital letters, as they fit together in complicated ways because of their inherent forms. Characters with straight stems such as 'I', 'J', 'E' and 'F', when placed together, require more space between individual letters than those with rounded shapes, like 'O' and 'Q', or those with diagonal strokes, such as 'A', 'V', 'Y' and 'W'. Letters in certain words may need adjusted spacing to compensate for the reduced space between characters, such as 'A' and 'V'. This is because the letters occupy different amounts of space, having varied widths.

Kerning allows for individual reductions or incremental increases to the letterspacing, whereas tracking increases or reduces space between words. Always trust your eyes.

## Word spacing

In display type, one way to gauge the amount of space to leave between words is the width of a lowercase 'i', but it will depend on the design sensibility. In some fonts, more than an 'i' space will exacerbate difficulties in reading.

↑ **Type in motion** Paula Scher's 1996 iconic poster design for New York City's Public Theater is a masterful example of text management that redefined designing with type for a generation of graphic designers. The movement of the dancer is embodied in the placement of the letterforms, creating enormous energy while managing a huge amount of information at the same time. Note the use of a controlled palette to assist the hierarchy.

⊕ **SEE ALSO:** THE ANATOMY OF TYPE, P64

READABILITY AND LEGIBILITY, P76

**Alignment:** The setting of text relative to a column or page.

**Centred:** Text that is aligned neither to the left nor to the right: symmetrical, with an even gap at the end of each line.

**Hyphenation:** The point at which a word is broken at the end of a line in continuous text and a hyphen is inserted.

**Justified:** Text that is aligned on both the left and right margins of a column (lines are equal in length).

**Kerning:** Adjustments to the spaces between two letters (used extensively for capitals).

**Leading:** Measured from baseline to baseline, leading is the horizontal space between lines of type. Related to the historical use of strips of lead in letterpress printing.

**Ligatures:** Two or more letterforms joined to create a single character.

**Optical adjustment:** Making adjustments to letterspacing by eye, not mechanically.

**Orphan:** A single word or line of text that overruns into the top of the next column, breaking how the text is read.

**Ragging:** When text is aligned left, some words at the ends of the lines might jut out further than the rest and cause uneven-looking paragraphs.

**Ranged (or Ragged) left/right:** Text that is aligned to a column, either left or right.

**Tracking:** The space between words, which can be adjusted.

**Widow:** A single word on its own at the beginning of a line. It should be typeset to sit at the end of the previous line.

# Theilowercaseiiiisiaigoodiguide

Word spacing is traditionally based upon a space equivalent to the body width of a lowercase 'i'.

Word spacing in text type also needs careful scrutiny, and typesetting style plays an important part. There are two basic setting styles for continuous reading: justified and ranged (or ragged) left. With justified setting, word spacing will vary because words are pushed out to fill the requirements of the measure. Space between words can become excessive, particularly if the chosen measure is too small or the typeface too large. Hyphenation (word breaks) can be adjusted to even out word spacing as far as possible, but justified setting is always tricky unless type size in relation to set measure is carefully considered. Setting justified text on a short measure with many long words is especially difficult, since fewer words end up on a line. This often occurs in newspapers.

With ranged-left setting, you have the advantage of being able to space words consistently. Many designers prefer this style for obvious reasons, although problems of legibility can still arise and ragging text (lines that jut out further than others causing unevenness) becomes a major issue. Type style also plays an important part in word spacing. Percentage adjustments can be made within the hyphenation and justification (H and J) settings of electronic page-layout programs, to accommodate closer or wider word spacing depending on the width of character of the typeface. In general, ranged-left setting

should not be hyphenated, except sometimes for shorter column widths; otherwise you can end up with lines of uneven length.

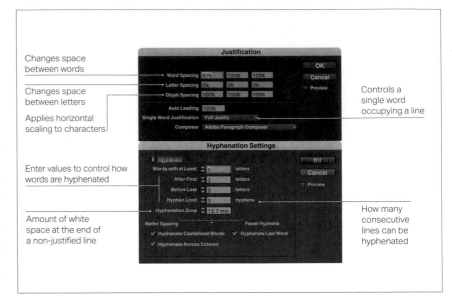

Changes space between words

Changes space between letters

Applies horizontal scaling to characters

Enter values to control how words are hyphenated

Amount of white space at the end of a non-justified line

Controls a single word occupying a line

How many consecutive lines can be hyphenated

⬆ **H and Js** Hyphenation and justification can be fine-tuned manually, giving an excellent level of control; here the dialogue boxes from InDesign are shown.

## Justification options

**1 No H and J** This justified setting has no word breaks. You can easily see the problem of excessive word spacing, which causes rivers of space to form.
**2 Hyphenation** Using hyphens can help to reduce the problem of excessive word spacing, but don't hyphenate too often in a block of text.
**3 Unjustified** Excessive word spacing can be made to disappear with the ranged-left style of setting. With no word breaks you can shorten lines, giving a ragged look.

1 With justified setting – that is, alignment on both the right and left of the measure – the word spacing will vary because words are pushed out to fulfil the requirements of the measure. Herein lies the problem. The space can become excessive, particularly if the chosen measure is too small or the typeface too large. The result is often bad word spacing, which can cause 'rivers' of space to run down the page.

2 Hyphenation can be adjusted to even out the word spacing as far as possible and avoid ugly spacing. Hyphenation specifications are sets of automatic hyphenation rules that you can create and apply to paragraphs. You can specify the smallest number of characters that must precede an automatic hyphen (the default is 3), and the minimum number of characters that must follow an automatic hyphen (the default is 2). These controls do not affect manual hyphenation.

3 With ranged-left setting you have the decided advantage of being able to space words consistently – the inherent difficulties of justified text can be avoided. For this reason, many designers prefer this style, though problems of legibility can still arise. As mentioned earlier, style of type also plays an important part in the amount of word spacing to have. Percentage adjustments can be made within hyphenation and justification (H and J).

### Leading

This term derives from 'hot-metal' typesetting, where strips of lead were placed between lines of type. Measured from baseline to baseline, it refers to the amount of spacing between lines of type. In display type, the designer will invariably have to adjust individual lines and not just rely on a constant setting. Each line of type is spaced differently, according to need. The role of leading becomes particularly important when setting large areas of text, notably in books. There are no clear rules regarding the adjustments of line spacing for display matter; it is a matter of skill in developing an even look and in letting your eye be your guide. Every time you use display type, analyse each case individually. For example, designers sometimes use negative leading (in which the leading has a lower numerical value than the type size). This can be effective in giving a dynamic visual appearance, but should be used with care. You can also set preferences for a baseline grid (a horizontal grid structure that helps guide text layout) and align your text to sit upon it.

All type settings are enhanced by the careful consideration of leading. Factors such as x-height, measure and weight of typeface will all influence the amount of leading you should employ

**ⓘ Left versus right**
Ranged-right text is considered harder to read than ranged-left text, because the eye travels to the end of the line and seeks a consistent location for the beginning of the next line. If the lines (on the left) are uneven, it's more difficult to do this.

### Ragging text

Creating ragging text, which is ranged left, takes time, practice and patience. The key is to create a 'soft' right-hand edge to the type by bringing words down onto the following lines and avoiding making harsh, obvious shapes – such as sharp diagonals – at the right edge of the text that distract the eye. A tried-and-tested rule of thumb is to alternate longer and shorter lines. Avoid putting in hyphenation to solve ragging issues; it is better to work with the natural flow of the words in the copy and only break where it's absolutely necessary.

**⬇ Ragging** This typographic event poster embraces ragged text. Ranged-left, the ragged speaker biographies continue the ragged title treatment.

### X-heights and readability

**Helvetica Medium, designed in 1957 by Max Miedinger, a Swiss type designer, is a sans-serif typeface that has a relatively large x-height in relation to its ascenders and descenders. This means that when setting text in this font you may need to add extra leading (space between the lines) to ensure maximum readability.**

**Set in 8pt, with 4 points of leading, or 8/12pt.**

**The same size of type in Futura Medium, designed in the mid-1920s by Paul Renner and based on simple geometric forms, has a relatively small x-height for a sans-serif typeface. However, its long ascenders and descenders (see the 'l' and the 'y') mean that when setting text in this font you may need to add extra leading to ensure maximum readability.**

**Set in 8pt, with 4 points of leading, or 8/12pt.**

This text is set in the same size of type, in the transitional serif typeface Times New Roman, designed specifically for *The Times* newspaper in 1931 by Stanley Morison. It has a smaller x-height in relation to its ascenders and descenders, and therefore an overall smaller appearance on the page, needing less leading.

Set in 8pt, with 3 points of leading, or 8/11pt.

The same size of type in the old-style typeface Bembo, originally cut by Francesco Griffo in 1496, has an even smaller x-height, although it is in the same size as before. This means that when setting text in this font you may want to reduce the space between the lines to ensure maximum readability. This typeface also looks less visually dense when set as text on the page, because the weight of its strokes is less heavy.

Set in 8pt, with 2 points of leading, or 8/10pt.

| PART 1 | PRINCIPLES |
|---|---|
| CHAPTER 3 | FUNDAMENTALS OF TYPOGRAPHY |
| MODULE 5 | **READABILITY AND LEGIBILITY** |

Debate continues between traditionalists and modernists as to whether sans-serif typefaces are more or less legible than serif faces. Traditionalists argue that serifs aid legibility by helping to differentiate letterforms, factors that keep the eye moving along the horizontal line. However, modernists argue that sans serifs do not really decrease legibility; it is just a question of readers becoming culturally acclimatised to the sans-serif face aided by electronic devices.

Certain rules have evolved about setting type and using letterforms that still apply. One rule is that long passages composed entirely of either capital letters or very bold text are difficult to read. Multiple capitals can be difficult to read because the words have similar visual shapes or outlines and all are the same height. Ascenders and descenders in capital and lowercase settings aid in the differentiation between words.

### Justified versus ranged left

Another perennially hot topic is the relative virtues of justified and ranged-left settings. Justified text may be no easier to follow than lines ranged left. Ranged-right settings force the reader to search for the beginning of each line, which can get very annoying over long passages and should generally be avoided. If you are reversing type out of black or a colour, then a sans-serif typeface might be a safer option than the alternative, with its finer lines and serifs. Of course, much will depend on the size of type, choice of colour and quality of paper or media.

Between 60 and 72 characters per line (on any given measure) is the best number for optimum readability. However, these parameters will change according to type size. When lines are too long, the eye loses its place; too short and the reader will become distracted by the constant returning to the start of a new line. The text throughout these paragraphs is set in Berthold Akzidenz Grotesk at 9 points, with a leading measure of 11 points.

**GLOSSARY**

**Justified:** Lines or paragraphs of type aligned to both margins simultaneously, creating different spacing in between words.

**Measure:** The length of a line of text on a page, based in inches, centimetres, points or picas.

**Ranged left:** Paragraphs or lines of text aligned to the left-hand side margin.

**Ranged right:** Paragraphs or lines of text aligned to the right-hand side margin.

⬇ **Systems** Changes in typographic styling, paper stock and size can be used as navigation devices that separate elements in the extended system: pagination, captions, body text and, in this case, a bold display type. All have distinct styles, but they work together.

➕ **SEE ALSO:**
UNDERSTANDING AND SELECTING TYPEFACES, P66

SPACING, P72

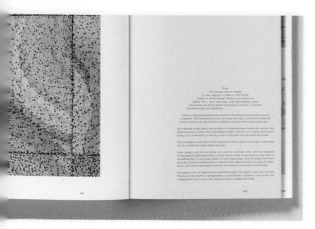

**◄ Structure and shape**
Justified type can be used decoratively, but the lines and the letters need to be managed line by line, as does the tracking and kerning on each word. When it's done correctly, the results can be very striking, as per this publication example by APFEL for the Venice Biennale.

## Key features: readability

Measure (line length), type size and leading (spacing between lines) work in concert and affect readability.

- We have established that the optimum number of characters per line is between 60 and 72. Any more and the eye has problems picking up the next line; fewer characters per line can interrupt reading flow. Of course, the needs of different design types will influence these decisions; in fact, context is everything. In magazines, measures tend to be shorter because readers dip into articles rather than reading from cover to cover. Novels, which have to satisfy a criterion of continuous reading, look very different to advertisements, where immediate impact is a primary concern.
Indeed, it is a useful exercise to ask why certain publications – newspapers, timetables, cookbooks, etc. – differ in their standards of readability depending on their function.

- Choice of type size and measure also depends on the amount of copy. Readers can cope with small amounts if the setting is smaller or on a narrower measure than the recommended optimum.

- Leading is a major element in readability. If there is insufficient space between lines, the eye will be hampered from moving smoothly to the next line. Increased leading is also required if the typeface is condensed, or if a serif typeface with a heavy or bold characteristic is being used.

- Typefaces with large x-heights have reduced ascenders and descenders, resulting in less differentiation in word shapes. Therefore, these typefaces need to have more leading.

**↑ Legibility** Legibility does not mean you cannot be playful with your design choices. A range of type scales, orientations and overlays can be used to communicate clearly as well as to add variety and pace. The most important consideration with this example by Matt Willey would have been printing proofs, to ensure information isn't lost or overlooked in the production process.

| PART 1 | PRINCIPLES |
|---|---|
| CHAPTER 3 | FUNDAMENTALS OF TYPOGRAPHY |
| MODULE 6 | **TYPOGRAPHIC EMPHASIS AND HIERARCHY** |

Knowing how to solve problems of emphasis using type is a critical skill. This involves considering the relationship between multiple elements – the size and weight of type, the position on the page, and the dynamic between elements – as well as developing an understanding of how these decisions call forth some contents while suppressing others. These kinds of typographic decisions relate to what are called hierarchies of information, since in any design some things will need to be read first, with secondary information to follow.

Before starting any design, it is crucial to understand where the main points of emphasis fall in terms of headings, sub-headings, intro copy, captions, quotes, and so on. These levels of importance are called hierarchies. Once established, hierarchies can be indicated in various ways: by space, weight, colour and form.

- Adding vertical white' space in the form of a one-line or half-line space above or below a heading, separating it from the surrounding elements, creates emphasis.
- The density of black ink creates its own visual emphasis. Sans-serif typefaces, such as Univers, are good for this because they typically have various weight combinations you can use: light with bold, medium with extra bold, and so on. Bear in mind that a smaller size of bold type is visually 'heavier' than a larger size of regular-weight type.
- Changing the typestyle is a third method – switching from roman to italics, for example. Italics add informality and movement to a design and are also effective for highlighting key phrases within text. Because of their more delicate form, you will probably need to increase the size proportionally for readability where needed.
- Changing some lowercase to capitals can add formality to a design. Capitals need more letterspacing, and so consume more space, though you don't have the problem of ascenders clashing with descenders. Small capitals provide an even more subtle shift of emphasis.

### The power of contrast

Other techniques involving the use of contrast can be applied to add emphasis effectively.

- Contrasting condensed with extended type can be effective, but use it sparingly with short, concise headlines. Remember that condensed type requires more leading, and that expanded type pushes out the length of the copy. Simple, effective paragraph styling adds emphasis, too, such as indents at the start of paragraphs or sections.
- Colour is a valuable tool and type does not have to be black and white to create contrast. Make sure that you have tested ink colour on the stock colour if you are printing. Transparent inks can compromise readability, and colours too close together in value or hue won't work. Colours with complementary values, such as red and green, can cause type to vibrate. When adding delicate colour to type, consider using a typeface with more weight, and provide a larger area of colour. Experiment with reversing out type or adding rules to draw attention to parts of the text.
- Changing type size or weight is a popular option. Again, when using shifts of size for emphasis, ensure that there is a substantial difference between the main text and the heading. If the sizes are too close, then the point is not well made. The difference in size has to be great enough to make the point.

⬆ **Refreshing** The striking use of a zesty green palette and the soft, sans-serif typeface complement the contents of this can. Evoking thoughts of the taste and the quenching of thirst cleverly represents the fizzy beverage and entices the buyer in.

**Contrast:** The difference between elements, which allows for comparison and emphasis. Contrast is closely related to hierarchy, since it allows different levels of information to be identified.

**Hierarchy:** In this context, the name for differing levels of text in a document. A page title, for example, is at the top of the hierarchy, whereas paragraphs of text are below.

➕ **SEE ALSO:** SPACING, P72

### Less is more

Try not to have too many means of emphasis going on at once. Too many techniques in one place will confuse the eye and detract, rather than add, to the concept. 'Less is more' is often a good principle when trying to work through problems of emphasis and hierarchy. Don't overstate your points by setting type in a large point size, bold, italics, underlined and at an angle. With computers, it is easy to change things, and you need to be disciplined to avoid creating a mishmash of weights, sizes, forms and indents. Resist the temptation to use all your techniques at once – and remember, you do not always have to shout to be heard.

### Type size

Your choice of font, weight of heading or amount of leading all depend on other decisions you have made. The same is true of type size: point size is an absolute measure of how

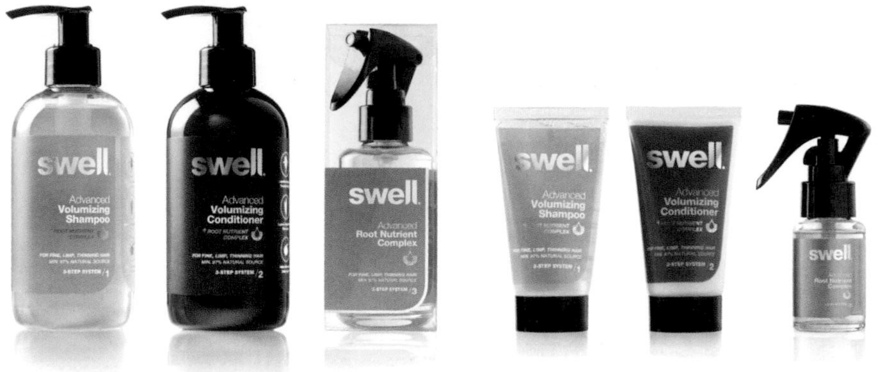
swell
Advanced
Volumizing
Shampoo
swell
Advanced
Volumizing
Conditioner
swell
Advanced
Root Nutrient
Complex
swell
Advanced
Volumizing
Shampoo
swell
Advanced
Volumizing
Conditioner
swell

**Customise and complement**
A slight parting in the negative space at the base of the logo's double letter 'l' is just enough to express the root-to-tip promise of great haircare products, designed by Aloof. Keeping the rest of the type clean and simple allows the subtlety of the logo to shine and stays true to the brand.

## Anatomy of a page

Work with your copywriter and your client to assign the page hierarchy before you begin your design work. If you have a system that repeats formats, as in book design, be sure to stay consistent in assigning fonts and weights to your style sheets.

(p 32 chapter 2 intro head)
Fundamentals of composition

(intro)
Good composition is an essential element of all art forms, graphic or otherwise, and should be considered the foundation of visual communication. Successful graphic designers are masters of the fundamentals that underlie all aspects of design. Elements on a page or on the web, in motion or in three dimensions, should always be led by concern for spacing, visual organisation, style and the size and format of the finished work. Graphic design projects use text and image in concert, with consideration for the relationships established between each of the elements. These compositions should also establish a visual hierarchy that directs the viewer's eye through a deliberate visual sequence.

(quote)
'Visual literacy also is an ability to view any image as an abstraction, to understand what is happening in purely visual terms as well as knowing and understanding visual terminology. It involves training the eyes to see minute detail and being sensitive to colour, shape, form and line. It has little or nothing to do with content or style'
Rob Roy Kelly

(p p 32 - 35 module head)
Part 1 Principles
Chapter 2 Fundamentals of composition

(Ahead)
Module 1 Basics of composition

(standfirst)
Composition refers to the visual structure and organisation of elements within a design. It concerns the process of combining distinct parts or elements to form a whole. Composition involves seeing the whole as greater than its parts, and is just as important as the individual elements that make up a design.

(B text)
Designers organise images and text – each with their own shapes, sizes, colours and textures – in many different media and in a wide range of formats; from two- and three-dimensional, black-and-white design, through full-colour work to web-based and time-based (moving) imagery. A practical understanding and exploration of composition is crucial for effective visual communication: it is the most significant tool in guiding the viewer through the complexity of visuals to the intended message. To create effective design work, no matter which medium you are working in, you must understand the principles of good composition.

(B head)
Theories of composition

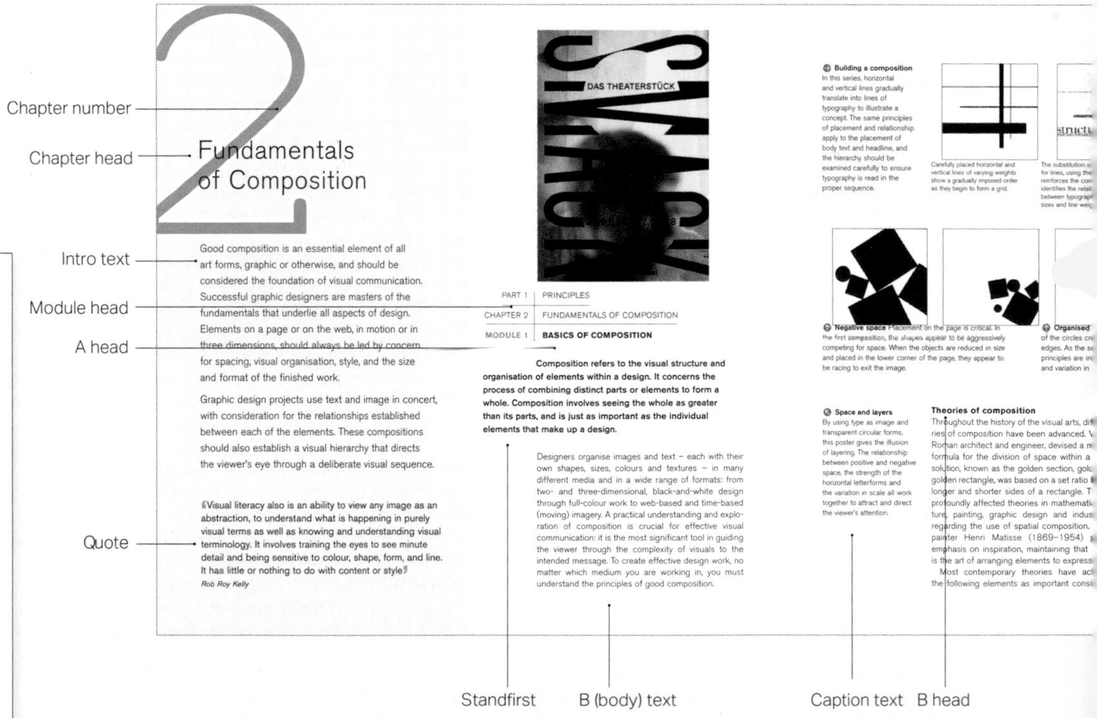
Chapter number
Chapter head
Intro text
Module head
A head
Quote
Standfirst
B (body) text
Caption text
B head
2
Fundamentals
of Composition
PART 1 PRINCIPLES
CHAPTER 2 FUNDAMENTALS OF COMPOSITION
MODULE 1 BASICS OF COMPOSITION
Theories of composition

big type is, but remember the same-sized type can look very different depending on other factors – the amount of space around it, the relative size of the text copy, the weight of font used, and so on. The central point about increasing type size is that it works as a strong form of emphasis, providing a focal point that attracts the reader's attention.

## Headings

Once agreement has been reached about the different levels of importance in the main text, they need to be translated into appropriate sizes and a format for the document should be designed. If headings are of varying levels of importance, try to make sure they are visually segregated.

There are numerous ways in which you can play with headings to improve the visual feel of a design.

- Breaking a line or word into different parts, or using alternating sizes with a heading, can look dynamic. For example, articles and conjunctions ('a', 'the', 'and', 'or') could be made smaller to give important words more stress.
- The logotypes of magazines (known as mastheads), billboards, newspaper headlines and posters are all working to catch people's attention in a short time span, so they often need to have large, well-differentiated typography to communicate effectively and quickly. Books, on the other hand, work on a slower timetable and their typographic presentation can be subtle.

⬇ **Small and bold** Small type does not necessarily mean small message. In this example, the numbers, titles and descriptions have small point sizes, and are only slightly varied, but the use of space allows these subtle details to pop, and help us navigate through the hierarchy of information.

⬇ **Big and subtle** In this example the large point size is not meant to be legible. Instead, the typography is being treated as an image for an audience to interpret and experience.

➡ **Hierarchy** Hierarchy is particularly important in poster design. You will have the attention of your audience for a very limited time, often in passing, so hierarchy must be used to signal the most important information at a glance. Supporting information is then investigated once you've grabbed their attention.

➡ **Balance** Typography is being used symmetrically in this example, mirroring the human form within the photographs opposite. The letters at the top of one page and bottom of the other have been inverted, to keep a structured rectangle form and add a unique twist, yet are still legible.

# Title 46pt
## Subtitle 28pt
### Subhead 18pt

Text                          10pt

caption                       8pt

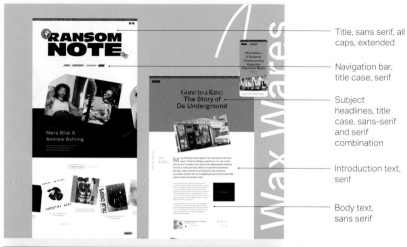

Title, sans serif, all caps, extended

Navigation bar, title case, serif

Subject headlines, title case, sans-serif and serif combination

Introduction text, serif

Body text, sans serif

↑ **Number series** Some typographers determine a hierarchy of sizes by using a Fibonacci series, in which each number is the sum of the preceding two. This may result in a sequence such as 8, 10, 18, 28, 46 or 8, 12, 20, 32, 52. Do the maths, if you like, but trust your sense of proportion and be true to the content.

→ **Establish a hierarchy** Choose a font family that gives you plenty of options such as light, book, medium, bold and Xtrabold weights, and good italics and numerals. Keep your choices limited to one to three fonts per layout.

← **Cohesion** Design, over multiple digital platforms, should be cohesive. As the user moves from one platform to another, they need reassurance that they are in the right place through repetition of typography and design elements.

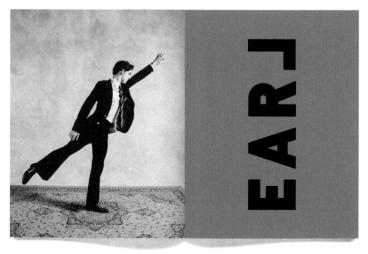

53

| PART 1 | PRINCIPLES |
| CHAPTER 3 | FUNDAMENTALS OF TYPOGRAPHY |
| MODULE 7 | **TYPOGRAPHIC RULES/BOXES AND ORNAMENTS** |

**Typographic rules (lines) and ornaments have been inherited from the letterpress tradition of setting and arranging type matter. They are still invaluable to the designer today since they serve both functional and aesthetic roles.**

Rules draw attention to specific parts of copy and break it into sections. Vertical rules can be used to separate blocks of text when other means of division are neither possible nor sufficient.

Generally, the weight (thickness) of the rules should match the tonal value of the text to which they relate. Horizontal rules work well for organising information and aiding readability. Examples can be found in tabular matter, such as timetables and contents pages, and sometimes between columns of text in newspapers and/or in books, where they can be used between each entry and to help direct the eye from item to page number.

### Highlighting text – rules and panels

Rules have gained in popularity since computer commands can underline a word or words. Some designers argue that there are more subtle means available if you want to emphasise typographic elements. Nevertheless, rules can be effectively used to highlight a piece of copy by placing them in the margin alongside the text, or as a dynamic component in the composition of a design. Widths available range from a 0.5pt (hairline) rule upwards, and are often measured in points, so that we might use a 1pt or 2pt rule.

Tinted, outlined or solid-coloured panels are popular in magazines for their ability to provide in-depth focus on a particular editorial theme, while relieving the eye from the potential strain caused by reading column after column of

◥ **Punctuate** The classic forms that serve as punctuation and ornament are celebrated as design elements in their own right. Given dimension and scale, they become the beautiful subjects of this article.

◀ **Exclaim** Paula Scher used matched weights of rules above and below each copy point to house each one in radiating shapes of near equal size. Note the control of the hierarchy through the point sizes and weights.

### GLOSSARY

**Ornaments:** Typed characters that embellish the page. Also known as flowers.

**Panel:** Device used to highlight information. Also known as a sidebar.

**Typographic rules:** Printed lines that direct the reader's eye.

Zapf Dingbats

↑ **Construct** Powerful words in tightly fitted boxes add sharp diagonals to this composition, and build an interlocked urban landscape of image and text.

← **Decorate** Printer's flowers and dingbats can be incorporated into a design system with great effect. The exuberance of these pages owes much to the enlarged ornaments that separate sections of information.

↑ **Creative glyphs** Glyphs are a fundamental part of type design. This type specimen poster showcases the variety and styles in the letterforms, and also the punctuation marks and diacritics. Elements are arranged creatively, resulting in an engaging composition.

main text type in a single size. These 'sidebars' are most effective when they contain supplementary information and are used to distinguish separate content. However, rules and boxes can easily overtake a design, particularly when they are used 'decoratively' rather than functionally.

### Rules in display type

In display setting, rules can create emphasis by drawing attention. The Constructivist art movement in early 20th-century Russia pioneered the use of rules in this way. Very heavy rules were used, running alongside, or at angles to, the copy. The popularity of the rule is still evident in today's designs.

### Ornaments

Ornaments have been in use since the origin of printing. They give a decorative feel to a layout and invoke a sense of tradition. They can also separate information, as in the title pages of traditional books. Zapf Dingbats is a well-known digital font made up of ornaments, as is Whirligig, by Zuzana Licko. However, as with rules and boxes or sidebars, overuse of ornaments should generally be avoided. If your content is unique, invent your own ornaments, icons or embellishments to enhance your type design and stay constant with your concept.

Poetica

➕ **SEE ALSO:** TYPOGRAPHIC EMPHASIS AND HIERARCHY, P78

♋ ♌ ♍ ♎ ♏ ♐ ♑ ♒ ♓ ✝ ℺ & ● ◗ ○ ■ □ ◻ ▢ ◻ ◇ ◆ ◆ ❖ ◆ ⊠ △ ⌘

Wingdings

➡ **Media as message** Paper letters are cut, stacked, blown and photographed to create a beautiful and truly unique composition. Letters can be constructed out of different media, reconstructed from found objects, hand-painted to become illustrations and handled in inventive ways to convey motion or other metaphors.

| PART 1 | PRINCIPLES |
|---|---|
| CHAPTER 3 | FUNDAMENTALS OF TYPOGRAPHY |
| MODULE 8 | **TEXT AS IMAGE** |

Contemporary designers know that type not only communicates specific meaning, but also possesses aesthetically powerful characteristics in its own right. If you think about how many expressive fonts are now available, and the way in which one can apply colour, weight, form and spacing to customise and achieve specific effects, it is possible to see type functioning as an image in its own right.

Illustrative, photographic, calligraphic and shaped text are further variations that add excitement to a design and effectively convey the mood and concept. Working with text as image requires an understanding of both the communicative and aesthetic properties of typography, and beautiful, illustrative typographic artworks are considered a collectable art form as well as a form of visual communication.

### Display type

Display type is chosen, in part, for mood, and each face has its own characteristics. Just as an artist can create mood through illustration, so can a typographer subtly illustrate meaning by choice of font, type size and weight. This effect of typography is normally seen at its fullest potential when type is used for display (above a certain size, for example 14pt), since smaller type is meant for reading. Display type exploits the specific characteristics of a given typeface.

### Symbolisation

Designers can exploit the familiarity of type by carefully manipulating suggestive letterforms so that they become images in their own right. This means that type can actually stand in for objects. Conversely, objects that resemble images can replace letters.

### Form matching content

Techniques for using type as illustration are numerous and transcend type as simple objects and vice versa. Certain words, such as verbs indicating action, particularly lend themselves to typography reflecting meaning. There can be word repetition; overlapping of characters; distorting characters to break them up, blur or roughen them; outlining or shadowing type; setting type along a curved path or in a circle; adjusting colour, weight or form; and so on. To be effective, however, positions and forms in type arrangement must reflect meaning and, as always, try to avoid clichés.

To be used effectively, our Latin alphabet, composed basically of straight lines, circles and part circles, has to be resourcefully manipulated. The decorative nature of shaped text transforms reading into a visual experience, and advertising and logotype design frequently use these techniques to give text enhanced visual impact to convey a specific message.

**Onomatopoeia:** In typography, the use of type to suggest the sounds of a spoken language, such as adding a large 'o' to the word 'open'. Marinetti and the Futurists were effective in employing onomatopoeia, in the design of books such as *Zang Tumb Tumb*.

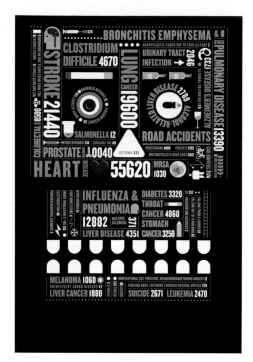

↑ **Information is beautiful** Peter Grundy's witty commentary on the statistics of death for *Men's Health* magazine arranges lines of type into a grinning and winking skull. Masterful scale management and excellent spatial relationships keep the illustration balanced, and establish the headline hierarchy by the highest numbers.

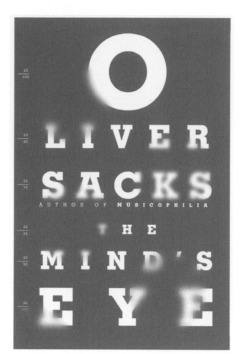

↑ **Intelligent design** This design concept by book designer Chip Kidd uses a recognisable typographic arrangement with a twist to illustrate points made by the author, Dr. Oliver Sacks. The book examines how the visual cortex processes visual information. The title was designed to evoke an eye-chart, then key areas were blurred in Photoshop.

↑ **Type and narrative**
With imagination, flat letterform shapes can be artworked into creative 3D objects. This quote, taken from the 1976 film *Carrie*, represents the 16-year-old protagonist's use of telekinetic powers to take revenge on her classmates for humiliating her. The design detail, eerie red palette and striking blue background give the composition a sense of chilling discomfort to reflect the storyline.

↑ **Interpretive typography**
Ergonomic glyphs and their composition have been created to mimic the body and movement using letterforms. The type specimen poster illustratively alludes to the concept behind this typeface by inverting the text onto a black background shaped like a moving figure.

# CHAPTER 3 ASSIGNMENTS

## ◘ Terminology

Using what you've learned about the anatomy of type in Chapter 3, annotate a premade typeface of your choice with the following anatomy. Repeat this exercise for five different typefaces, making a note of the similarities and differences in the forms and structure.

- An ascender and the ascender line
- An uppercase (cap) and the cap heigh.
- A lowercase, x-height and the baseline
- A descender and the descender line
- An eye, a bowl and a counter
- A cross stroke and a crossbar
- An ear, leg, link and loop
- A bracket, terminal and beak
- Whether your typeface is serif (highlight the serif) or sans serif

## ◘ FontStruct

FontStruct is a free, online font-building tool. You can easily create fonts using geometrical shapes, and generate TrueType fonts, ready to download and use in any application.

**1** Begin by documenting the typography on your route to work or school. Take pictures and make sketches of everything you see. Once you have a full camera or sketchbook, lay out the typefaces, identifying interesting moments within the letterforms. This could be serif flares, elegant descenders or ascenders, or interesting graphic forms within other symbols, such as ampersands or asterisks. Select one of these interesting moments and sketch out the 26 letters of the alphabet (upper A–Z and lower a–z case) following this style.

**2** Within FontStruct you are limited by a grid and series of geometrical shapes to construct your letterforms. The modules can be rotated, repeated, but not scaled or distorted beyond these parameters. This exercise asks you to design your own typeface in a simple manner. Working with modules in this way will help you understand the architecture of letterforms and the coherence and harmony intrinsic to type design.

Look for repetition in the letters. Where can you repeat your designs, and what letters are unique? Once complete, repeat this exercise with a different starting point from your collection of found type.

**3** Additional task.
Create a type specimen poster for your new typeface. This should display the complete set of letters, its name and some supporting text outlining the concept behind it. It should include examples/mock-ups of how the type can be used and arranged. Make sure that the text used relates to the concept of the typeface.

## ◘ Great expectations

This assignment is based on the project Page 1, by GraphicDesign&. It is an unusual typographic experiment designed to explore the relationship between graphic design, typography and the reading of a page. It collects the responses of 70 international graphic designers to the same brief – to lay out the first page of *Great Expectations* by Charles Dickens, a text that directly references lettering as Pip searches for clues about his family from the letterforms inscribed on their tombstone. Contributors were invited to explore, challenge or celebrate the conventions of book typography. Each layout is accompanied by a short rationale explaining the designer's decision-making process.

### Kerning
Kerning is the process of adjusting the spacing between characters in a proportional font, usually to achieve a visually pleasing result. Kerning adjusts the space between individual letterforms, while tracking adjusts spacing uniformly over a range of characters.

**1** Practise kerning at https://type.method.ac/

**2** Type and print out the words below in a typeface of your choice. Cut the letters up and rearrange them, kerning them tightly, loosely and somewhere in between. Make a note of how kerning changes the way in which the words are communicated, and select the strongest version to stick down permanently on a separate piece of paper. Repeat this exercise with two additional typefaces.

- GREAT
- EXPECTATIONS
- great
- expectations

### Leading
Leading is the distance between two baselines of lines of type. The word 'leading' originates from the strips of lead hand-typesetters would use to space out lines of text evenly.

**1** Type and print out the sentence below in a typeface of your choice. Cut the lines of text up and adjust the leading tightly, loosely and somewhere in between. Make a note of how leading changes the way in which the text is communicated, and select the strongest version to stick down permanently on a separate piece of paper. Repeat this exercise with two additional typefaces.

'My father's family name being Pirrip, and my Christian name Philip, my infant tongue could make of both names nothing longer or more explicit than Pip. So, I called myself Pip, and came to be called Pip.'

### Paragraph
Line length is the width of a block of typeset text. A block of text or paragraph has a maximum line length that fits a determined design. If the lines are too short, then the text becomes disjointed; if they are too long, the content loses rhythm as the reader searches for the start of each line.

**1** Type and print out the paragraph below in a typeface of your choice. Adjust the paragraph to short line lengths (5 words per line), long line lengths (20 words per line) and somewhere in between. Which do you think is more legible, and why? Make a note of how line length changes the way in which the text is communicated, and select the strongest version to stick down permanently on a separate piece of paper.

'As I never saw my father or my mother, and never saw any likeness of either of them (for their days were long before the days of photographs), my first fancies regarding what they were like, were unreasonably derived from their tombstones. The shape of the letters on my father's, gave me an odd idea that he was a square, stout, dark man, with curly black hair. From the character and turn of the inscription, "Also Georgiana Wife of the Above", I drew a childish conclusion that my mother was freckled and sickly.'

**2a** Hyphenation is the automated process of breaking words between lines to create more consistency across a text block. In justified text, hyphenation is mandatory. In left-aligned text, hyphenation evens the irregular right edge of the text, called the rag.

Pick up today's newspaper. Can you highlight the hyphens in the text? Now, using the paragraph text from the previous exercise, adjust the paragraph so it is fully justified with hyphenations. Each line should be the same width (120mm per line). What does this do to the text? Make a note of how hyphens and justified text change the way in which the paragraph is communicated and select the strongest version to stick down permanently on a separate piece of paper.

**2b** Rivers, or rivers of white, are gaps in typesetting, which appear to run through a paragraph of text, due to a coincidental alignment of spaces. Distracting rivers are considered poor typography because they draw the eye's attention away from the words and instead towards the spaces in between them.

Pick up today's newspaper. Can you highlight the rivers in the text? Now, highlight the rivers in the outcome of the previous exercise with your pencil. Can you see them? Are they distracting?

**3** An orphan is a single word, part of a word or very short line, except it appears at the beginning of a column or a page. This results in poor horizontal alignment at the top of the column or page.

A widow is a very short line – usually one word, or the end of a hyphenated word – at the end of a paragraph or column. A widow is considered poor typography because it leaves too much white space between paragraphs or at the bottom of a page.

Pick up today's newspaper. Can you highlight the orphans and widows in the text? Now, highlight the orphans and widows in the outcome for the previous exercise with your pencil. How do they impact the way you read the text?

**Page**
Using what you have learned from the previous exercises, use the entire text from the first page of *Great Expectations*, or a text of your choice, and cut and place designs for pages that communicate the following themes:

• Timid
• Loud
• Curious
• Strict
• Simple
• Complex

## ◼ Technical annotation

Create a technical annotation for three pages from books, newspapers or magazines. For example, you might want to label elements of type design, typesetting, type hierarchy, grid systems, layout, page architecture, colour schemes, colour theory, image making, book design, book formats, binding, cover design, printing processes, paper stocks or something specific to the book theme/content, etc.

Design each technical annotation as a black-and-white A3 page.

## ◼ Further reading

Stephen Coles, *The Geometry of Type: The Anatomy of 100 Essential Typefaces*, Thames & Hudson, 2016

Steven Heller and Lita Talarico, *Typography Sketchbooks*, Thames & Hudson, 2012

Jost Hochuli, *Detail in Typography*, Hyphen Press, 2015

Sarah Hyndman, *Why Fonts Matter*, Virgin Books, 2016

Robin Kinross, *Modern Typography: An Essay In Critical History*, Editions B42, 2019

Robin Kinross, *Unjustified Texts: Perspectives on Typography*, Editions B42, 2019

Ellen Lupton, *Thinking with Type*, Princeton Architectural Press, 2010

Ellen Lupton, Farah Kafei, Jennifer Tobias, Josh A. Halstead, Kaleena Sales, Leslie Xia and Valentina Vergara, *Extra Bold: A Feminist, Inclusive, Anti-racist, Nonbinary Field Guide for Graphic Designers*, Princeton Architectural Press, 2021

Lindsey Marshall and Lester Meachem, *How to Use Type*, Laurence King Publishing, 2013

Yulia Popova, *How Many Female Type Designers Do You Know?*, Onomatopee Projects, 2020

# Fundamentals of Colour

**To understand how to choose or assign colour for a specific purpose, designers must first develop knowledge of how colour works, how colours are classified, and the terms used to describe them.**

A thorough understanding of colour is essential to expert design, and is one of the most important tools in graphic design. There are infinite variations of colours at the designer's disposal, and endless ways of combining them across many media, from printed inks to screen-based colours, each with their own characteristics.

Colour has a unique, complex language, and the ability to change its meaning when partnered with other colours. When choosing colours to incorporate into your design, you will need to consider issues of contrast and harmony, and how these might affect legibility in typography. You can also set the mood of a design by using the psychology of colour, but you must be sure your selected colours convey the correct message at an unconscious level, and that they are suitable for the audience your project is intended to reach.

Colour is differentiated in three main ways: hue, tone and saturation. 'Hue' refers to the colour's generic name – for example, red, yellow or blue. A single hue will have many variations ranging from light (tint) to dark (shade). This is called tone or value. A single hue will also vary according to its saturation or chroma (also known as intensity). Saturation ranges from full intensity to low intensity, or from brightness to greyness. Colour can also be described by its temperature and movement. Hues in the red spectrum appear warmer and closer to the viewer than hues in the blue spectrum, which appear colder and further away.

Complementary colours, such as red and green, lie opposite each other on the colour wheel, whereas analogous colours, such as green and blue, lie adjacent to each other. The former are associated with contrast; the latter are linked to harmony. Certain colours have a profound effect on each other when combined. They can vibrate or blend, appear vibrant when partnered with one colour and muted when placed with another. The more you experiment with colour, the more you will understand how to select and group various hues for meaning.

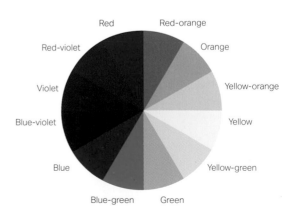

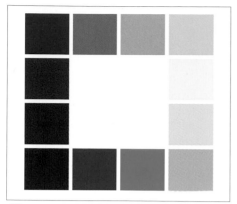

⬆ **Hue** distinguishes one colour from another. It is the generic name of the colour – red, say, as opposed to blue.

⬆ **Tone** (or value) is the relative lightness or darkness of a colour. A colour with added white is called a tint; a colour with added black is called a shade.

⬆ **Saturation** (or chroma) is roughly equivalent to brightness. A line of high intensity is a bright colour, whereas one of low intensity is a dull colour. Two colours can be of the same line but have different intensities.

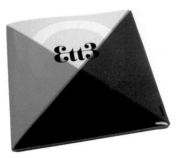

⬅ **Colour wheel** Primary, secondary and tertiary colours of pigment are shown on the wheel. The primary colours are red, yellow and blue. Secondary colours are made by mixing any two primary colours together, producing orange, green and violet. A tertiary colour is produced by mixing a primary colour with the secondary colour nearest to it on the wheel. The tertiary colours here are red-orange, yellow-orange, yellow-green, blue-green, blue-violet, and red-violet.

⬆ **Subtractive colour** An acetate envelope printed with transparent primary colours transforms the cover of a publication and creates multiple triangles in varying hues and tones as it is removed. This same effect can be viewed digitally by working with transparencies and adding layers to your file. Experimenting with colour will help you learn to control the hierarchy in page design, create readability in typography, and set the mood and pace.

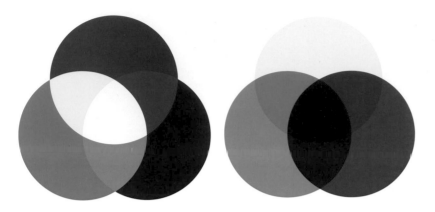

← **Onscreen colour** Additive primaries and RGB light are used to create colours on computers, televisions and monitors. Combined, the additive primaries result in white light.

← **Printing primaries** Subtractive primaries and CMYK – cyan, magenta, yellow and key (black) are the primaries used in printing. When combined, subtractive colours make black.

**Advancing and receding colour:** Colours in the red spectrum appear to advance toward the human eye, whereas those in the blue spectrum appear to recede.

**Colour modes:** The expression of colour in numerical values that enable us to mix them efficiently: CMYK, LAB, RGB.

**Simultaneous contrast:** The human eye tends to differentiate between two neighbouring colours by emphasising their differences rather than their similarities – background colours affect foreground colours (the image).

**Vibration:** Complementary colours of equal lightness and high saturation tend to make each other appear more brilliant, and cause the illusion of motion along the edges where they both meet.

**Weight:** Colours differ in perceived 'weight'. For example, if a man were to move two large boxes equal in size, one pale green and the other dark brown, he would probably pick up the green one because it appeared lighter. It is generally assumed that blue-greens look lighter whereas reds appear stronger, and therefore heavier.

### Additive and subtractive primaries

To understand how colour works, the most important point to know is that coloured light (additive colours or the RGB system) and coloured pigment (subtractive colours or the CMYK system) do not work in the same way. To put this differently, if you are working with your computer, the colour on your monitor (RGB system) will not be the same as the colour that is printed (CMYK system). This phenomenon creates problems for printed projects, since colours on screen appear brighter than in print.

With printed matter you will be working with subtractive colour. Here, each colour printed onto a paper stock subtracts from white, and if the three primaries overlap, black results. The colour wheel shows primary colours; the subtractive primaries are red, yellow and blue. Secondaries are a mix of any two primaries, resulting in orange, green and violet, and tertiaries are a mix of an adjacent primary and secondary colour. The term 'full colour' refers to four-colour printing and to achieve a full range of colours printers use cyan, yellow, magenta and black (known as CMYK; K = black = key colour).

### Pantone

An additional colour used in a project is called a flat colour or sometimes a spot colour. When selecting colours for this, you should use a universal matching system known as Pantone Matching System (PMS). Pantone colour is mixed from 15 pigments (including black and white) and is primarily used for print colour matching. This system is different from the CMYK system and few colours can be matched between them. For more information, see pages 132–133.

### Process charts and modes

When printing in full colour (CMYK), you will find it useful to identify and specify the exact colour that you want to see printed by using a printer's process colour guide. This will show you all of the colours that you can make by specifying and combining different tints of cyan, magenta, yellow and black. When designing for print on a screen, be sure you are working in CMYK mode, not RGB. Once you have chosen your colour, you can make a new swatch on your document, specifying the different tints. This is the only accurate way to specify the printed colour that you will achieve when ink goes onto paper.

➕ **SEE ALSO:** PRINTED COLOUR, P132

### Printer relationship

A good relationship with a printer is fundamental for getting the most successful outcomes. Software is in a continuous state of updating, so it is easy to be left behind and have to address software conversion issues between computers. As a result, simple design elements such as colours, fonts, bleeds and pagination can all go wrong after the file is sent. Becoming familiar with a limited number of printers not only means they are aware of your preferences, but you'll also have someone that is willing to catch mistakes before production.

### Communication

Communication is key; if your printer is using terms you are unfamiliar with, ask them to elaborate. When your printer says 300gsm cover stock or 4/4 perfect bound, do you know what they are talking about? Basic print terminology is important to come to terms with, not only for avoiding mistakes but also for understanding the print options available to you.

### Preparation

Pre-press and file preparation can vary from printer to printer, so it is important that you have a conversation about file formats, colour palettes and bleed in advance of printing your work. If in doubt about your choices, ask the printer for a mock-up, although this usually comes with an extra fee.

### Calibration

If you are working on a project that requires very specific colour specifications you should talk to the printer about the possibility of calibrating your computer screen to the print machines, or being aware of the variety of colours when using different printers.

### Loyalty

And finally, loyalty is important. Printers do not usually turn a profit when dealing with student projects; you are an investment, so make sure you bring custom to them when you are working in the professional world.

⬇ **Greyscale** Squares in tones of black and white create halftones and can define light and shadow in both an abstract and a representational way. Subtle variations in the value of each square will create gradients that blend seamlessly.

⬇ **Movement and contrast** Reds, yellows and orange values come to the foreground of the composition, and blues and greens seem to be further away. This example adds scale change to colour theory to complete the effect of motion.

⬇ **Vibrating edge** When complements in red and green are adjacent, the eye perceives a faint white line along the edge. Vibrating edge is used to stunning effect in this design, but the same technique can render typography unreadable.

⬅ **Fluoro** The use of bright fluoro colours in this poster and set of business cards creates an attention-grabbing set of visuals. Using a very bright palette can provide a variety of different visual solutions for varying formats, while still being bold and cohesive.

| PART 1 | PRINCIPLES |
|---|---|
| CHAPTER 4 | FUNDAMENTALS OF COLOUR |
| MODULE 2 | **COLOUR LEGIBILITY, CONTRAST AND HARMONY** |

Knowledge of the context in which finished work will be viewed is fundamental to the use of colour in graphic design. How that colour is perceived, and how legible it is, will vary greatly depending on whether it is viewed on a screen or in a print-based medium. Colour has a dramatic effect on legibility and needs to be considered very carefully. Contrast and harmony are ways in which a design can be further enhanced.

⬆ **Pastel tones** Super Garden's herb packaging uses an extensive pastel palette to evoke an organic/health-orientated product line. The gentle colour treatments result in a delicate touch throughout, distinguishing and unifying the individual products while being aesthetically pleasing.

➕ **SEE ALSO:**
READABILITY AND LEGIBILITY, P76

COLOUR TERMINOLOGY, P88

If you are designing a website or an onscreen project such as film credits, you'll be working with additive colours in the RGB mode. These are somewhat reliable monitor to monitor and have the lumens associated with onscreen colours. Very subtle variations may go unnoticed on screen, and care should be taken to avoid additional vibration when combining colours. If you are designing for print, be sure you are working in CMYK mode. This will enable you to come reasonably close to your intended selections, but test printing is the only reliable way to be sure your colours are correct. As explained in Module 1, problems can occur on translation to print in subtractive colours. Both clients and designers can be misled into expecting printed colours to have the same saturation and tonal range as those approved on screen. Don't rely on your monitor unless the finished design work is intended for the screen. Request scatter proofs and view your work in the same context as your intended audience to determine if your colours are successful before the final print run.

### Colour legibility

Legibility refers to how clearly something can be read. Many factors can influence colour perception and legibility; for example:

- lighting and viewing conditions in the reading environment will have a clear effect on the legibility of both print- and screen-based work – compare viewing a monitor in a darkened room and under direct sunlight;
- selection of colours;
- background colours and textures on which colours are printed; and
- size and shape of type or image used.

Good colour legibility is achieved when ground and colour have contrast – for example, deep violet (the colour nearest to black) on a white ground. The legibility decreases by moving the image colour towards yellow, however, because violet and yellow are complementary and may cause a vibrating edge. Changing the contrast is key to legibility, which means using your knowledge of the colour wheel.

## Contrast and harmony

Colour should both contribute to and support the content of a design, and it should reinforce the ideas you are giving visual form to. Therefore, it is important to understand how colour can work in contrast and in harmony. Both are related to legibility and colour associations, and affect design function and perception.

Allocating colour proportion is a critical decision. For example, a small amount of bright red in a complementary scheme can have a stronger impact than equal proportions of red and green. Equal amounts of a saturated red and green can actually result in unpleasant visual discord, and may bisect your composition in undesirable ways. You can avoid this by varying the saturation levels of the hues. By using a greater proportion of green with less saturation and a red with good saturation, the red is given extra emphasis. You can reduce the vibrancy of a hue by adding a bit of its complement to it, greying the colour effectively enough to change the relationship between your selections. With analogous schemes, the hues tend to have less vibrancy and therefore similar proportions can be used to pleasing effect.

Designers who develop an understanding of the complex and subtle ways in which colours interact will be able to explore new ways to express graphic ideas. Practical needs, such as legibility and the requirements of the work, should always be considered as a fundamental part of the design process. Experimentation will further your colour expertise; try a design project without using black or white, and use the values, tints and hues of colour to solve your design challenges.

**⬆ Limited colours** By keeping the colour palette to a minimum, you can create a striking, complementary visual. For the event Night Light for The Black Woman is God series, the designer has used a limited palette of orange, black and white. The colours create various areas of focus, including the sharp white text on the heavy black background that draws the viewer to the important text on the design.

**⬇ Layers and texture** The use of subtle colour schemes and the layering of textures creates an alluring design for Silk Events. The solid blocks of colour and typographic shapes combined with the cloudy overlay create dynamic and deluxe visuals.

## GLOSSARY

**Analogous:** Similar, comparable, alike; for example, two colours that are near to each other, such as grass green and leaf green, are analogous.

**Contrast:** Differentiation between two or more elements, in this context, of image colour. For example, high contrast is between black and white, or blue and orange; low contrast is between two similar shades of blue, for example cyan and cornflower.

**Harmony:** Image with a balance of two or more colours that work together – for example, taupe and grey.

| PART 1 | PRINCIPLES |
|---|---|
| CHAPTER 4 | FUNDAMENTALS OF COLOUR |
| MODULE 3 | **COLOUR ASSOCIATIONS** |

**Why are certain colours preferred, or seen to be more effective? It is because colours have, throughout history, come to hold particular associations that most likely derive from nature, and have, over time, become rooted in human psychology. They have come to possess cultural, symbolic and often personal associations. To use it well, you need to understand how colour works both as a language and as a system of signs, and how it creates an emotional response.**

↑ **Seeing red** The colour red is associated with caution in most Western cultures, but with good fortune and luck in China. This bilingual logotype uses the brilliance of a nearly primary red to evoke the imprint made by a traditional Chinese ink seal and to announce an American exhibition of contemporary Chinese artists. The strength of the colour also allows the viewer to see the letter 'I' in ink, even though it is bleeding off the edge.

Intelligence, memory, experience, history and culture all play a part in colour perception. Although individuals may perceive colours with slight variation, colour perceptions have different meanings depending on psychology and cultural background. Colours have symbolic associations in all societies, depending on context, and different cultures assign different meanings.

• Black is the colour of mourning and death in the industrialised West, whereas in China and India the colour of mourning is white.
• Red does not have the instant conventional association with 'stop' in those countries where cars are less pervasive, and is associated with good luck in China.
• Green was associated with poison in the 19th century through its links with arsenic, whereas today it is seen as the colour of spring and environmental awareness.
• Blue is associated with postage in the US, where the mailboxes are blue, whereas in Sweden or Britain you would look for the colour red.
• Yellow is the colour of courage in Japan.

The meaning of colour can change over time and across different cultures. If you are designing for international markets, you need to be particularly aware of such differences.

### Colour in emotion and language

While colour associations are highly subjective, despite local differences, colours and hues may have some universal characteristics. Reds, oranges and yellows stimulate the senses and tend to be perceived as warm, capable of exciting feelings of cheeriness, good health or aggression. Opposite on the colour wheel, blues and greens are seen as cool, with connotations of calmness, peace, safety and/or depression.

There are other dimensions that also influence perception. For example, compositions close in value may seem hazy, vague or introspective, whereas dark combinations might evoke night, fear or mystery. High colour intensities are dynamic and create a feeling of movement. Clearly, colour perceptions are rooted in psychology. They are even used figuratively to describe feelings. 'Seeing red' or 'singing the blues' are common descriptions of states of mind.

↑ **Colour schemes** The use of a flamboyant colour scheme can be impactful and eye-catching. When designing with any colour combination, place an emphasis on the contrast between background and foreground elements to ensure that each element is easy to see and read.

→ **Multiple palette** This vibrant poster series has a consistent design that allows for a flexible colour palette, while remaining recognisable. This one-off approach makes the posters stand out and more memorable to an audience.

## Colour theorists

**Josef Albers** (1888–1976) proposed that colours are never stationary; that is, they are constantly changing in relation to the colours surrounding them.

**Johannes Itten** (1888–1967) created colour experiments based on contrasts such as temperature or hue, and associations based on seasons.

**Wassily Kandinsky** (1866–1944) developed his colour usage in terms of spiritual moods and relations to musical instruments and sounds. His paintings are a synthetic colour expression of sound.

**Wilhelm Ostwald** (1853–1932) set up an order of colours based around the concepts of harmony and disharmony.

**Mary Gartside** (1765–1809) had her work on colour theory published privately under the disguise of traditional watercolouring manuals. Art Historian Alexandra Loske claims she is the only woman known to have published a theory of colour until the 20th century due to gender issues with regard to publishing, self-promotion and the intellectual activity of women artists in the early 19th century.

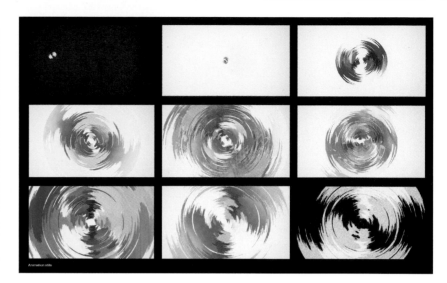

↑ **Bright palette** The right palette can immediately associate the viewer with the intended message or product. This colourful display of sound waves and vibrations has a palette inspired by the energy of music. The moving image sequence allows the colours to blur together, furthering the concept of movement and sound.

↓ **Muted palette** Sophisticated, muted values have previously been associated with a higher price point in retail packaging, but are more commonly linked with organic or natural materials. Natural colour values and repeated forms combine with a sudden pop of vibrant orange in this anti-plastic packaging campaign, to add an edgy element to an environment-conscious treatment.

**Future Folds**

When did it become accepted for something as perishable as food to be contained in something as indestructible as plastic? The convenience of supermarkets have distanced us from the origins of our food, where even we become disgusted by the things we consume. Inspired by South East Asian leaf folding craft, we invite you to revive your sense of curiosity and explore the potential of banana leaves as a sustainable packaging alternative.

## GLOSSARY

**Associations:** Connections between colours and emotions, culture, experience and memory.

**Connotations:** A colour's broader associations, for example: green – jealousy, naivety, illness, environment, nature.

**Denotations:** What the colour literally means, or is; for example, a red rose is a green stem with red petals.

⊕ **SEE ALSO:** COLOUR TERMINOLOGY, P88

| NORTH 10 | SOUTH 76 | EAST 130 | WEST 182 | CENTRAL 224 |
|---|---|---|---|---|

| PART 1 | PRINCIPLES |
|---|---|
| CHAPTER 4 | FUNDAMENTALS OF COLOUR |
| MODULE 4 | **COLOUR AS INFORMATION** |

Colour is a powerful tool, especially in information design, where it is used to help the designer organise data into various structures, and to aid the experience of 'reading' a design. Psychologists have proved that the colour of an object is seen before its shape and details. Because colour works at this basic level, it is very good at keeping things defined, reinforcing informational hierarchies, guiding the eye through complex systems and data, and aiding navigation through physical spaces.

← ↑ **Charting information**
Beautifully organised, well designed information grabs the attention and is likely to be examined thoroughly. Here, a simple colour system is used in an infographic for London beer. The chart follows a clear, five-colour coded system for the easy navigation of the geographical location of both breweries and public houses.

Systems are anything that contain a flow of complex information – maps, signage, sections, structures, web pages. Colour helps to categorise that information. Environmental graphic designers specialise in designing wayfinding systems, architectural signage, exhibition design and data mapping, and rely on colour as an important organisational tool for this.

• Complex buildings, such as hospitals and airports, need excellent signage systems to help people navigate through large, complicated architectural spaces. Colour is an obvious means to correct paths. Many shopping centres are so large that parking zones are now colour coded – a memorable way to help you remember where you left your vehicle.
• The London Underground map, developed by engineer Harry Beck, is one of the most famous maps in city transport. Beck used colour to differentiate lines, so that routes could be readily identified. The map is schematic: it is a simplified diagram that uses abstract graphic elements (lines) to represent a complex real-world situation. This most original of designs is a model copied in various forms throughout the world, including on maps for the Paris and New York City metro systems.

• In finance, colour has traditionally been used in many ways. Debits in balance sheets would be in red to denote arrears, hence the phrase 'in the red'. This custom is still in use to separate trading figures from year to year.
• Charts apply colour to quantitative and statistical information, where differing quantities of data need to be reinforced.
• Catalogues and books often have different colour-coded sections to aid navigation through pages. Penguin Books introduced the first paperbacks in Britain in the 1930s using a bright orange background. This colour quickly became fused with the books' identity. Later, the same publisher introduced another imprint, called Pelican, whose books were given a blue background. Customers quickly came to recognise the differences through the use of colour. Such visual associations can also help to delineate sections within a body of text and highlight a number of different levels of importance. The designer can set crucial parts in a bold typeface and use a different colour from the rest of the text. The eye picks up this difference very quickly.
• Web designers use colour to help people navigate through the structure of a site.

**GLOSSARY**

**Data:** Facts or pieces of information of any kind.

**Diagram:** Drawing or plan that explains the parts of something, or how something works.

**Quantitative:** Related to quantities of things, or measurements (numerical).

**Schematic:** Simplified diagram or plan related to a larger scheme or structure.

**Statistical:** Related to the collection, classification and organisation of (often numerical) information.

↑ → **Finding the way** Navigating a city requires an organised map. The London Underground map, originally developed by engineer Harry Beck in 1931, was the first to use this schematic system and has served as the model for cities all over the world. The colour-coded navigation system in Shibuya Station in Tokyo, Japan (above), has a circuit board-like diagram and is seen by 2.4 million passengers on an average day. The colour coding extends to the directional signage in the Tokyo subway system (right).

↑ **Diagrams as information** The use of diagrams to convey information is a simple way to communicate complex messages. In this example, a clear style of diagram and illustration is developed over a series of sketches and iterations to test the success of the message.

→ **Colour language** Colour is a great way to communicate. In a setting where many languages are spoken, such as an airport or a hospital, colour-coded pictograms and information systems are useful communication devices.

# CHAPTER 4 ASSIGNMENTS

## ◘ Colour dictionary

**1** Create a colour dictionary in a format of your choice. This could be a small publication, a poster or even a website. List each of the terms below with a supporting definition and a one-colour icon.

Additive colour; advancing colour; analogous colour; associations; calibration; CMYK; colour legibility; colour wheel; connotations; contrast; denotations; gamut; greyscale; harmony; hue; movement; palette; Pantone; primary colour; receding colour; RGB; saturation (or chroma); secondary colour; simultaneous contrast; spot colour; subtractive colour; tertiary colour; tone (or value); vibration; weight.

**2** Additional task
Continue to build your dictionary as you come in contact with more terms, but more importantly, research the historical, societal, cultural and political role of colour. Do you know where colours originate and why they might be in common production in your own country? Do you know why certain colours are featured on national flags or political campaigns? Colour is a fascinating device, with layers upon layers of history behind it.

## ◘ Contrast and balance

**1** With a photograph of your own, use Adobe Photoshop to edit the colour mode to monotone. Make three versions of this photograph that are red, yellow and blue. Add the text COLOUR in a typeface of your choice, and using only the three colour ways, experiment with contrast and legibility of colour combinations. Once complete, try black, grey and white typography.

Make a note of the clearest combination on screen. Now print the combinations. Are there differences? Why do you think that is?

**2** Use the same photograph, this time creating three versions that are green, orange and purple. Add the text COLOUR in a typeface of your choice and, using only the three colour ways, experiment with contrast and legibility of colour combinations. Once complete, try black, grey and white typography.

Make a note of the clearest combination on screen. Now print the combinations. Are there differences?

**3** Repeat this exercise with no restrictions on colour combinations. You can apply a red photograph with purple text, or an orange photograph with black text. Make as many combinations as you can, and write a small reflection on each experiment, outlining what works and what doesn't in terms of legibility, but also which tones and moods are generated through these colour combinations.

Make a note of the clearest combination on screen. Now print the combinations. Are there differences?

## ◘ CMYK

CMYK is a scheme for combining primary pigments. The C stands for cyan (aqua), M stands for magenta (pink), Y for yellow and K for key. The key colour in today's printing world is black, but it has not always been. This assignment takes you through the process of setting up a file for printing processes that require each colour to be layered on another to complete the final image, such as lithography, screen printing or risograph printing.

**1** Using one of your own photographs, use Adobe Photoshop to edit the colour mode to CMYK (Image ModeCMYK).

**2** Click on the Channels panel to reveal the colour channels. If the Channels panel is not visible you can locate it in the Window menu. Select the Cyan channel to reveal the greyscale channel.

**3** Select all of the image on the canvas using the Selection tool and then select Copy.

**4** Go back to the Layers panel and create a new layer. Click on the Edit menu and Paste the greyscale channel. Now, turn this new layer off, by clicking the eye icon to the left of the layer key, and select the original image again.

**5** Click back onto the Channels panel again, and select Magenta. Repeat the process as before: select all and copy. Paste the channel as before. Rename each layer as you go, to note which file matches which separation and avoid confusion.

Once you've completed the process for all channels, you have now successfully created the four colour stencils to simulate the CMYK process. To prepare them for printing, follow the next set of steps.

**6** Starting with the new Cyan layer, click on the fx symbol at the bottom of the Layers tab. A drop-down will appear. Click on Colour Overlay. A new window will open. In the Colour Overlay tab, change the Blend Mode. Click on the drop-down and select Screen.

**7** To change this colour, double-click on the rectangle. A new window will appear. Select the ink you want in the Swatches tab, then OK. Do the same for each colour layer, by selecting the ink you want to print with.

Cyan: C=100 M=0 Y=0 K=0
Magenta: C=0 M=100 Y=0 K=0
Yellow: C=0 M=0 Y=100 K=0
Key: C=0 M=0 Y=0 K=100

**8** Once you have chosen your colours, convert each layer to Smart Object. It is important to do this one by one.

**9** Select the four colour layers and choose Multiply in the drop-down. Now you can see a simulation of the printed outcome. If you want to change the colour of a layer, double-click on the one you want to edit to open a new window. A new window will open, with a .psb version of your layer.

**10** Double-click on Colour Overlay to open the window and change the colour. Do the same as before by choosing an ink in the Swatches tab. To see this change implemented in your main working file (with all the colour layers), you have to save the changes in this file.

**11** You can now see the updated layer in your first file. Once you're happy with the inks, save each layer as a separation. To save your first colour stencil, double-click on the layer to open the new window again. Turn off the Effects, then Flatten your image.

**12** Now you are ready to save this file. Go to File and Save As... Name your file appropriately with Your name/Project title and the ink colour assigned to the artwork. The format should be PDF, and you need to untick all the boxes. Select the preset High Quality Print and untick Preserve Photoshop Editing Capabilities. Click Save and you should be left with a file under 10MB.

**13** Additional tasks
If you have access, it is recommended you use these stencils to create a screen for screen printing, or a master for risograph printing. However, it is very interesting to experiment with your home or office digital printer. Start by printing the lightest colour, yellow. Reinsert your print into your printer and print with magenta. Repeat this with cyan and finally the last layer of key. How did it turn out?

**14** CMYK are the inks used in digital printing. Other forms of printing open up exciting opportunities to experiment with other colour combinations as you have done in earlier assignments. What happens if you were to swap magenta for a fluoro pink spot colour? Or yellow for a metallic gold? Experiment with these processes to gain a better understanding of ink mixes and colour combinations.

## ◘ Colour audit

Begin by investigating, researching and exploring a single colour of your choice, ready to compile a collection of visual information based on the colour for presentation. Select a colour that you have a strong connection with, whether that is one you like or dislike, a colour you see all the time or one you've never seen before.

**1** Data
Collect visual examples of your colour being used or referenced in the following areas:

Architecture; art history; consumer culture; contemporary art; emotion; the environment and environmental issues; the everyday; graphic design; history; literature; music; non-Western art; print making; politics; popular culture; society and societal issues; and any other category you can find.

**2** Physical swatches
Collect at least 100 physical – not downloaded – 10-cm (4-in) square swatches of your colour: for example, squares cut from magazines and newspapers, paint sample cards, fabric cuttings, printed photographs, ephemera, found items, screen-printed offcuts, ceramic shards, painted and unpainted signage, food packaging, etc.

**3** Digital swatches
Repeat this task using only digital swatches: for example, screengrabs taken from digital logos, films, animations, websites, social-media channels, swatches constructed on digital software programs, digital photographs, etc.

**4** Organisation
Brainstorm and sketch ways in which you can bring this information together. What is the most interesting finding you have come across? Is it an individual piece of information, a combination of pieces of information or something about the pure volume of information you have unearthed? What is

it about this information you find interesting and how could you communicate this to someone who is unfamiliar with your colour?

Create a printed catalogue of your research and a publication that communicates something of interest to your peers. These two outcomes must feel part of a set.

## ◘ Further Reading

Sean Adams Noreen Morioka and Terry Stone, *Color Design Workbook: Real World Guide to Using Color in Graphic Design*, Rockport Publishers, 2017

Josef Albers and Nicholas Fox Weber, *Interaction of Color*, Yale University Press, 2013

Aaron James Draplin, *Draplin Design Co. Pretty Much Everything*, Abrams Books, 2016

Regina Lee Blaszczyk, *The Color Revolution*, The MIT Press, 2012

Alexandra Loske, *Colour: A Visual History*, Ilex Press in association with the Tate, 2019

Richard Mehl, *Playing with Color: 50 Graphic Experiments for Exploring Color Design Principles*, Rockport Publishers, 2013

Ruben Pater, *CAPS LOCK: How Capitalism Took Hold of Graphic Design and How to Escape From It*, Valiz, 2021

Ruben Pater, *The Politics of Design: A (Not So) Global Design Manual for Visual Communication*, BIS Publishers, 2016

Kassia St Clair, *The Secret Lives of Colour*, John Murray, 2018

Chris van Uffelen, *Designing Orientation: Signage Concepts & Wayfinding Systems*, Braun, 2020

Victionary, *You Are Here: A New Approach to Signage and Wayfinding*, Victionary, 2013

Victionary, *You Are Here 2: A New Approach to Signage and Wayfinding*, Victionary, 2022

Banker Wessel and Richard Baird, *Process – Visual Journeys in Graphic Design*, Counter-Print, 2022

# Practice

In this part, you will be introduced to the tools and techniques of design, which form a key group of skills for professional practice in any field. You may use powerful digital tools regularly in the production of work, and it is essential that you familiarise yourself with the industry-standard technologies that designers utilise. However, these tools cannot generate the idea, nor can they execute the design for you, and the kinds of conceptual, intellectual and formal skills you bring are what will differentiate you from other designers. In short, you need both an excellent understanding of principles alongside outstanding technical skills. Being able to design formally and/ or conceptually eloquent and innovative work is only half the story, since you then need to get the work into print, on screen, in three dimensions or across multiple platforms, and so on. 'Design is the battle, but printing is the war' used to be the designer's battle cry, describing the problems designers may face when getting a design from the sketch stage to a final, printed piece of work. Those problems still exist, but designers now need to be able to deliver graphics that will be viewed in multimedia applications, the screen being pre-eminent. Chapter 5 introduces basic image making and sourcing, followed by an overview of the key technical and software skills used in design today, including Photoshop and InDesign. In Chapter 6, various production issues, including colour for print, PDFs, paper stocks and press checks, are introduced. Chapter 7 is dedicated to design for digital applications, and

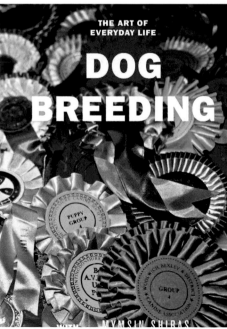

summarises the specific technical skills, tools and languages these platforms require. Here, you'll find design considerations for different styles of website, key software tools and how to bring creativity to an 'off-the-peg' CMS (and the acronyms are explained, too!). There is even a tick list of questions to ask a client during the website planning stages. Chapter 8 overviews seven of the key areas of design, including editorial design, web design and motion graphics. These 'tasters' aim to give a sense of the key skills and aptitudes needed to work in each field, and of the highs and lows of each profession, and to provide pointers to additional resources, including 'Best in the business', which highlights some of the most influential practitioners in that area of design.

PART

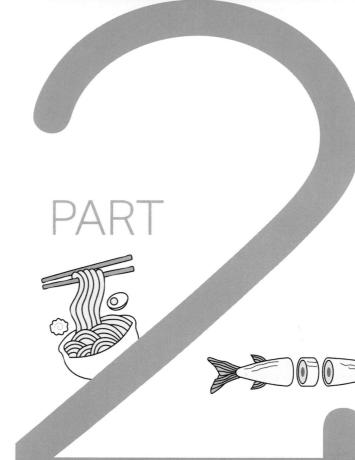

2

# 5 Tools and Technologies

Graphic design production and practice is almost completely digital, and dependent on changing technologies. Previously, typographers would set type, pre-press production would be crafted by specialists at a printing company and designers would commission a photographer. Now, one person can do all of these jobs on a computer, under the gamut of desktop publishing (DTP).

This chapter introduces you to the software applications and tools that are most commonly used in the graphic design industry. Each module focuses on a specific medium, such as photography, or a specific software application, such as Photoshop, grounding you in its unique tools, history and terminology and giving you the opportunity to explore further. New applications, and updated versions of the ones in use now, will continue to be adopted into the practice of graphic design. The best way to prepare for a constant learning curve is to recognise the commonalities in the way they function, and gain proficiency through practice.

➜ **Layers** Thoughtful framing and the clever use of reflection, darks and lights can add depth and drama to an image.

**Photography and image making/sourcing are key skills for graphic designers. Not all designers are good photographers, but an understanding of the skills needed to compose and shoot images is essential. Your photograph may only serve as a placeholder, but having the image to hand will help you work out rough proportions, assign and design a composition, and can serve as research for drawing and/or digital illustration.**

Fortunately, the rules of good design – composition, contrast, hierarchy, rule of thirds and colour theory – don't change much for different design disciplines. Frame your photos the way you would approach any assignment, and compose each shot with purpose.

**Types of photography**
There are many broad categories of photography and image production that are relevant to designers. For our purposes, we'll focus on the most common, which are:

• objects and products
• portraits and images of people
• landscapes and buildings
• ephemera and texture
• reference and research

Consider the purpose of your design challenge and what your needs might be before you shoot. Make sure the resulting images fit the purpose, and that you have considered all aspects of your image as it relates to your design work. For example, product images are generally brightly lit, sharp and clear, whereas landscapes and portraits may have a variety of styles and convey a specific mood.

Your designs will be more powerful if you learn how to spot an effective, well-composed picture and can recognise a good tonal range. Think about how the image can combine effectively with typography, colour treatments and other illustrations.

There are many reasons why one image will make you stop and stare and another will make you turn the page without stopping to look at all. It certainly helps if a picture is in focus, correctly exposed, placed where it is shown off at its best and has some interesting content, but images can be a powerful form of expression within a design. Try to capture images that reflect the design sensibility you need to communicate your message, and note that there are limits to how much you can alter them electronically in post-production.

← **Asymmetry** Positioning the focal point off-centre breaks the traditional layout of a photograph, capturing the attention of the viewer by adding a sense of dynamism to the composition.

← **Symmetry** Centred and still, a symmetrical composition can evoke calm and emptiness. Drama is intensified in this case by the use of an ominous monochromatic palette.

↙ **Perspective** The variance in distance and the use of the perspective of the viewer within this photograph evoke powerful sensations of being inside the construction, at the location itself.

↓ **Contrast** The strong contrast in black-and-white photography can create a compelling and striking composition. In this instance, exaggerated shadows and light within the environment pull the focus to different areas of the image.

→ **Rule of thirds** The rule of thirds involves mentally dividing up your image using two horizontal lines and two vertical lines, and positioning the important elements along those lines, or at the points where they meet. In this image, the face and yellow bag lie roughly where the lines would meet, and therefore pull in your focus. The black column of colour on the left runs down a vertical line of this grid, creating an aesthetically balanced composition.

⬆ **Composition** Composition plays a big part in what is being communicated. The design detail in the identity across this stationery range is amplified through the composition of the arranged objects. As a result, the organisation's message is clear, aesthetically pleasing and professional.

⬇ **Cropping** By cropping photographs you can alter the impact and composition for application. By applying this thinking and the use of bold typography, the covers for *The Art of Everyday Life* series are very engaging and intriguing, persuading the audience to learn more.

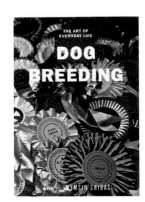

➕ **SEE ALSO:** FUNDAMENTALS OF COMPOSITION, P32
FUNDAMENTALS OF COLOUR, P88
PHOTOSHOP, P110
PHOTOMONTAGE AND COLLAGE, P113

## Which camera?

Digital cameras and smartphones enable high-quality, high-resolution images to be created instantly and with ease. Digital cameras and smartphones are immediate, versatile and capable of taking reasonable-quality images in less-than-ideal lighting conditions. Most have great storage space, and you can select and delete unwanted images immediately. Many smartphones have great internal cameras that offer instant availability and the option to email or upload the photo to social media as soon as you have taken it, but the quality may not have the tonal range you need for a final image.

To take a good picture you will need a decent camera. If possible, beginners should use at least an 8 megapixel digital SLR (single lens reflex) with a 22–80mm zoom range, a viewfinder or viewing screen, and a macro setting option. A macro setting will allow easy focusing for close-ups and detail. Good SLR cameras allow you to shoot what you see, and choose where to focus the image and exactly how to compose it. Automatic digital cameras calculate lighting, focal distance and aperture settings with no input from the photographer, setting up a point-and-shoot attitude with reasonable results. For manual digital photography, a knowledge and understanding of how the camera works is necessary to give the photographer far

greater control. Practice and study will allow you to create unorthodox and striking images.

## Light and colour, composition and cropping

If you are creating photographs for illustration work, you want the initial photograph to feature as much detail and clarity, and balanced lighting, as possible. Further effects can be added electronically or manipulated in Photoshop, if desired, but you are always limited in post-production. You can always blur a clear image, then return to a clear image, but a blurred photo will be of limited use. Consider what you need from the photo before you shoot. You might be thinking in terms of high-saturated colour, black and white, or sepia tone, but always shoot in colour first to give yourself the option to experiment with all types of colour manipulations in post-production. Also consider the lighting: direct bright sunlight may bleach out the image, whereas overcast conditions will flatten the contrast. Most cameras have a built-in light meter. When composing your shot, make sure that it is as close to the centre of the contrast range as possible. To crop an image is to select only a part of the final shot. Often, cropping is used to take out an unwanted part of the picture. It is a useful tool that can help improve composition and eliminate superfluous information to strengthen the image.

## Which lens?

Different lenses extend the capabilities of the camera.

- A normal lens on a digital or film SLR is 35mm, considered to be near enough to human vision.
- A macro lens captures sharp, extreme close-ups of objects.
- A wide-angle lens captures a wider vision, but with perspective distortion.
- A telephoto lens captures objects at a distance.

## Archiving your images

The storage of digital images needs care. It is not enough to have them saved only on a computer; they also need to be backed up on portable external hard drives or a cloud-based (virtual) system of digital storage, such as Dropbox, iCloud or Carbonite. If a negative is scratched, it can still be printed and retouched, but the failure of a hard drive will result in complete loss of all your images.

## Sourcing images

When making decisions regarding what images to use, the principal point to consider is whether the brief, timetable and fee allow or justify producing an image from scratch, or if it might be necessary to source, or purchase, a ready-made image from elsewhere. The Internet provides the quickest way to source stock images, from websites such as iStockphoto, Getty Images or Dreamstime. These images can be purchased and downloaded from a website on a royalty-free basis using a credit system, and are usually priced by usage. For example, on some sites a picture of a dog can be purchased for one credit for a 72dpi image, acceptable for a web-based illustration, or for five credits as a 300dpi image, for a print-based illustration.

Images can be bought either for specific time periods or outright. A drawback to purchasing a temporary licence is that there is no guarantee that other designers will not use the same picture in their designs. Your client may prefer that you purchase the picture outright, which will cost more. Customising the image is always the best creative option. You can select the elements you need and create your own image through collage or retouching.

## Tips and terms

Take time to check and adjust your settings, and always bracket your shots – adjust your f-stop up and down as you take multiple versions.

- **Depth of field:** The zone of sharpness in an image from the nearest point to the furthest point that appears to be sharp. Lens aperture, focal length, point of focus and distance from the camera will all affect this zone of sharpness.
- **F-stop/focal length and aperture:** Size of aperture or 'iris' inside a camera, which controls the amount of light that hits the film or pixel sensor; the range on a general camera is f4 (large aperture) to f22 (small aperture). A large aperture (f2, for example) brings more light into the camera and results in a softer image; a small aperture (f16, for example) allows less light into the camera but gives a sharper image.
- **Filter:** Plates of glass or plastic attached to the front of the lens in order to accentuate different qualities. For example, a polarising filter cuts down light glare, while a colour filter enhances different colours. This is also a term that has carried over to various software applications and social-media outlets as a post-production tool.
- **SLR:** Single lens reflex. These types of camera use a viewfinder and mirrors so that the photographer's sightline goes through the main lens and results in a what-you-see-is-what-you-get image.

➡ **Depth** The use of depth and distance in this image pinpoints two areas of focus. The first is the cyclist, who is more in focus and vividly coloured. The second is the landscape in the distance, which is less sharp to suggest the expansiveness and remoteness of the area.

### GLOSSARY

**ISO:** International Organisation for Standardisation. This sets a standard range for virtual film speeds in digital cameras: ISO 100, for example, works best in good lighting conditions for stationary objects; ISO 1600 works best in poor lighting conditions and for mobile objects.

**Placeholder or FPO ( For Position Only):** A temporary or low-resolution image in place of the high-quality counterpart during the design process.

**Resolution:** The resulting output from a digital camera. Digital cameras and some top-of-the-range camera phones have up to 12 megapixel sensors and can produce less pixelated, sharper and higher-quality images.

| PART 2 | PRACTICE |
|---|---|
| CHAPTER 5 | TOOLS AND TECHNOLOGIES |
| MODULE 2 | **INDESIGN** |

**InDesign is the industry-standard page assembly and desktop publishing application. The software allows you to bring all your lessons in composition, page layout, contrast and typography into play. Elements you create in vector software (Illustrator), or the imagery you edit in raster-based applications (Photoshop), can be combined with text and images to create brochures, magazines, posters or multi-volume publications for print and interactive application.**

Adobe InDesign is the industry-standard desktop publishing software and updates on a regular basis. Generally, Adobe files will open in any edition of the software; however, if using a higher upgrade of InDesign that will then be opened in a lower upgrade, you will first have to save it as a mark-up or IDML file. There are many features that overlap in Adobe Illustrator, Photoshop and InDesign, but it is vital you are using the correct software. For example, typography should be handled in Illustrator, as this is a vector-based design program, and photographs in Photoshop as this is a pixel-based design program. Everyone has their own unique way of using these software applications; the key is finding what works best for you.

## Work area

The main toolbar sits to the left of the screen, the canvas in the centre and the secondary toolbars to the right.

**⮕ Main toolbar**
InDesign localises its main tools into one long toolbox. Mirroring many of the functions found in Illustrator and Photoshop, the tools in this panel can be accessed by clicking the icons or utilising the keystrokes assigned to each item, such as 'V' for the Selection Tool, 'P' for the Pen Tool and 'G' for the Gradient Tool. Note that some of the items with a small arrow also reveal other fly-out tools such as Rounded Frames, the Fill Tool and the Measure Tool.

## Useful tools and features

InDesign has many tools full of features and functions to help create compositions. Here are some of the more basic yet powerful tools that are the mainstays of any InDesign user. The keyboard commands for each tool are shown in brackets.

**1 Selection Tool (V)**
Selects the entire shape or line, which can then be stretched, rotated or moved anywhere on the page.

**2 Direct Selection Tool (A)**
Selects and manipulates specific lines, path points or handle ends distinctly to change the position of individual lines, points or curves of a shape.

**3 Pen Tool (P)** Enables you to create straight or curved lines by selecting two points on the page and 'bending' to your desired shape. By clicking the Pen Tool, you can reveal the Add Anchor Point, Delete Anchor Point and Convert Direction Point Tools to manipulate the points that make up curves and lines.

The Control panel can be docked at the top or bottom of the screen, as well as float freely, like all of the panels

Master pages are the page templates upon which you can program elements such as grids, header and footer elements, and automatic page numbering

Click on Popup windows to activate

⬇ **Swatches panel** This is where all the colours used in a document are located.

A simple coloured icon to the right of your swatch indicates if the swatch is CMYK or RGB colour

To modify a colour's mix – either by typing in its numerical values or PMS number – double-click a swatch to reveal the Colour Mixer. You can also alternate between CMYK and RGB in these settings.

⬆ **Popup windows** Window organisation is important, because the amount of panels and tools necessary to do a job can easily fill up your screen. The Adobe CC applications help reclaim screen real estate by allowing users to 'dock' and minimise panels as they see fit. With a variety of options available under Window > Workspace, you can select one of the pre-organised panel arrangements or create your own. There is also a handy option to reset these workspaces if you lose something.

Standard colour swatches that accompany every document are 'None' or empty, 100% white, 100% black and Registration. They cannot be modified in InDesign. Registration black is formed by all four CMYK colours for printing on plates, as opposed to 100% black. It's called this because it is used to print the registration marks, which are those marks that the printer uses to align the four plates once your job is on press.

⬅ **Info panel** Displays layout information for the document or selected objects, including values for position, colour, size, text and rotation. For viewing only – you cannot enter or edit the information in the panel, but you can ascertain many qualities of an on-page object by hovering over it with your cursor.

**4 Type Tool (T)** Used in the creation of text boxes and edits the type within them. By working in conjunction with the Control panel and Type panels, this tool will allow you to select and modify text to create headlines, paragraph blocks and captions.

**5 Control panel** Provides a customisable array of functions for the tool you have selected from the main toolbar. The Type Tool, for example, allows you to adjust the font, leading, tracking, text weight and style, paragraph alignment, column count and margin spacing.

**6 Rectangle Frame Tool (F) and Rectangle Tool (M)** Both create rectangular, polygon and rounded forms: the Rectangle Frame Tool creates frames to insert graphics and imagery; the Rectangle Tool is for drawing shapes to fill or outline with colour. Precise adjustments to size and position are made with the Transform panel.

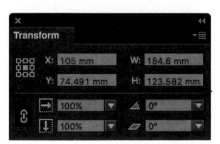

## Page layout

Creative layout design utilises different on-page items such as text boxes and image boxes to help place imagery and content, and assign colour in compositions on a generated pasteboard. These compositions can be sorted into a virtual pagination structure, comfortably up to hundreds of pages. The program also manages issues such as page size, orientation and output. The following tools are standard.

➡ **Guides** Imaginary rules are pulled over the page and viewed upon request. They do not print, but help in creating layouts and grids and lining up items. Usually gutters, margins and baseline grids are set with guidelines in the Master Pages.

❗ **Bleed**
When preparing imagery, remember to compensate for the bleed. If any of your pictures go to the edge of the page, remember to add about 3–5mm (dependent on print requirements) to that side of the image to be clipped off at press-time. This goes for background colours and lines as well.

Reoccurring graphics can be set up in Master Pages

Page numbers and running heads are set in the Master Pages

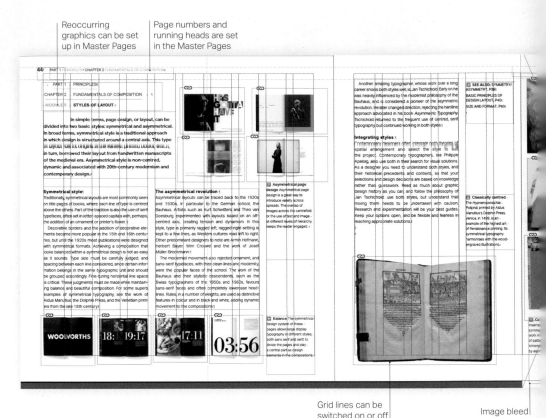

Grid lines can be switched on or off

Image bleed

## Page layout concepts

Beyond placing and sizing imagery, the designer can use desktop publishing programs to express content meaning with extensive control of typography. Through automatic flowing of text from multiple columns to multiple pages, hierarchy and information organisation is easily controlled and experimentation and changes are easily handled. Creative composition and invention in text layout require manipulation of the page items, and will cause countless ragging and adjusting. Make it part of your process to address this and leave time to fine-tune your typography when the document is completed. Magazines and newspapers around the world use desktop publishing programs to get as many words as is comfortably legible and aesthetically pleasing on a page, with grids, layouts, templates and columns to make this happen.

Master Pages and Style Sheets will help you to create almost any composition and project. In Master Pages, you can create formats to be repeated throughout a multi-page document – for example, headers, page numbers and call-outs. In the Style Sheet palette window, you can select your typographic hierarchy and set it to be constant throughout the document.

**⬇ Master Pages** These template pages, upon which predefined pages mimic grid elements and on-page template elements such as text block items, header and footer elements, and automatic page numbering, are usually found at the top of the Pages or Page Layout panel. These pre-styled layouts help in creating uniform changes throughout a large document, but can be specifically changed on a per-page basis when necessary. To unlock a Master Page item select Command/Ctrl + Shift + click.

**Style Sheets** Design and typographic styles such as colour, size, leading, position and decoration may be applied to text automatically with Style Sheets. Selections of text may be tagged with certain predefined meta-information at the click of a button. By naming a series of elements Headline, you can globally affect the styles and attributes of each selection, which is helpful and time-saving for last-minute design changes.

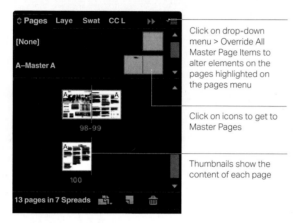

Click on drop-down menu > Override All Master Page Items to alter elements on the pages highlighted on the pages menu

Click on icons to get to Master Pages

Thumbnails show the content of each page

**❗ Page numbering**
On a Master Page, create a text box and go to Type > Insert Special Character > Markers – Current Page Number. Now, that same text block on each page will reflect the appropriate page number.

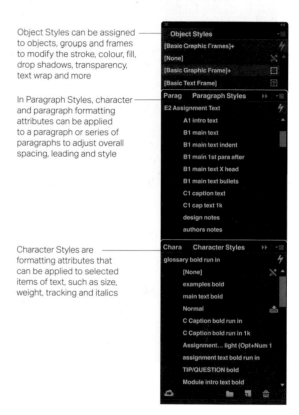

Object Styles can be assigned to objects, groups and frames to modify the stroke, colour, fill, drop shadows, transparency, text wrap and more

In Paragraph Styles, character and paragraph formatting attributes can be applied to a paragraph or series of paragraphs to adjust overall spacing, leading and style

Character Styles are formatting attributes that can be applied to selected items of text, such as size, weight, tracking and italics

## Holding page

InDesign is a holding page. Unlike Photoshop and Illustrator, InDesign links images from the folders on your computer. If you move or rename these folders the links will break and will not export correctly. It is therefore vital that you are organised and have a good file management system (i.e. a folder for images, a folder for typefaces, etc.). To relink a broken link, select Window and Links. You will see a small icon alerting you to the broken link.

## Packaging

Exporting documents for proofing – most commonly with PDFs – and file preparation for publishing with an outside printing vendor are important details usually handled well by page-assembly programs, but you should know what vendors are looking for. Packaging allows you to group your updated InDesign file, PDF for proofing, and all the assets and links to the file, including a folder of imagery and a folder of all fonts in use. Make sure you check your font and image licensing before sending files to your printer.

**➕ SEE ALSO:** PHOTOSHOP, P110

ILLUSTRATOR, P114

PREPARING FILES FOR PRINT, P124

| PART 2 | PRACTICE |
|---|---|
| CHAPTER 5 | TOOLS AND TECHNOLOGIES |
| MODULE 3 | **PHOTOSHOP** |

**Photoshop is the industry-standard software for raster-graphics editing and manipulation, and is frequently used for collecting images and to select elements for montage or photo retouching, both for print and digital. It also has the ability to perform basic 3D modelling, basic animation and a variety of output-for-web options.**

Photoshop replaces and enhances darkroom techniques such as retouching and editing brightness and contrast, and allows for ease of cropping while providing a cleaner, 'dry', chemical-free environment for editing. The most common tools used in Photoshop for photo editing are the Spot Healing Brush, the Clone/Stamp Tool and the Patch Tool. These allow the editor to remove imperfections and unwanted objects.

Photoshop's major advantage is that imported images can be moved, edited and layered over a potentially infinite canvas without loss of information, quality or resolution. Photoshop documents with multiple layers can get quite large and may compromise the memory allocated on your computer. Be sure you save and archive the original PSD version, and flatten and save the document correctly. All Photoshop artists must have knowledge of all the selection tools available, and an understanding of layering and saving options.

### 🚫 Scanning

One way to import images into Photoshop for modification and incorporation into a design is to scan them. Most scanners will provide their own software, designed to work seamlessly with Photoshop. Options can range from the most simplistic image capture to a full range of customisable colour settings, and resolution options for photos, line art, documents or pre-screened printed material. Many scanners will allow the capture of actual objects if the depth of field is not too great. For example, if you need an image of a key, you can place a key on the scanner bed and capture the image, which can then be altered like any other photographic subject.

### Work area

This section shows the general layout of Photoshop. Additional pull-outs can be accessed through the 'Window' menu on the header bar.

➡ **Main toolbar**
This bar has easy icon access to all of the main tools, some of which also have keyboard shortcuts.

Foreground/background colour selection. Clicking on the squares selects the colour, whereas the 'X' key swaps them over

### Useful tools and features

There are five main tools that enable you to edit an isolated area of pixels without altering the rest of the image. Each of these can be accessed through the main toolbar, and many have additional options to customise the tool, located at the top of your screen in the header bar. The keyboard commands for each tool are shown in brackets.

**1 Marquee Tool (M)** Selects an area or sets up a boundary within the layer that is being worked on. Different Marquee Tools can select rectangles and ovals, and, when holding down the Shift key, geometric circles and squares can be selected. This tool also allows you to select a one-pixel-width line down or across the entire layer. This is useful when making a striped page pattern or creating a boundary line.

**2 Magic Wand Tool (M)** Selects pixels of the same colour with the Tolerance option set to 1, but within a range of colour with Tolerance set to more than 1. If the Contiguous box is unchecked, the tool will select all the pixels in the entire document that are of the same colour value, regardless of whether they are joined together or not. Use the Shift key to add pixels to the selection and the Alt key to subtract.

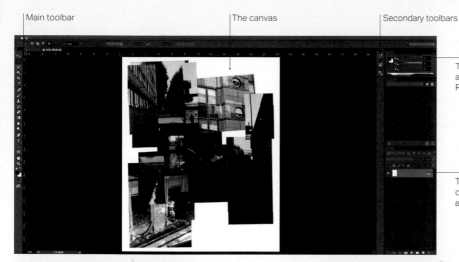

Main toolbar | The canvas | Secondary toolbars

The colour pull-out lets you adjust the colour by altering the RGB or CMYK measures

The Layers pull-out details each canvas layer and which filters or additions are on each layer

**Shortcuts**

These keyboard shortcuts are helpful and save time:
• ctrl or ⌘/C Copy
• ctrl or ⌘/V Paste
• ctrl or ⌘/Z Undo
• ctrl or ⌘/M Marquee
• ctrl or ⌘/+ Zoom In
• ctrl or ⌘/- Zoom Out
• ctrl or ⌘/W Magic Wand
• ctrl or ⌘/T Free Transform
• Space key + mouse movement: move canvas around in window.

**❗ Tablet**
A tablet with stylus pen is the preferred tool of many Photoshop artists. The pen gives the designer free range of hand movement and pinpoint precision by emulating the feel of using a brush or a pencil. The most common brand of tablet is made by Wacom.

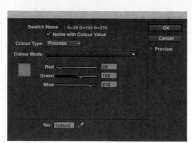

**← Colour editor** The Photoshop Colour editor when set to the CMYK (cyan, magenta, yellow, key/black) range is used for print colour. The RGB (red, green, blue) colour editor is used when designing for the Web/television. Each range has different effects on the colour usage.

**← Preset colour swatches** The swatches are used as a standard range of colours, for example black, white, 10%, 20% and 50% greys. If you have mixed your own standard swatch, or have been set a range in a brief, you can save and keep it to select when working on a design.

**3 Pen Tool (P)** Creates vector-based lines and curves with control points (see Illustrator, page 114). These points can be dragged over the layer for a better fit, converting them from fixed points. An area enclosed by the Pen Tool boundary can be affected by various fill functions or made transparent to add texture and depth.

**4 Lasso Tool (L)** Draws and selects freehand shapes. Use the Shift key to add a new selection or the Alt key to subtract. The Polygonal Lasso draws straight-line sections. Use the Alt key to toggle between the Lasso and the Polygonal Lasso Tool, and the Shift key to draw perpendicular or 45° angles. The Magnetic Lasso is the fastest way to outline and isolate a shape. The Magnetic Lasso will attach to the pixels that describe the outer edges of any photographic subject, making it a simple matter to eliminate a background or copy and paste the object into a different layer or file.

**5 Brush Tool (B)** The size, shape and colour of the Brush Tool can be changed, as can its hardness and scatter range. Alter the brush's flow rate or opacity to achieve different effects for use in retouching, adding texture or digital painting. The Brush Tool options can be found under the header bar.

## Pixels

The best way to describe a pixel is as a tiny square in a grid of squares on the monitor screen. Each square is lit by different intensities of red, green or blue light (RGB) to form the entire gamut of colours. These pixels can be modified either on their own or as a group. If these pixels are tiny enough, they merge together to form a smooth picture. Another name for this is a raster image.

---

**⊞ SEE ALSO:** INDESIGN, P106

**➡ Animation** Creating a GIF requires only a few frames to make something attention-grabbing and dynamic. These vivid illustrations are brought to life with a quick and simple animation technique.

## Resolution

Image resolution is a key area of knowledge for a graphic designer. The most common measurement of resolution is dots per inch, or DPI. At 25dpi an image is heavily pixellated; at 72dpi (used for all web-based imagery) it is clearer but not a high-enough quality for print. The standard resolution for photo quality and print images is 300dpi, or for large posters, 600dpi. Be sure your image is at 100% scale, and at the right DPI. If you enlarge a small 300dpi image by 200%, it becomes 150dpi, and will not print at a high quality. You can easily adjust a high-resolution image, e.g. 300dpi, to a low resolution, e.g. 72dpi, in Photoshop. But you cannot increase a low resolution to a high resolution, e.g. 72dpi to 300dpi.

### Animated GIF

An animated GIF can be created using a limited amount of animation, and is designed to catch the viewer's attention. Visuals can be easily animated in Adobe Photoshop by displaying a sequence of static images or 'frames'. Timing can be adjusted to further control the presentation. Animated GIFs must comply with established standards relating to overall file size, limiting the number of animation slides and controlled rotations. Typically, animations are set to loop continuously. The artwork is supplied in the GIF or Animated GIF file format. In this example, the Slug Club letterforms slightly expand and contract to give the sense of a living organism.

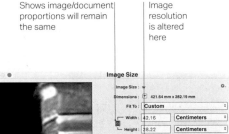

Shows image/document proportions will remain the same

Image resolution is altered here

Checking this box ensures the document proportions are kept the same or 'constrained'

### GLOSSARY

**Canvas:** The virtual 'ground' that images are placed onto in Photoshop.

**Collage:** Derived from the French word for 'to glue', involving the assemblage of elements of texture, found materials and newspapers.

**DPI:** Dots per inch; the common form of resolution measurement. Designers typically use 72dpi-sized images for web images and 300dpi-sized images for photo-realistic prints.

**Ephemera:** Objects such as newspapers, bus and train tickets, and other found textures and typography.

**Juxtaposition:** The process of putting two or more unrelated or opposite elements or objects together to create different effects.

**Montage:** Derived from the French word for 'assemble'; a picture made from pieces of other pictures.

25dpi

72dpi

300dpi

## Layering

Photoshop can layer different images and elements so that each one can be worked on separately without altering the rest of the image:

**Opacity** Changes how translucent each layer is.

**Presets** Adds colour styles and textures to the layer.

**Layer styles** Adds effects such as shadows, strokes, glowing edges and textures to the layer.

**Blending options** Changes the properties of the layer.

**Layer > Merge/Flatten** Merges all or some of the layers together.

**Filter** Applies effects such as blur, sharpen, lighting and textures.

Use these to adjust the size, resolution, colour values and white balance of each layer:
**Image > Adjustments > Hue/ Saturation**
**Brightness/Contrast**
**Image Size/Resolution**
**Canvas Size**

**Click and hold** on a layer to drag it to different positions, bringing it to the front or moving it behind other layers.

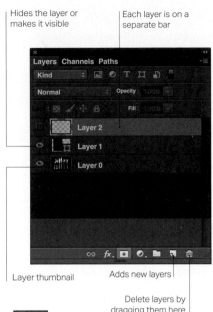

Hides the layer or makes it visible

Each layer is on a separate bar

Layer thumbnail

Adds new layers

Delete layers by dragging them here

## MASKS

Quick Mask selects and masks out an area that needs to be protected from editing. Using a selection tool, outline the area you want to edit, then select the Quick Mask option from the main toolbar. To add to the selection, paint in black; to subtract, paint in white. When you select the Standard Editing mode, the selection will reflect the edits made in the Quick Mask mode. Layer Mask creates an isolated section of the existing image to which more effects can be added. When you select the Layer Mask it will tell you that you are in 'layer mask edit mode' in your filename. Remember to check the status of your layer before you alter the image, otherwise you may be working outside the masked area.

## Photomontage and collage

Photomontage and collage are historical artistic methods, in which fragments of photographs, images, elements, textures and typography are brought together to create new meanings and new images. Photoshop extends this process by making it possible to hide the methods of assembly, creating a seamless picture. Photomontage is a process concerned with manipulation of photographs and is historically associated with graphic artists such as Hannah Höch and John Heartfield, as well as contemporary illustrators such as Dave McKean. The process pulls in and reassembles fragments to construct images that appear seamless, or that leave the edges exposed for a handmade look. Collage is a process more concerned with the assemblage of ephemera, textures and typography, and can be seen in the work of artists Kurt Schwitters and Romare Bearden. Many of these images are based on found objects or materials, and result in abstract assemblages and patterns that are rich with texture and aesthetic qualities but do not, necessarily, convey any particular meaning.

⬆ **Collage** By using colour, image, texture and scale, you can create beautiful compositions by hand or on a computer, like these dynamic collages by Alfred Cassels.

### GLOSSARY

**Photomontage:** The assemblage of various fragments of photographs.

**Pixel:** The smallest element of a computer screen or printed image. The word 'pixel' is an amalgamation of picture (pix-) and element (-el).

**PPI:** Pixels per inch.

**Raster:** Assemblages of pixels on a 2D grid system that can be viewed on computer screens or print media.

**Resolution:** The clarity of a digital image. A low-resolution image (25dpi, for example) will have clearly visible pixels; a high-resolution image (300dpi, for example) will not.

| PART 2 | PRACTICE |
|---|---|
| CHAPTER 5 | TOOLS AND TECHNOLOGIES |
| MODULE 4 | **ILLUSTRATOR** |

Adobe Illustrator is a vector-based package used for illustrative, logo and page-layout design, because of its shape-rendering and text-editing capabilities. Its linear handling complements Photoshop's pixel-based format, and most designers have knowledge of both programs.

**⬆ ➡ Vector illustration**
Illustrator's vector-based format allows for a variety of image-making techniques, object edits and custom typography, which makes it an excellent format for many illustrations, such as this striking one by Engy Elboreini.

Illustrator's main advantage is the resizing of vector-based illustration without loss of detail, from its 'point and line' function. For example, at billboard size a raster image becomes pixellated and blurry, whereas a vector image retains design by angle geometry and proportion, and remains sharp.

For the graphic designer, Illustrator offers a clean, crisp edge to the produced objects and brushes, and mapped along 'paths' can be moved, edited and recoloured easily. As in Photoshop, you can build layers of illustration using textures and transparencies, and typography, and create finished artworks to import into a desktop publishing program.

## Useful tools and features

Many of the tools found in Photoshop are duplicated across the Adobe range, such as the Selection Tools, Lassos and Pen Tools. Here are five of the most commonly used tools in Illustrator. The keyboard commands for each tool are shown in brackets.

**1 Pen Tool (P)** Creates vector-based lines and editable points.

**2 Type Tool (T)** The most useful tool in the best program for creating crisp logos and typographic solutions.

**3 Rectangle Tool (M)** Creates customised shapes.

**4 Warp Tools (Shift + R)** These tools change the geometry of vector objects. The Warp Tool drags a specific area of an object. The Twirl Tool changes the local geometry/colour into a spiral. The Crystallise Tool changes the local geometry/colour to splines.

**5 Mesh Tool (U)** Creates colour graduations within a 2D vector object. For example, making a star with the Star Tool and clicking within the shape with the Mesh Tool sets up a gradient, which can then be edited.

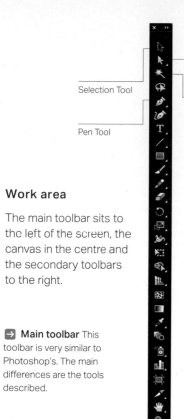

Selection Tool

Direct Selection Tool

Pen Tool

Magic Wand and Lasso Tools

Main toolbar

Header bar

Palettes, including Swatches and Layers

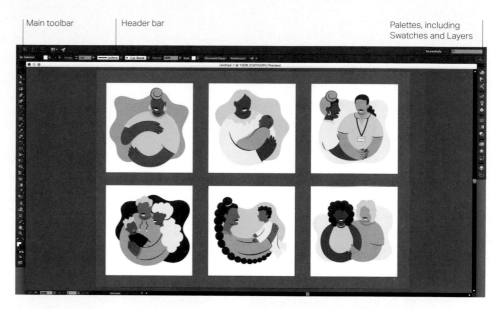

## Work area

The main toolbar sits to the left of the screen, the canvas in the centre and the secondary toolbars to the right.

➡ **Main toolbar** This toolbar is very similar to Photoshop's. The main differences are the tools described.

Stroke/Fill colour selector. Clicking on the squares swaps them over, as does the 'X' key

⬇ **Pathfinder** Use these boxes to transform simple shapes into more complex ones, through merging, overlapping and subtracting parts.

⬇ **Align** Clicking on these options will realign selected objects into the formations shown or add space evenly between objects as desired.

➡ **Flat design** Illustrator offers a platform to generate flat design, which is a series of minimalist, stylistic elements that give the illusion of three dimensions (such as the use of vectors, shadows, gradients and textures). This is particularly useful when designing for websites or applications since it enables interfaces to load faster and use less memory.

❗ **File types**
There are three main file types: PDF (Portable Document Format); EPS (Encapsulated PostScript); and AI (Adobe Illustrator Artwork). Generally, PDF format is used for final images sent for print or submission, whereas EPS and AI are file formats kept in-house.

❗ **CMYK**
Illustrator documents need initially to be set to CMYK in preparation for the output to be delivered to print.

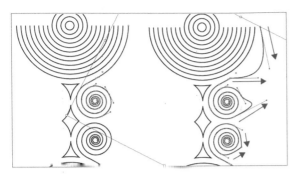

⬆ **The Bézier curve** in Illustrator with anchor points at either end and handles (straight blue lines) that control the curve.

⬆ **Anchor points and handles** In Illustrator these are constructed as mathematical algorithms, as opposed to pixels. This means that a small drawing in Illustrator can be enlarged to any size without losing quality. The versatility of this type of design works well for Team Romania, who have a variety of outputs and colour schemes.

Illustrator has many great functions worth investigating further; these include changing type into an image, live tracing accuracy and setting up files for CAD (laser cutting/engraving, vinyl, etc.).

## Vectors

Bézier curves are mathematically determined paths or vectors created between two points, which can be manipulated by anchors at either end. These curves, popularised by Pierre Bézier in 1962 from Paul de Casteljau's algorithms, provide the backbone of objects produced in Illustrator, and are found in the Adobe range as paths and anchors or handles created by the Pen Tool and lines, objects and type guides in InDesign. They are also the basis for digital type used in publishing, text-editing

software and 3D software programs. To manipulate a typeface, select the bounding box with your Selection Tool, click type and create outlines. This will turn your letters into vectors with visible paths and anchor points.

## Clean control

Precise adjustments and easy scaling are perfect for logo design work, whether the logo is pictorial or typographic. Vector.eps images are used because they can be enlarged to fit a billboard or scaled down for a business card without loss of detail. Customised typography should always be done in Illustrator; because the resolution does not change with size, typography will always be crisp.

➕ **SEE ALSO:** COLOUR TERMINOLOGY, P88
INDESIGN, P106
PHOTOSHOP, P110
PREPARING FILES FOR PRINT, P124

⬅ ⬆ ➡ **Versatility** The use of vector shapes and vector typography allows the designer to experiment freely with form. The Medisound logo has been drawn in Adobe Illustrator, which will allow the client to apply it at a small scale on a business card or resize it to fit a billboard with ease.

**Application of Illustrator** This example shows how fundamental and versatile Illustrator, along with other programs, can be in establishing a corporate identity, and how it can be applied at a large scale without losing quality.

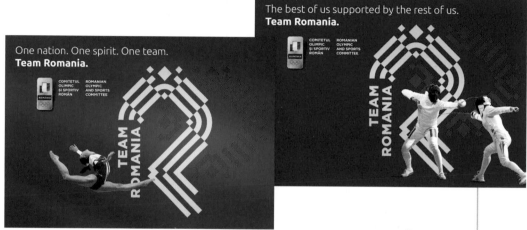

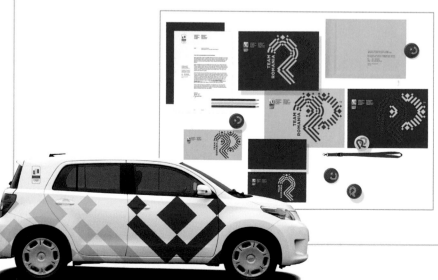

| PART 2 | PRACTICE |
| --- | --- |
| CHAPTER 5 | TOOLS AND TECHNOLOGIES |
| MODULE 5 | **ANIMATE AND AFTER EFFECTS** |

Adobe Animate and Adobe After Effects are two of the main software packages for the creation of time-based presentation. Both compose 'moving imagery' for screen or web, use timelines and keyframes, and incorporate both pixel and vector graphics. They differ in how material is rendered in the program and how it is delivered to the audience.

## Animate

Known for many years as Flash, Animate excels with vector graphics, and is used for interactive web-based applications and animation, with a range of features. It uses Action Scripting, which dramatically extends the functionality and interactivity features of the application.

- Illustrator images can be imported, then animated, or created in the design stage, then output to virtually any format (including SVG, PNG/JPEG sequence, FXG graphic interchange format, QuickTime movie and animated GIF).
- Complex animations are built one stage/movement at a time using keyframes. 'Tweening' then creates transitions between two keyframes. A higher number of frames per second (common frame rates are 24fps, 25fps and 30fps) creates a smoother transition. Unlike After Effects, transitions between different scenes or forms need to be built in by hand.

- Animate supports ActionScript, an object-orientated programming (OOP) language that is designed specifically for website animation and interaction.
- Open-source community libraries of script are there to be utilised by a user for assembling into the desired forms. Animate is prevalent on the Internet, in the form of animations, navigation and video, due to its discreet file size. And, unlike Flash, Animate incorporates native HTML5 Canvas and WebGL support to leverage web standards.

## After Effects

After Effects uses both vector and raster graphics, from either stills or video clips imported from Photoshop, Illustrator, video cameras or animation packages, and is used primarily as a post-production effects and compositing tool. As a stand-alone product for viewing (.mpeg or .qt [QuickTime] file formats), clips and stills are organised on tracks similar to video-editing programs like Adobe Premiere Pro and Final Cut X.

## Useful tools and features

The Animate interface is set up in a similar way to most of the Adobe software. The After Effects interface is less similar to the Adobe range, which reflects its use as a motion graphic, animation and compositing application. Here are some tools and resources that stand out from both programs.

**1 Animate: Bone Tool** The Bone Tool can be used for inverse kinematics (IK) – in other words, to link several elements on the canvas with armatures, so that movement of one element will translate back through the link and respond as if the elements are connected by bones.

**2 Animate: Packaging**
Much like the package file option in InDesign, Animate allows .OAM packaging, which is a compression .zip format allowing you to package up assets to import into other Adobe tools like Muse or Dreamweaver.

**3 After Effects: Cartoon Effect** Creates a cartoon aesthetic. Import live footage into the work environment, go to Effects and choose Stylise. Collapse Stylise and select Cartoon Effect. Drag and apply to the footage in the timeline. Tweaking the presets parameters changes the overall look and feel of the imported footage.

Main toolbar menu. Tools that are used daily are situated in this toolbar menu

Composition Workspace is one of the most important panels in After Effects: this is where you can see the progress of your work

The Character panel is used to manipulate text. There are many panels in After Effects, which can be found from the Window menu

Layers are used to organise the workspace. Labelling layers with colours is an easy way to stay organised in After Effects

The audio icon indicates that the audio is present in the timeline

Audio waveforms. The height of the line indicates the strength of volume in the audio: long vertical lines indicate loud audio, small vertical lines describe quiet audio

### ⬆ Deconstructed Circle

The storyboard shows the key sequences for compositing the final animation. Deconstructed Circle was produced by Zak Peric in After Effects, and the animation can be seen using the weblink https://vimeo.com/85708559.

Transitions, effects and presets can be drag-and-dropped between compositions that will then render using computer RAM Memory (more RAM memory means quicker rendering times). After Effects has many filters, effects and presets, such as film scratches or blurring, to create a mood or tone in your project. What makes After Effects popular and powerful is the range of third-party plugins that can be used to extend the functionality of the

application (e.g. Red Giant Trapcode Suite and Boris FX Boris Continuum Complete), although it can be argued that AE Scripts website (http://aescripts.com) is the most complete repository of current plugins available for After Effects and other animation, 3D and compositing applications.

### 4 After Effects: Puppet Tool

Excellent for creating bone structure in bitmap images. Select the Puppet Tool and place pins in order to create hierarchy. Each pin can be animated separately to create complex movement.

**5 After Effects: Mocha** This stand-alone application, which comes with After Effects, enables you to motiontrack (planar track) objects within a film so that words, images or symbols can be spliced into the film, even if the film tracks fast or is blurred. For example, you could track a different billboard image onto a billboard as a car passes and the camera pans to follow the car. This method of tracking is called planar track (which is similar to the four-corner pin-tracking technique).

**6 After Effects: Animation Presets Menu** Ideal for those who are new to animation and compositing, After Effects features pre-animated presets that can be utilised in any project. The benefit of using these presets lies in their flexibility and speed. (Each preset keyframe can be changed to create a new effect/visual outcome.)

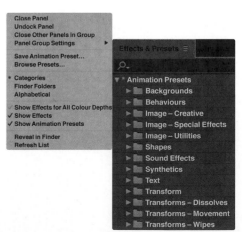

# CHAPTER 5: ASSIGNMENTS

There are endless tutorials available online that will help you navigate your way around the most up-to-date version of Adobe Photoshop, Illustrator, InDesign, Animate and After Effects. The Adobe site itself has the most comprehensive at https://www.adobe.com/uk/. Use these tutorials to build confidence and learn the correct terminology. When you are ready, complete the tasks below. Remember, you can always return to the tutorials or search for anything you specifically want more practice with.

## PHOTOSHOP

### ◻ Editing images

'You have to begin somewhere,' he once said, 'so you put something down. Then you put something else with it, and then you see how that works, and maybe you try something else and so on, and the picture grows in that way.' Artist Romare Bearden is best known for his collage and photomontage work. Study Bearden's images, looking particularly at the use of smaller, individual images combined to make a larger, more comprehensive image.

**1** Using the last ten images you took on your smartphone, create a collaged image of a domestic scene, including the inside of a home and people.

**2** Open Photoshop and edit your ten images. To edit an existing image, select File > Open [your image].

**3** It is important to establish the output for your work before starting; if in doubt, always set up as if you are printing to high quality, since it's much easier to reduce than increase image size and quality. Select Image > Image Size > Resize to 300p/inch (not cm). Note: p stands for pixel, the basic unit of programmable colour on a digital image.

**4** Similarly, knowing if your work is going to be screen- or print-based will alter the way you set up the Colour Mode. To set Colour Mode, select Image > Mode > RGB (Screen), CMYK (Print), Greyscale, Mono/Duotone – you will need to set your Colour Mode to greyscale first before having the option to

Mono/Duotone it. Note: The specific colour that a pixel describes is made from red, green and blue, which produces the screen format RGB. Printer colours are made by combining cyan, magenta, yellow and black – CMYK – and won't look the same on screen as when you print them. For this project, set your images to CMYK.

**5** Once you are happy with your edits, select File > New and enter the 20 x 20-cm (8 x 8-in) dimensions of the canvas you will be working on.

### ◻ Selection tools

Photoshop layers are like sheets of stacked acetate. You can see through transparent areas of a layer to the layers below. When you move a layer into position the content on the layer slides like a sheet of acetate into a stack. You can also change the opacity of a layer to make content partially transparent.

The selection tools (Quick Selection, Magic Wand, Marquee/Lasso, Magnetic Lasso, etc.) isolate one or more parts of your image. By selecting specific areas, you can edit and apply effects and filters to portions of your image, while leaving the unselected areas untouched.

It's also possible to make selections based on a range of colours in an image using Select > Colour Range. Using the Eyedropper Tool, choose the colour you want, then alter the settings in Colour Range to increase/decrease the selection. In addition to pixels, vector data can also be used to make selections. Use the Pen or Shape Tools to produce precise outlines called paths, which can be converted to selections. Once a layer or selection is created, that area is now isolated and can be duplicated, moved or edited in some way. Explore the adjustment options for hue/saturation, opacity/brightness and contrast, etc.

**6** Spend time experimenting with the selection tools, cutting shapes from your smartphone images. When you are happy with your edits, Save As > EPS to save the transparent background. Make multiple shapes from each image, aiming for roughly 50 images (5 from each original).

### ◻ Collage

**7** Open a new Photoshop document, select File > New and create a 20 x 20-cm (8 x 8-in) document. Make the resolution 300dpi, so you can print it, and name the file Collage 1.

**8** Under the Layers tab, select Background and change it to Layer 0.

**9** Import all the shapes, with each having its own layer. Using the Move Tool, you now can reposition or scale any of your imported images. Hold down the Shift button to scale your images without distorting them.

**10** Create a Bearden-inspired collage, placing your cut shapes thoughtfully to make one composition. Experiment with filters to affect the colours, and revisit the cropped shapes in their original files if you need to adjust anything.

**11** When you have a file you are happy with, save it with all the layers intact. Then, flatten the image, crop it to your liking and, using the Save As selection, rename the file and save the compressed version with a different name. It will be smaller and easier to import, but always save the original, layered version in case you want to make a change.

### ◻ Outsourcing

**12** Repeat the same exercise, but instead of using your own cropped images, source them from images generated collectively by your class. This time, create a domestic scene with people on the outside of a home.

**13** Repeat the exercise, but instead of using your own images, source them online through royalty-free platforms such as Unsplash. This time, create a domestic scene of your choice.

In practice, you should only outsource an image if you cannot make it yourself. No matter how complicated, look upon this as a creative problem to be solved. You could stage a scene and capture your own image or capture a series of elements and compile an image in Photoshop.

**14** Additional task
It is good practice to organise and store imagery for future use. Whether you print things out or keep them filed away on a computer, creating a visual reference library will result in much more scope and ideas for image making. Set up a platform to archive your visuals, perhaps a sketchbook or online platform such as are.na or Dropmark. Make sure you always have a camera, whether it be digital, film or a smartphone, so you can take images you find engaging and could use for future projects.

## ILLUSTRATOR

### ◘ BIG alphabet

**1** This assignment, inspired by Jon Dowling's book *BIG TYPE*, requires you to turn a typeface into a vector and manipulate its shape to fill a whole A3 page. Look at the typefaces you have on your computer, or a typeface you can purchase and download online. You can use a free typeface, but remember these are not always reliable in terms of consistency, legibility and spacing. Once you've selected a typeface, study it in detail, looking at the anatomy and how the letters sit alongside each other in the alphabet.

**2** Open Illustrator and create a landscape A3 canvas. Select the Type Tool and, at the bottom of the canvas, type the letters of the alphabet in uppercase in your chosen typeface. Increase/decrease the size so A-Z can fit along one line.

**3** Select the text box with the Direct Selection Tool and click Type > Create Outlines. Illustrator has just turned your letterforms into vector shapes. This technique is often used when printing vinyl or creating screen prints; make sure you keep an un-outlined version to one side in case you need to go back and edit.

**4** Using the Direct Selection Tool, you will notice the letter now has handles. Grab the handles and start moving them around to experiment with how the letterform changes.

**5** Using the various Pen Tool options, add and subtract handles and add and remove curves to expand the top of your letters – you are aiming to stretch the letters from the bottom of the canvas, all the way to the top.

**7** Repeat this exercise, this time with a portrait A3 canvas and letters running down the left side.

Now you have grasped how vectors are moved and shaped, experiment with your new vector letterforms and vector shapes. You can draw shapes freehand with the Pen Tool or use existing shapes available through the Rectangle Tool and others. You can also use the Pen Tool to join handles or overlap your two letters and select Pathfinder > Shape Modes: Unite to create a single compound shape. Explore and experiment with the Transform and Pathfinder Tools and other effects available through Illustrator.

**9** Vectors can be used in a variety of contexts due to their scaling abilities. If you have access to the resources, explore some of these outputs: large format printing, laser cutting and digital embroidery.

## INDESIGN

### ◘ Interactive

Using the letterforms you have just manipulated in the Illustrator assignment, you will now create an interactive type specimen poster for your typeface.

**1** File management
The most important thing to remember about InDesign is that it does not hold information you place in the file, but links it from an external source. If you rename or delete the original file, the InDesign link will be broken and it will not appear in your InDesign document. Therefore, it is always advisable to set up a file management system. Create a folder called Single Page Poster. Within this folder save the InDesign file and create subfolders for text and images.

**2** Set-up
Open InDesign and select File > New > Document (command+n). On the top tab select Web and select the 595.276 pixels width by 841.89 pixels height (A4) option from the blank document presets. Ensure the Portrait option has been selected using the icon and untick Facing Pages. You can also adjust Columns and Margins here if you wish, although there is another option once you're inside the program. Click OK/Create.

**3** Layout
Select Layout > Margins and Columns > to set your margins to 10mm, except for the bottom margin which should be set at 15mm. You may need to double-click the Lock icon to enter different values. Select Layout > Create Guides > where you can set your columns. Set three Rows to four Columns to the Margins. Click OK.

**4** Add images
Import your experimental typeface. One way to do this is to select File > Place and draw to grids. Alternatively, as your typeface is vector-based, you can copy and paste it straight from Illustrator. Arrange the typeface (A–Z) so it fits the entire page with space for a description.

**5** Hyperlink
Using the Selection Tool, right-click/control and click the first letter of your typeface to open a menu. Select Hyperlinks > New Hyperlink to open a dialogue box. There is a drop-down menu with options to create a hyperlink from a URL, file, email, page, text anchor or shared destination. For this assignment, create a hyperlink from a URL, copying a website from a typographer you admire. Repeat this with each letter of the alphabet.

**6** Export
When you are happy with your final design and your hyperlink is in place, select File > Export. Name your file in the top of the dialogue box and select Adobe (Interactive) from the format drop-down. The Export PDF dialogue box gives you a multitude of options. Look through and make amends where you feel appropriate. Make sure you export your document as pages so the poster stands alone. Reopen your PDF once exported to check the layout and that the hyperlink works.

# CHAPTER 5: ASSIGNMENTS CONTINUED

## ▣ Print

In this assignment, you'll be creating a double-page spread using the collages generated in the Photoshop assignment.

### 1 File management
To set up a file management system (see Interactive: Step 1, page 121), create a folder called Collage. Within this folder, save the InDesign file and create subfolders for text and images.

### 2 Set-up
Open InDesign and select File > New > Document (command+n). On the top tab select Print and select the 210mm width by 297mm height (A4) option from the blank document presets. Ensure the Portrait option has been selected using the icon and tick Facing Pages, which allows you to design spreads for a publication rather than a single page. Enter 4 into the Pages box. If you select More Options you will see there is space to enter values for Bleed. This allows printers to control elements that run flush to the page; the standard tends to be 3–5mm, but always check with your printer first. Enter a value. You can also adjust Columns and Margins here if you wish, although there is another option once you're inside the program. Click OK/Create.

### 3 Layout
Follow the instructions for Interactive: Step 3, page 121.

### 4 Master pages
Once inside the program and looking at the blank document, it is time to start thinking about setting up a framework. If you select Pages from the right-hand workspace, you will see the Master at the top. If you cannot see Pages, go to Window > Workspace > Essentials – you may need to 'reset' Essentials if you're using a public computer. Anything edited or added to a Master page or spread will be implemented throughout the whole document. Double-click both pages on the spread to begin. Any amends you make should have both spreads selected to apply them to both pages.

### 5 Add text
Now you have a framework set up, start to lay out a 250-word paragraph describing what the typeface is to be used for. In the toolbar, select the Type Tool and draw a text box to fit one of your columns. You can type directly into InDesign or import your text by using File > Place and locating the Word document. Your text will appear in the box, but it may not all fit. If there is more text, you'll see a small red plus symbol (+) in the lower right corner of the box. With the Selection Tool, click on the symbol and draw another text box on your page. The text will flow from the first box to the other, and will indicate the connection with a thin blue line that connects each box.

You can now edit your type for size, font and location – for more options, select Window > Workspace > Typography. Change it at least once, just to see the differences in the type flow and word count per line. Add a headline and subheads, if you need them. Give the text a title and typeset the heads in a way that complements the body copy you originally wrote. Think about how these four elements work together. Have you left negative space, and have you used both pages in an inventive way that complements each other?

### 6 Add images
To insert your collage image or individual images, select File > Place and draw to grids. Alternatively, create a shape and, while it is highlighted, select File > Place and the image will fill the shape. Use Control + Click > Fitting or use the Direct Selection Tool to experiment with how the image occupies this shape. If you need to alter the colours in your photo or make any edits, go back into Photoshop and change it; as long as you save the file in the same place with the same name it will update automatically. If in doubt, replace the image.

### 7 Personalisation
Now that you are getting to grips with the fundamentals, experiment with the colour of the document using various tools. Add a title page and a back cover. Could you add more pictures? Or do something inventive with the typography? It is always difficult to design on a computer, so take a step back into your sketchbook.

### 8 Export
When you are happy with your final design, select File > Export. Name your file in the top of the dialogue box and select Adobe (Print) from the format drop-down. The Export PDF dialogue box gives you a multitude of options. Have a look through these and make amends where you feel appropriate. Make sure you export your document as spreads so the pages sit alongside each other. Reopen your PDF once exported to check the layout.

## ANIMATE/AFTER EFFECTS

## ▣ Animation presets

*Set by Zac Peric*
In this assignment you will create a six-second typographical animation using the After Effects animation presets feature.

### 1 
Select Composition Menu > New Composition and, from the Presets drop-down menu, select HDV/HDTV 1080, 29.97. Change the time of the animation by editing the duration to 0;00;06;00 (i.e. six seconds) – see image 1, opposite.

### 2 
Use the Type Tool (see image 2) and in the main Composition 1 (Comp 1) type the words: 'This is my text'. Position your text to the title safe option by finding Title/Action Safe at the bottom of the main composition window (see image 3). Position your text to the bottom of the Title/Action Safe line.

### 3 
Find the Effects & Presets Menu (see image 4), then collapse Animation Presets Menu > locate Text folder > Animate In > Typewriter preset. Drag and drop Typewriter to your composition. Note that when you add the typewriter preset, your text will disappear in your main comp.

### 4 
Test the animation, making sure that you are at the beginning of the timeline (see image 5). Press the spacebar to play the animation. Your written text should fully appear in two seconds and 15 frames.

### 5 
To manipulate this animation, click the disclosure triangle next to the text layer to reveal the animation properties of that layer (see image 6). You will see an

additional property called Animator 1, which has the Range Selector 1 animation property (see image 7).

6 In the next step you will use already added keyframes (diamond shapes in your timeline) to manipulate the speed of the animation. Shorter distances between keyframes means a faster animation; longer distances means a slower animation. Move the last keyframe to four seconds (moving it to the right of the timeline). Press the spacebar to play the slower animation. Moving the last keyframe to the left of your timeline (to the one-second mark) will make this animation faster.

7 Go back to the Effects & Presets Menu and locate the folder called Animate Out, situated in the Text folder of the Animation Presets. Click on the disclosure triangle to collapse that menu. Find the preset called Fade Out Slow. Before you drop it onto your text layer, move your timeline (blue tooltip) to the four-second mark. Drag and drop this preset to the text layer (see image 8). Press the spacebar to test the animation, which will start to fade out at the four-second mark.

8 Go to File > Export > Export to Render Queue. You will be presented with a new Render Queue window with three options highlighted – Render Settings: Best Settings; Output Module: Lossless; and Output To: Not Yet Specified. Click on Not Yet Specified, which will open a new finder window. The file will be called Comp1.mov. Save the animation to your preferred location. When the Save button is pressed the window will disappear.

9 Click on the Render button in your Render Queue window. After the render is complete the movie will appear wherever it was saved to, as in the previous step. Play your final render to test the animation in a movie player (such as QuickTime).

## Further reading

Kelly Anton and Tina DeJarld, *Adobe InDesign Classroom in a Book*, Adobe Press, 2022

Molly Bang, *Picture This: How Pictures Work*, Chronicle Books, 2016

Conrad Chavez and Andrew Faulkner, *Adobe Photoshop Classroom in a Book*, Adobe Press, 2022

Russell Chun, *Adobe Animate CC Classroom in a Book*, Adobe Press, 2022

Jon Dowling, *Big Type: Graphic Design and Identities with Typographic Emphasis*, Counter-Print, 2022

Nigel French, *InDesign Type: Professional Typography with Adobe InDesign*, Adobe Press, 2018

Lisa Fridsma and Brie Gyncild, *Adobe After Effects Classroom in a Book*, Adobe Press, 2022

Val Head, *Designing Interface Animation: Meaningful Motion for User Experience: Improving the User Experience Through Animation*, Rosenfeld Media, 2016

Robert Klanten, Hendrik Hellige and J. Gallagher, *Cutting Edges: Contemporary Collage*, Die Gestalten Verlag, 2011

Austin Shaw, *Design for Motion: Fundamentals and Techniques of Motion Design*, Routledge, 2019

Brian Wood, *Adobe Illustrator Classroom in a Book*, Adobe Press, 2022

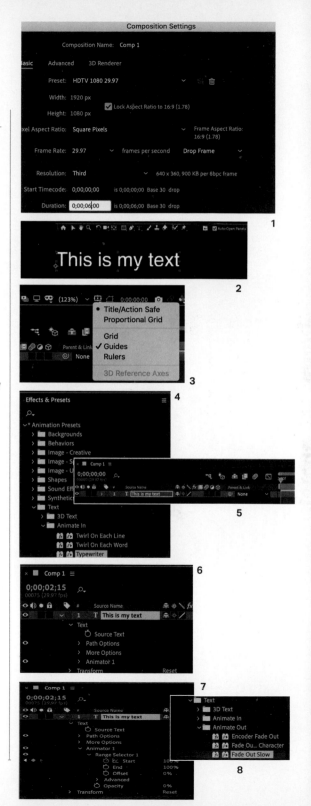

# Print Production and Presentations

When working in the realm of printed media, print production is the last stage in the design process, but it can be the first to be overlooked by the junior designer focusing intently on 'design'. It is really the final oversight of the creative decision-making process, and there are still options to be considered, even with the most detailed planning. If you have considered the project carefully and chosen colours, paper stocks and processes to suit, this final phase becomes a shared creative experience between designer and vendor.

Familiarity with print-production techniques and issues is vital to ensure the final printed job looks and feels the way it was intended. Planning for the use of a special-effect ink, stock or particular finish will only be achievable if you have a thorough (and up-to-date) understanding of the print-production process and a good relationship with your printer. Make it a habit to make a plan or enlist your production representative early in the process. Whoever takes on the task can provide dummy booklets on various stock samples, help to adjust packaging templates, solve bindery and fastening challenges, and provide ink-on-paper samples (ink draw-downs) so you can see how a Pantone ink colour might behave on coloured stock.

**⬇ Proofing** Print your PDF files and check them for typos, scale and colour fidelity, and assemble them to a finished artefact to avoid mistakes. This book cover, for example, should be printed to scale and wrapped around a book of the exact dimensions to assess the impact of the design over three dimensions.

Keeping your digital work habits pristine will restrict to an absolute minimum the need to tidy up files just before sending them. By this stage your bleeds should be set, your colours checked against samples and swatches, all photography should have been purchased/prepared, page items should be aligned, ragging adjusted, and the spell check complete. Creating a positive workflow, from design stage to finished product, will help ensure a successful outcome every time. A true measure of a designer is not only apparent in your conceptual design and typographic skills, but also in your handling of the process from start to finish, including preparing and sending out files to service bureaus and print vendors.

After a final proof is signed off by the client, many issues often remain before work can be printed. Remind yourself that because every piece of design work is unique, each can create a unique set of problems, and this stage is your last chance to check your work before handing it over to a printer.

## PDF advantages

- Highly compressed files can be generated – with optimised imagery and fonts embedded – to create a very close copy to the original working document. This condensed and mobile format can be easily emailed *en masse* to clients and co-workers for feedback, with edits and mistakes more easily caught during the production process.
- To print, the recipient needs only the free Adobe Acrobat Reader download. Many systems have this pre-installed, but it is always best to get the latest version.
- Newspaper and magazine publishers often receive ads as high-resolution PDFs only, with properly embedded fonts and images at the correct resolution and profile. Advanced tools in Adobe Acrobat Professional, such as Preflight, optimiser and fix-ups, can be key to achieving a successful run.
- Email and Internet creators can link files to web pages for online viewing or attach files to emails.

**Note:** Keep in mind that you cannot easily edit a PDF document. Any changes that might be needed after a PDF leaves your computer will require the original document for editing. That means edits can only be done by the designer, in the original format, unless you provide the native file to your vendor, but be aware of image and font licensing when you do this.

## PDF options

When Preflighting, you can bring your PDF to PDF/X and PDF/A standards. These file types, defined by the International Organisation for Standardisation (ISO), adhere to standards that facilitate reliable PDF transmission. They apply the wills and will-nots of a file. Using a PDF-X1, a file generated from Acrobat Preflight (a recognisable preset option in the Pre-Flight menu), is considered the best way to ensure that your file is correct and secure, and is an option in InDesign.

- Be meticulous. It is your responsibility to check everything from tint specifications and image colour spaces to tidying up unused colours in your palette menu, style sheets, unintentional indents on justified edges, extra spaces and missing fonts. Programs such as InDesign have spell check, an option to show hidden characters (such as spaces and paragraph breaks) and Preflight capabilities.
- Have a conversation with your printer about printer's marks, crop marks, bleeds, single pages and other export options.
- Printers are often sent postscript or PDF files – lockcd documents including all fonts and images – thereby reducing the potential for error. PDFs play an important role these days in near-instant proofing, and are the primary format used for sending files.

## The role of PDFs

The Portable Document Format (PDF) has come a long way from the aim of the 'paperless office', and is now a means to instantaneously review in-progress drafts and final sign-offs (or soft proofs) with clients, vendors and colleagues. PDF has become the standard for version editing, as well as submitting ads and media to newspaper and periodical publishers; the final output for the printer is itself a high-resolution PDF.

Many programs create reliable PDFs automatically, ensuring correct colour profiles and linking to final images and fonts. In creating PDFs using Acrobat, InDesign or Illustrator, you should start the press optimisation process using predefined settings. In InDesign you can go to Adobe PDF Presets > Press Quality. To customise the PDF settings, first go to File > Export and choose your format for print from the drop-down window. When you select Save,

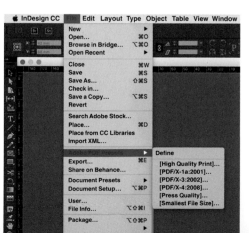

**PDF presets** Select the correct PDF Preset setting for your file. Choose low-resolution, 72-dpi formats for sending files for email review, and high-resolution files for production.

another option window will allow you to select Compression > Do Not Downsample; then select Marks and Bleeds to set your crops, bleeds and printer's registration marks. Always double-check the PDF in Acrobat to make sure everything is correct.

**Font embedding** When a font is not embedded, it is usually because it is missing from the document folder or has vendor restrictions; when opened or printed, a generic typeface might be substituted. Nothing is worse than opening a publication with your client's advertisement – a masterpiece in Gill Sans, say – and being greeted with a horror dripping in Courier. Proper embedding during your process prevents font substitution at the viewing stage, and ensures that vendors reprint the text in its intended font. Preflight tools in InDesign and Illustrator usually help you steer clear of errors before reaching PDFs, and you can always check Properties when viewing PDFs to check that fonts are embedded.

## What to send

When collecting a project for output, essentially you are mirroring requisite elements that make up the design: fonts, images and page layouts. However, you are also augmenting these with as many items as possible to help translate to your vendor what you are trying to achieve in production. You can do this by including a satisfactory comp (comprehensive) printout to be used as a guide.

Traditionally, elements such as images and fonts were strung together in desktop publishing programs such as InDesign; these included a suite of Preflight and Packaging capabilities to check and collect everything for output.

## File types and compression

Different applications store and compress data in various ways. Misunderstand or misuse these formats and you are heading for trouble. For example, you might spend hours scanning-in files and creating artwork for a magazine, only to save your hard work in the wrong format. At best, this will cost you hours; at worst, the job. A working knowledge of file formats and the process of compression could go a long way in preventing this scenario.

Electronic files appear to travel many distances around the city or around the globe, when in fact one computer is just copying from another. During this process, corruption

### Print checklist

**To send a file electronically, be sure to include all of the following.**

❯ **Your final approved document** (InDesign: .indd; high-res pdf and an .idml mark-up if your printer is not using the most up-to-date software.)

❯ **A folder of all linked images** (.eps, .tif, .pdf), entitled either 'links' or 'images'. You should also include original files in .psd or .ai, in case your printer needs to make an adjustment.

❯ **A folder of all fonts** (PostScript, TrueType, OpenType). Be wary of typography sharing licences.

❯ **Printer instructions and profiles** (included in the Preflight and Packaging options).

❯ **Output or a low-resolution PDF** for the printer to use as a guide, clearly labelled as such to avoid confusion.

❯ **A detailed comp dummy** that tangibly demonstrates folds and sequences.

❯ **Ink swatches**, additional material samples and a paper sample, if needed.

❯ **A note to the vendor** that may include specific instructions, a copy of any relevant correspondence and job numbers.

❯ **Email information** reiterating agreed-upon specifications with the files attached or a notice of online upload.

can occur, especially to page layout and font files. Compressing files before sending via email or FTP (File Transfer Protocol) is an effective way of preventing this.

Most files that are not native application formats can include some sort of compression to facilitate use in other programs or transmission via the Internet. The amount and type of compression, especially with imagery, video and audio projects, can affect the quality and performance of your final file.

.ZIP compression file types reduce the number of bytes by removing the redundant areas of underlying code that make up every file. These repeated and replace-able areas are put back into the file using a program such as WinZip or Stuffit to 'unzip' or 'unstuff' the file back to its original format. The final, expanded file is identical to the original before it was compressed. Macs and PCs natively create and open ZIP files, whereas Stuffit file creation and expansion needs a separate program.

## File naming

- Do not put any spaces in the name or extension; if you need to separate words, use an underscore: 'my_file.jpg'.
- Use lowercase, not uppercase, characters.
- Use only alpha (abc) or numeric (123) characters. Avoid characters such as @%^&*(), and use a full-stop (.) to separate name and extension.

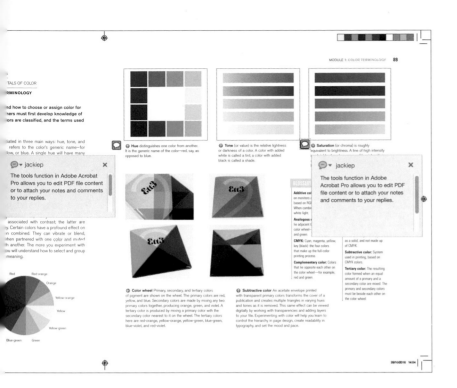

Sometimes called archives, these compression formats are in all walks of design and production because they speed up and simplify data transmission across the Internet. Used primarily to send large files within emails, many studios and companies utilise an FTP set-up on their web server to easily transfer files online.

There are many online transfer sites that enable you to send large files and avoid compression. Dropbox and Google Drive are file-sharing programs, so will update in your recipient's folder when you update them in yours. WeTransfer is a great resource for sending one-off files.

**PDF Tools** PDFs are commonly sent as email attachments for approval and opinion during the design process. The Tools function in Adobe Acrobat Pro allows you to edit PDF file content or to attach your notes and comments to your replies.

## Key graphic file formats

 **PSD** and **AI** are the file formats for Adobe Photoshop and Adobe Illustrator used for image creation.

**Compatible with:** Photoshop, Illustrator and InDesign with minor restrictions.

**Tip:** Make sure you always save an unflattened master version of your Photoshop files to fall back on, and save Illustrator files with unoutlined text.

 **EPS** used to be the most widely used file format in artwork preparation for print. It can contain either vector or bitmap information and is best used when dealing with logos and illustrations as well as vinyl printing and one- and two-colour jobs.

**Compatible with:** Illustrator for edits and InDesign for layout.

**Tip:** EPSes themselves can contain font data that may need to be backed up with a font file at the collection stage, or font outlines can be created.

 **TIFF** creates one of the largest files because it saves an alpha channel in the file, which allows for transparency at the art's edge, not at the pasteboard's edge. Best when dealing with monotone, greyscale or watermarks for colour toning, TIFF is the highest-quality image format for full-colour photography as well.

**Compatible with:** Photoshop for editing and InDesign for layout.

**Tip:** Make sure you check with your printer as to whether they accept files with LZW compression, which is an option while saving.

 **JPEG** is a format that uses lossy compression – meaning that a certain amount of the image quality is lost during the saving process. With a complex photographic image this would usually remain unnoticed (unless the image is over-compressed).

**Compatible with:** Photoshop for editing and InDesign for layout.

**Tip:** Nowadays, most digital cameras save as large JPEGs, which can be resaved as high-quality images for print due to advances in image resampling and printing. For large, high-quality reproduction, you should be using .tif files.

| PART 2 | PRACTICE |
|---|---|
| CHAPTER 6 | PRINT PRODUCTION AND PRESENTATIONS |
| MODULE 2 | **CREATING A CONVINCING PRESENTATION** |

It is critical that your client approve the final version of the electronic file, usually a PDF document, but presenting the idea clearly at the concept approval stage can influence the client's choice on which concept to produce. A comp, or comprehensive, is the designer's finished concept shown in the closest possible approximation to the produced product as is possible. Good craft skills are essential and, although a bad concept can't be saved by good craft, a great concept can sometimes suffer if it is poorly crafted.

⬆ **Presentation** Packaging prototypes for retail, food and beverages should represent how they will look and function at the point of purchase. There are software packages that will render images onto a digital object, but your client may want to simulate the consumer experience to help them decide.

### Colour

Electronic output from a high-quality desktop printer can come very close to matching the four-colour process intended in production. Matching Pantone colours can be trickier. Colours on screen can be misleading, and will only come close if your monitor is perfectly calibrated. A Pantone number encoded in your document will ensure the colour ink that prints, but to show that exact colour to your client in comp form you may need to depend on a custom blend that adjusts the colour for comping only. Make a separate file named 'Comp' and adjust your colours there. That way you won't send the wrong document to the supplier. Although expensive, it is worth investing in a Pantone swatch book so you can show the client the exact colours without having to pay for Pantone scatter proofs.

### Format

With your colour perfected, you need to assemble the document into whatever form the product will take, such as booklet, poster or package design. Output papers come in various weights, and some colour printers will accept the stock you intend to use in production. If you can, print on stock samples, which will give you and your client the best representation of the final product and will show you how duotones and tritones will be affected by the stock colour.

Unfortunately, it's nearly impossible to register output on both sides of the paper, so you'll need to use a dry mastic sheet, like 3M mounting material, to glue – or dry mount – the sides together. Always leave some bleed and printer's registration marks, and trim your pages after you have assembled them. Cut and score the paper for folding after the assembly is completed in a clean, dry studio space.

### Craft

Some techniques can't be imitated digitally and need to be done by hand. Die cutting will require careful handwork with a thin utility knife, and practising your cutting and comping skills will lead to cleaner presentations. Metallic stamps will need to be hand cut and applied, also. In some cases, a poster, or board, of your intended materials and colours can help in the presentation, but there's no substitute for a clean comp.

← ↙ **Design formats** When presenting to a client, it is important to create visuals that can help lead your conversation. Be sure to make the presentation available to your audience once finished, and an added bonus would be to bring professional mock-ups so they can see your design skills both on and off screen. Once the project is complete, it's equally as important to get professional photographs of your work for your portfolio.

→ ↘ **Presentation mock-ups** If you are presenting or pitching a physical design, such as signage, pay particular attention to the quality of the finish. Simulate the print process you plan to use and consider the colour and materials throughout all of your designed elements.

⊞ **SEE ALSO:** PRINTED COLOUR, P132

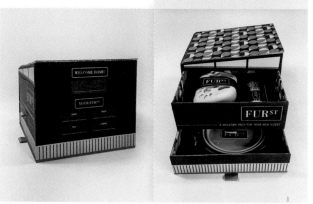

← **Finishing** Processes such as embossing, debossing and die cutting can add a luxurious, sophisticated quality to your designs. In this example, the pared-back colour palette draws more attention to these finishing details.

| PART 2 | PRACTICE |
|---|---|
| CHAPTER 6 | PRINT PRODUCTION AND PRESENTATIONS |
| MODULE 3 | **PAPER STOCKS AND FINISHING** |

Paper is absolutely part of the picture, and it can enhance or diminish the vibrancy of your imagery. Paper stock is manufactured in a large assortment of weights, colours, textures and finishes, and selecting the correct one can really add to the success of the finished product. Sampling is the ideal way to determine whether or not a particular stock will work for you. You should also be aware of the common terms used to describe paper, including the various attributes and how they apply to a particular job.

⬆ **Add flavour** Deeply textured cover stock in cocoa brown is a tantalising entrée to the individually packaged chocolates on the inside of this package design. Beautiful typography and delicate matt colours partner to establish the brand as a luxury item.

Paper is produced from pressed pulped wood, cotton or recycled paper. Seven standard attributes describe different characteristics.

• Weight describes the density of the fibres that make up the sheet, and is measured in grams per square metre (gsm or g/m2) or pounds (lb). Letter weights vary from 60 gsm to 300 gsm cover weight. Speciality stocks can be even heavier.
• Thickness is measured in caliper (inches) or millimetres; however, greater thickness does not mean better quality.
• Texture depends on the size or quality of wood fibres and the method of construction. Tightly pressed, fine fibres result in a smoother paper normally used for writing or printing; less pressed, bigger fibres form board and fibrous card.
• Strength (tension and resilience) is affected by texture, density, weight and thickness; for example, tissue paper and cardboard are both used for packaging, but in different contexts.
• Opacity depends on density and thickness, and refers to how much text or image on the overleaf page can be masked. Vellum paper is highly translucent and is made by immersing good-quality paper in acid, which alters the fibres.

• Brightness depends on how much the paper has been bleached before it is pressed. Brighter stock reflects more light and results in a fresher look to a page. Environmental concerns have resulted in a return to unbleached paper in recent years.
• Colour is produced by dyeing the fibre pulp before it is pressed. Coloured stocks can be more expensive than white stock.

### Matt, satin and gloss surfaces

Different paper qualities affect the intensity of printed ink – there is a stark difference between printed matt and gloss surfaces. When ink adheres to matt paper, it is absorbed and has no shine. Matt finish is used for printed-word texts such as newspapers and books. It is usually easy to read, but does have a tendency to make images and colours duller. However, ink printed onto gloss paper stays on the surface, so more light hits the paper below and bounces off, giving a deeper, more intense colour. This quality is used for book covers, magazines, brochures and packaging. Satin paper (or dull coat) comes somewhere between the two, giving a slightly less intense colour than gloss but without the shiny surface.

⊕ **Paper samples**
Printers and paper suppliers have a range of paper samples to distribute to existing and potential clients. Each booklet has samples of the available colours, weights and surface finishes on each sheet. The big suppliers, such as GF Smith and Fedrigoni, make beautifully designed publications that are worth getting your hands on. Alternatively, some design magazines advertise paper stocks inside their issues.

❶ **Going green**
Concerns about sustainability mean that many designers now use recycled papers, or sheets made from cotton, not wood pulp. This is not the only concern for sustainable design; there are also environmental issues based around paper bleaching and certain inks, all of which are important considerations when designing.

## Finishes and coatings

Finishes and coatings are added either to protect printed ink, or in patches to emphasise an area of ink.

• Varnishes are coatings applied 'on press', either with other inks or as a separate run, and can be matt, satin or gloss, and tinted with added pigment.

• UV coatings are spread on as a liquid, then hardened with ultraviolet light. They can be matt or gloss, and applied accurately in spot form or as complete coverage.

• Aqueous coatings – matt, satin and gloss – are relatively expensive and are laid at the end of a run. As such they cannot be controlled to be put in specific areas, only as a complete coat.

• Laminates are layers of sheet plastic or clear liquids that bind into the paper to protect it.

• Paper can also be embossed and debossed to emphasise lettering or an image, and it can be stamped with metallic foil or glossy, flat or shiny colour, a beautiful effect on matt paper. It can also have a painted edge, which is a particularly beautiful addition to publication design. It can also be laser cut or die cut to expose pages underneath. These are beautiful but expensive techniques, so be sure your budget allows for the technique you choose.

### GLOSSARY

**Coated:** A hard, waxy surface, either gloss or matt, and not porous (ink sits on the surface).

**Coated one side:** A paper that is coated on one side and matt on the other.

**Gloss:** A shiny form of paper, used for magazines, books and so on.

**Gsm:** Grams per square metre, or g/m2.

**Laid:** A paper that has lines on its surface from its means of production. Often used for stationery.

**Linen:** Similar to laid, but finer lined.

**Matt:** A dull, non-shiny quality of paper, used for newspapers, for example.

**Ream:** Standard quantity of paper; 500 sheets.

**Satin:** A form of paper between matt and gloss.

**Stock:** A generic form or type of paper, such as tracing paper or matt coated.

**Varnish:** A liquid sprayed or spread onto paper to give it a hard-wearing surface so that printed ink stays intact.

**Wove/Smooth:** A smooth, uncoated paper that is very porous (ink sits under the surface).

---

⬇ **Texture and light** Die cuts add surprising pops of colour and use light and shadow to add detail to an extended system. Consult your print vendor or paper merchant to choose the right stock for your project.

↗ **Surface texture** Business cards are personal items. Adding a tactile element, such as a raised embossing, adds memorability and delicate light and shadow to the surface of the design.

⬆ **Impression** Add texture and tactility to your composition by embossing or debossing the surface of your stock. Uncoated, textured stocks work well, with or without ink coverage.

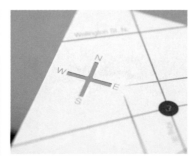

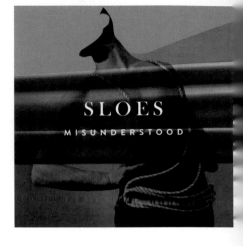

Various factors determine how many colours you use to produce a job. Aspects such as aesthetics, budget and branding come into play when you make your selections, and you want to be sure the colours you choose are the ones that appear accurately on the finished product.

↑ **Pantone Colour Bridge** This not only shows you what a particular solid PMS colour will look like, but also its full-colour printed counterpart, while giving the CMYK, RGB and hexidecimal formulas for typing it in.

↓ **PMS book** Keep one of these books to hand when designing, attending client meetings and going on press checks as a guide to help choose and validate colour.

Any printed image we see is an illusion of light, paper and patterns of ink that rely on the visual cortex 'blending' the information our retinas perceive into a logical image. Many different kinds of printing types have been created in order to mass-produce this 'illusion'.

Single-colour (monotone or monochome) printing can be used when there are budget constraints or when there is a particular colour that must be used. For instance, many companies specify a particular Pantone ink for consistency across all their printed work to ensure brand recognition.

Two- and three-colour printing allows for interesting mixtures of Pantones: overprinting two translucent inks can generate a third colour, and printing black-and-white images in two colours (duotone) and three colours (tritone) can enhance their effect.

Four-colour process printing uses cyan (C), magenta (M), yellow (Y) and black (K) inks specified in percentage tints to create a huge variety of other colours. This more popular method is used for reproducing full-colour imagery, photographs or flat colours.

### PMS

The Pantone Matching System consists of colour reference manuals, or books, used for selection and input, either by PMS number or by precise CMYK formulas. Printers have copies of these books and the corresponding matching inks.

Pantone colours, or spot colours, have different ink options, since colour reacts differently with different printing processes and surfaces. To help approximate this, PMS swatch books come in many versions, made for different papers such as coated and matt, and in solid or process colours.

### Workspace, monitor and calibration

The key to consistent colour is to work in a well-lit room with a properly calibrated monitor. Using colour conventions such as PMS and composing colours using CMYK breaks helps you achieve correct colour from screen to press. When in doubt, do it by the numbers.

With colour you can mix cyan, magenta, yellow and black in any image-making program or by selecting colours from an image. This approach mimics the pioneer press person's experimentation with inks that forged the path for printing today. However, PMS is a more reliable way to ensure you are going to get the colour you choose.

**Calibrating your monitor** The best place to begin a successful colour workflow is with the monitor. Correct calibration and profile usage ensure that what you see on screen is what turns out in print. Reliable translation of material from scanner or camera to monitor and printer means proper communication from one device to the next. Many modern monitors come with presets and programs to help you get basic values, but in recent years colourimetres have become readily available to ensure every colour point and setting is consistently and dependably adjusted to standard. Colourimetres cycle through a series of modes to read the current state of display and adjust the video card correctly, creating a new profile, called an ICC profile, for the monitor to create colour from.

◀ **Tints and opacities** Screen colour doesn't always translate exactly in print. Proofing your design on the actual stock will give the best indication of the final outcome. This example contains a number of transparency layers and halftones, and the only way to gauge the success of such a composition is to proof it. Liaise with your printer for more information about costing a printed proof into your budget.

❶ **Global standard**
GRACOL is currently the standard colour profile, but ask your service bureau which profile they prefer you to work with – they may even have created their own.

Every device has its own set of ICC profiles. Set up by the International Colour Consortium, these standards facilitate the translation of colour information of an image from one device to the next. When a screen, scanner or camera is recalibrated, each is given a new profile and the image produced picks up that profile. Images opened in Photoshop can be reviewed; if a profile setting is different or missing, then the working profile of the monitor is used.

## PMS and Pantone book paper choices

### PMS
- **Solid** Over 1,000 PMS spot colours are contained in either the fan guide or the chip book, with speciality versions for metallic colours, pastels, neons and tints.
- **Process** Over 3,000 Pantone Process Colours with their CMYK percentages are contained in these books.
- **Colour Bridge** Formerly known as the Solid to Process Guide, this book provides a larger colour swatch and tint comparison showing how solid colours will look in CMYK, and gives print and web formulas.

### Pantone
- **Coated** This book contains PMS numbers followed by a 'C', indicating that a colour can only be matched by printing on a coated (glossy) surface.
- **Uncoated** This book contains PMS numbers followed by a 'U', indicating an uncoated (matt) surface.

### GLOSSARY

**DPI:** Dots per inch is a measurement of printer resolution that reveals how many coloured dots are available to create a square inch of an image. The higher the DPI, the more refined the text or image will appear.

**LPI:** When printing halftones, such as in one-colour newspapers and reproductions, the lines per inch is the number of lines that compose the resolution of a halftone screen.

**PPI:** Pixels per inch or pixel density is interchangeable with DPI, but usually refers to the resolution of an unprinted image displayed on screen or captured by a scanner or digital camera.

➕ **SEE ALSO:**
FUNDAMENTALS OF COLOUR, P88

❶ **RGB to CMYK**
Printers often insist that you give final image files converted to a CMYK format. Generally, it's best to keep images in RGB format until you are ready to send the file to the printer, since image-manipulation programs such as Adobe Photoshop work best with RGB files for correction and effects. Printers recommend the Image > Mode > CMYK function to change an image from RGB to CMYK. They may also prefer to do their own pre-press production check to ensure files are prepared to their satisfaction.

➡ **Limited colour** These examples of publication spreads use limited palettes of two or three colours. Stripping the information back in this manner allows the content to provide most of the hierarchy, as well as creating a simple yet beautiful, no-fuss composition.

◀ **Surface and ink** Coated paper allows the ink to sit on the paper surface so the shine of the stock is evident. On uncoated stock, the ink sinks into the paper fibres and dries to a matt finish. PMS coated and uncoated swatch books show you the differences on each PMS numbered ink.

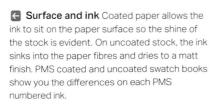

| PART 2 | PRACTICE |
| --- | --- |
| CHAPTER 6 | PRINT PRODUCTION AND PRESENTATIONS |
| MODULE 5 | **PRINT MEDIA** |

**Despite the fact that digital printing is considered much easier, traditional printing methods continue to thrive, partly because of the textures, visuals and detail created by the process, which cannot be replicated in digital, no matter how hard we try. There is also the joy of the craftsmanship itself to consider: nothing is more rewarding than printing through traditional means.**

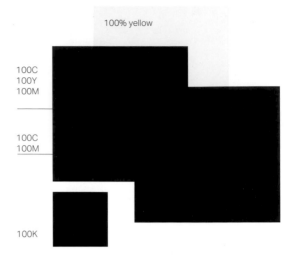

⬆ **Full-colour printing** CMYK is the most popular form of print used daily in book and magazine production. Be aware that 100C 100Y 100M combined does not equate to 100K.

### Colour

In traditional printing techniques (that is, everything except digital printing), your digital artwork needs to be separated into the constituent colours in which it will be printed. The printing process needs to be done in layers, one colour at a time, and alignment therefore plays a very important role in production. You will have two options: the first is to keep all your coloured layers separate, with no overlaps, giving you complete control of the colour onto the background. The second option – which can be difficult to set up, but is perhaps more rewarding and less time-consuming if done properly – is to have overlaps of colour. This process means you have fewer layers to create as you are relying on colour mixes to create your image. For example, if you print two yellow circles, followed by a layer of two blue circles,

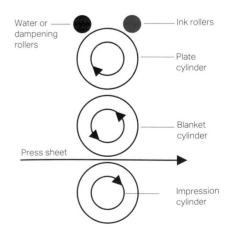

➡ **The principle in action**
This press diagram shows an exposed plate wrapped around the rotating plate cylinder, where the image is dampened and inked before being transferred onto the blanket cylinder.

⬅ **On a roll** Most presses feed one sheet of paper through at a time, but larger web presses, which are used for long runs, draw paper from a roll.

## Offset advantages

- High-quality images can be achieved by providing a higher-resolution print.
- Works on a wide range of print media such as paper, fabric, plastic, wood, metal, leather and glass.
- Cost per printed piece decreases as the quantity increases.
- Quality, cost-effectiveness and bindery finishing are fully controllable in large-run jobs.
- Modern offset presses use computer-to-plate technology, increasing economy and quality.

↑ **Full black** Choose this process when your halftone photographic subjects have significant expanses of black and a full greyscale range to add richness to the subject. Printed body text and fine lines should be printed in as few colour separations as possible to avoid registration issues. Use 100K or choose a Pantone black.

**❶ Black**
Many designers and printers prefer the 'mega-black' or 'super-black' formula for large areas of black. This formula, at 60C, 40M, 40Y, 100K, should be used in imagery, not text, and provides a much richer interpretation over 100K alone to create black.

overlapping one yellow circle with one blue circle only, you should be left with a yellow, green and blue circle. Three colours, with two layers. Interestingly, the Adobe program Photoshop is designed to use layers, mimicking these traditional print processes.

### Offset lithography

Lithography is the process of printing from a flat surface, which has been treated so as to repel the ink except where it is required for printing. To separate your coloured layers in traditional lithography, the printer will make plates, a separate one for each of the four-process ink colours, or an individual plate for each Pantone, or spot colour. Most large presses have room for at least six inks and can accommodate varnish as part of the process. Requesting too many spot colours may cause the job to run through the press more than once, and can strongly affect printing costs.

This printing process is based on the principle that water and oil do not mix. The digitally produced printing plate is treated chemically so that the image will accept ink and reject water. The simplified diagram (opposite) shows an exposed plate wrapped around the rotating plate cylinder, where the image is dampened and inked. The inked image on the plate is then transferred onto the blanket cylinder.

The rubber blanket transfers the image onto the stock, which has been carried around the impression cylinder (adjusted depending on the stock used). This planographic process is rapid, and the plate is inked on each rotation.

Although considered a traditional method, this process is still widely used by commercial printers due to the higher quality of printing produced, and is most cost-effective for quantities over a few hundred – and even more so with quantities of higher volume.

→ **Surface printing** There are many ways to transfer your designs onto different materials and products, so consult your vendor and printer to discuss the various options. Consider how many colours you will be printing and how many impressions you need. Most surfaces can be offset-printed, screen printed or have vinyl applied, but new digital technologies are rapidly adding even more options.

## Screen printing

Screen printing is a printing technique that uses a mesh screen and ink. It is often referred to as silkscreen because originally the mesh screen would have been made of silk fibres. However, over time, synthetics such as polyester have replaced the silkscreen, and the term has been changed to screen printing to reflect this.

The mesh screen is made from tiny woven fibres, resulting in several miniscule holes. When ink is applied to the screen, it passes through these holes to reach the printing surface. The role of the graphic designer is to design a stencil to block these holes, so creating an image through the unblocked areas.

The blocking process can be achieved with a paper or plastic stencil, or more commonly with a blocking agent such as filler or photosensitive ink. When the photosensitive ink has dried and been exposed to halide light, the screens are washed out with a pressure washer, ensuring that unwanted blocking ink is removed.

Each colour in a screen-printed design needs its own screen; therefore it is considered more efficient to use screen printing when running large numbers of prints.

As a reproduction technique, screen printing has many wonderful qualities: little equipment is needed; prints can be made quickly, by hand, with no electricity; it is cheap to mass-produce; smaller set-ups can be portable; and, perhaps most importantly of all, it is easy to learn. Screen printing is an obvious choice when you are looking for ways to create a lot of prints to reach a lot of people.

## Risograph

Risograph was formally the name of a company in Japan, who in the 1980s created a digital duplicator, which is a printer designed mainly for high-volume photocopying and printing. Now known widely as Risograph or Riso printing, this was not always a mainstream printing technique. As digital printing developed, there was a pull back to more environmentally friendly and cost-effective methods of printing, and in many ways a desire for more nostalgic and DIY-aesthetic printing techniques and detailing.

Risograph is very similar to screen printing, in that the original image file is sent to the machine and burnt onto a master. The master is then wrapped around a print drum. This drum rotates at high speed, which pushes the ink through the screen and onto the paper as it is sent through the machine.

Unlike offset lithography, it only takes a single print for the screen to be fully inked and ready to print in large numbers. It is therefore very energy-efficient and generates a minimal amount of waste.

In terms of colour, unlike offset lithography, screen printing, and relief printing/letterpress, Risograph doesn't have

**Screen print** The use of a mesh, as opposed to a printer, makes screen printing an ideal option for printing onto fabric or unusual surfaces such as this transparent, limited-edition vinyl sleeve.

**Multiple runs** Screen printing is most cost-effective when prints are created in large numbers. This typographic T-shirt, for example, would cost less per unit the more T-shirts that were printed.

a Pantone system, so you will need to contact your printer for samples before you create your designs. The colours available to Risograph are unique and offer something that digital printing simply cannot recreate. Be aware, though, that colours can vary depending on the paper stock.

Risograph printing does not offer perfect results and, in most cases, this is actually why it is a desired printing technique. Prints will be different to your designs on screen, and individual prints will also alter slightly from one another. The machine automatically creates a halftone effect, so avoid heavy blocks of ink or anything that requires perfect registration. Risograph is most often used to create artist publications, invites, flyers, posters, illustration prints and zines.

## Relief printing/letterpress

Relief printing involves applying ink to a printing block, plate or matrix. You can carve/etch your designs onto the surface, leaving raised and sunken areas. The raised areas will take ink, and the sunken areas will not. When pressed onto a surface, the raised areas will transfer the ink and the sunken areas will remain ink-free. Pressing can be done with a printing press, with a brayer/roller or by hand.

Relief-printing techniques include variations of woodcut, metalcut, wood engraving, relief etching and linocut, which are authentic ways to create illustrations and imagery. However, as a graphic designer, you are more likely to concentrate on traditional text printing – movable type/letterpress (a variation of woodcut and metalcut). Used with a printing press, movable type is arranged, set and locked into the bed of the press – in much the same way you would do it digitally – and many copies are produced by repeated direct impression of the inked, raised surface of the letters.

Invented in Germany by Johannes Gutenberg in the mid-15th century, letterpress remained the main means of printing and distributing books and newspapers until offset lithography was developed in the United Kingdom and America around the 20th century. More recently, letterpress printing has seen a revival in an artisanal form.

**Risograph** Like screen printing, Risograph printing was originally created for high-volume photocopying. Due to recent trends, Risography is now back in fashion and offers a cheap solution for printing large runs of a design.

WE ARE OUT OF OFFICE

**Rise of the Riso**
Risograph printing is widely considered to have a granular quality that is difficult to achieve with other printing techniques. It is more environmentally friendly and cost-effective than other methods of printing, and is also growing in popularity.

**Riso colours**
Due to the set-up of a Risograph printer, the use of minimal colours in designs is not only more cost-effective, but often makes it easier to set up your files. It is also quicker to print large runs of your design.

| | |
|---|---|
| PART 2 | PRACTICE |
| CHAPTER 6 | PRINT PRODUCTION AND PRESENTATIONS |
| MODULE 6 | **DIGITAL PRINTING** |

With conventional offset lithography almost a century old, digital presses – emerging in the early 1990s with the ability to create print directly from a digital file – have opened up new frontiers. Forward thinking printers have embraced any technology that enables them to provide more options for their customers. Different than traditional offset, from speed to price to flexibility, digital printing has worked its way into the workflow of many designers and print houses as clients' needs, wants and timeframes accelerate.

75dpi at actual printed size

Digital presses reproduce documents through a process of toner-based electro-photography – a technology inherent in the common desktop laser printer. This not only speeds up the process, but also removes a variety of margins for error.

Generally used for print runs of fewer than 1,000 pieces, for economy, digital printing also opens up per-piece customisation for direct mailing, variable data jobs and frequently updated publications such as newsletters and timetables. Personalised printing and printing on demand are therefore growth industries, allowing for print-on-demand books and other items of varying printed details, page quantities and binding techniques.

Vendors include online-and-on-demand service bureaus, traditional sheet-fed and web-offset printers, screen printers, sign manufacturers and point-of-purchase display producers. Allow yourself and these agencies a margin for error in production stages as you prepare and oversee your digitally printed project. Always check a digital proof and discuss the options with your printer.

300dpi at actual printed size

◀ **CMYK and resolution** When a full-colour image is needed for print, it must be generated as a CMYK file. For full-colour, duotone and greyscale images, image size is reproduced and digital file resolution should be twice the lines per inch (lpi). The standard for high-resolution print is 300dpi.

### Ink versus toner

With digital printing the toner does not permeate the paper like conventional ink, but instead forms a thin layer on the surface. Some designers and printers believe that digitally printed colour can appear more saturated. This happens due to lack of light absorption by the paper when ink 'sinks in', as in traditionally printed items. It is not necessarily a bad thing, because 'more saturated' to a printer can also mean 'more vibrant' to a client. Make sure you discuss project adjustments to match your intended output more closely, since some newer presses use a combination of toner and ink to achieve more exact colour values.

Some digital presses that use toner may produce large areas of solid colour with banding and blending problems. Ask your printer to run samples, so you can review for yourself what may or may not work.

### Time frame

Digital printing cannot be beaten for production timing, since there is no set-up and clean-up of the press for each job. Some offset print houses are now offering shorter print-timing by utilising such techniques as gang-run printing or shift-scheduling. Newspaper Club, for example, have litho and digital print runs on certain days, with certain turnaround times and costs to reflect both jobs.

## Digital or offset options

- **Quantity** Short-run jobs can prove more cost-effective with digital printing; larger quantities are likely to have a lower per-unit cost with offset printing. The rule of thumb is: over 1,000 pieces – go to offset.

- **Colour** Digital presses are like large four-colour process (CMYK) desktop printers. With monotone or duotone printing, offset printing may offer a more cost-effective solution. If Pantone colours are needed, traditional offset is the only way to go. However, digital printing may offer economical and scheduling advantages when it comes to full-colour pieces.

- **Paper and finishing** Special paper, finishes, surfaces and unique size options are increasing every year for digital, but offset printing still offers more flexibility because of the variety of print surfaces available. Also, most digital presses can only handle 35.5 x 50-cm (14 x 20-in) press sheets, whereas offset goes up to 100 x 70cm (40 x 28in), increasing the number of impressions you can group on a sheet.

- **Proofs** Digital offers more accurate proofs, since you receive a sample of the final printed piece using the exact process and paper that will be used for the intended final run. In offset printing, the proofs are generally being produced by digital printers.

### Personalisation

Database-driven variable data printing allows digital printing to offer the most economical way to customise marketing materials, direct mail pieces, newsletters and other items with different information or designs on individual printed pieces. Finally, all that information that companies have been collecting for years can be easily used in print.

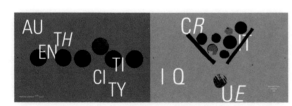

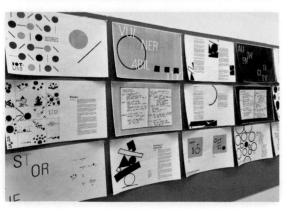

**↖ ↑ Multiple formats**
Digital printing can be used for all types of projects as long as you are working with digital files in CMYK mode. Printing can be done in many formats, including large-format printers that accommodate much bigger surface areas for packaging, posters and banners.

**← Block colour** Printing solid blocks of colour on a home or office printer is not recommended, even for mock-ups, since this is not what it was designed for. For mock-ups of dense imagery and colour, it's worth investing in a printer's proof. That way you can assess the colour before final production.

**❶ Desktop printers**
Desktop digital printers are essential for printing comprehensives for client approval. A good-quality inkjet or laser printer will also help you to check your work-in-progress and simulate your intended printing effects.

| PART 2 | PRACTICE |
|---|---|
| CHAPTER 6 | PRINT PRODUCTION AND PRESENTATIONS |
| MODULE 7 | **CORRECTING COLOUR PROOFS AND PRESS CHECKS** |

The arrival of colour proofs from the printer is second only to the arrival of a finished printed piece of work you have created. However, at colour proof stage, it is still possible to correct some flaws in photographic reproduction, both digital and conventional.

Your proof should be carefully examined for density, colour, registration and dots or spots that may appear on the surface, in addition to any potential text errors you or your client may have missed. It's better to catch them at the proofing stage, when they can still be corrected fairly inexpensively, than during the press check. Keep your comp with you and check the proof to be sure the trim, fold and assembly have been detailed properly. Whenever possible, ask for a proof on the actual stock you will be imprinting, so you can check the colour accurately. Circle anything that worries you, and ask your printer about it.

**Press check**

Printers are usually very receptive to clients overseeing their jobs at the beginning of the press run, and this almost always turns into a learning experience. It is especially helpful when aesthetic judgment is needed. The press person will pull a sheet off the press for you to review, approve and sign off on. At this point you should take your time, pay attention, ask questions and have a checklist to keep you focused.

Remember that at a press check time is expensive – egregious errors such as misspelled words and unaligned edges should have been handled at the proof stages. This will help to avoid any extra correction costs, set-up charges and rescheduling for you and your client. When you are 'on the floor' in the press room, you should focus on overall aesthetic considerations, although a keen eye is always on the hunt for an errant inch-mark instead of an apostrophe, or a random double space.

Greyscale density patches are printed in steps from no tint through to black. They are used to check black-and-white photography and black text in a similar way to that of a colour control strip

The colour control strip tells the designer whether the proof is faithful to the film being proofed. For example, if the printer has used too much yellow ink, so that the proof looks too yellow when the film is correct, the colour bar will help to show this

Check trim marks for position and that the bleed allowance is correct

Check registration marks to see if the job has been proofed in register. If it is correct, all you will see is black. If it is out of register, one or more colours will show next to the black

⬆ **Striking colour** The front cover of *Selvedge* magazine is rich with colour and detail. It is vital that colour proofs are analysed in great depth to ensure the production matches the high-quality visions of the photographer and creative director. The solid red background and smaller details of colour and texture in the fabric, accessories and make-up are the key focal points in this composition, and therefore must be produced and printed to a high standard to carry the concept of the magazine.

**Linen tester (loupe)** A magnifier called a linen tester, or a loupe, is used to check colour separations, transparencies and proofs. It will clearly show the dot screen of your halftone images and will allow you to check the sharpness and dot registration easily. The built-in folding stand keeps the lens at the exact right distance from the sheet surface and leaves your hands free, so no fingerprints are confused with potential flaws.

### ❶ Printer's marks

When setting up a file for printing, a number of marks are needed for the printer to determine where to trim the paper, check calibration and dot density, etc. To add crop, registration, colour bars, page information, bleed and slug, in the Export dialogue window select Marks and Bleed and select either All Printer's Marks or individual marks.

### ❶ Checking proofs

Tints, transparencies and overlays can be deceiving if you only check them on screen. Be sure you are satisfied with the effects you see on the proof. On press, you can ask the printer to hold back slightly on individual CMYK colour values but it will affect the whole sheet, not just the image in question. The best practice is to make the adjustment to the proof before the plates are made.

## Press check checklist

Be prepared; bring these with you.
- An extra copy of electronic files or, even better, a laptop you can work directly from (with requisite fonts and imagery installed).
- The Pantone book (coated/uncoated, or spot or process). See page 133.
- The colour proof that you signed. Although many vendors may want this back, be sure to ask for it again at press time.
- A linen tester or loupe to check for such things as registration, dot bleed, dot gain and font clarity. It usually has a folding stand to hold the lens at the correct distance from the page.
- Patience. A press check on a multi-page document can be lengthy, especially on large print runs. Be prepared for down time, and settle in for the long run.

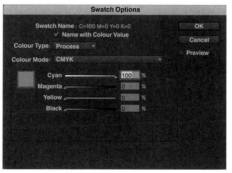

**← InDesign** Check the swatch colours in your native files if they need adjusting. In the InDesign main menu under Window > Colour > Swatches, you can see the four-colour breakdown of your tint.

**+ SEE ALSO:** PREPARING FILES FOR PRINT, P124

PRINTED COLOUR, P132

On first specifying a tint, always give percentages of the process colours, obtainable from a tint chart, rather than a Pantone colour swatch or reference number to match, because many special colours cannot be achieved from the four-colour process. The tint on the proof can then be checked against the tint chart. Watch out for mottled tints, which can be caused by the film or plate being exposed out of contact

## Backgrounds

If a common special colour or tint background is required for several pages in a publication, the designer should be aware of problems the printer might have in maintaining consistency between pages. For example, if a taupe background is used, consisting of a percentage tint of process yellow, and there are some pages that require a heavy weight of yellow to be run for the pictures, the tints on those pages may be heavier than on the other pages. The use of a special fifth Pantone colour for the backgrounds only should prevent this problem – but it is more expensive to run five colours than four.

### GLOSSARY

**Dot gain:** A printed dot that becomes bigger than intended due to spreading, causing a darkening of screened images, mid-tones and textures. This varies with different paper stocks.

**Quality control strip:** Usually incorporated in printed sheets outside the grid to monitor the quality of plate-making, inking and registration. Checking black sections helps point out colour casting.

**Registration marks:** Hairline marks at the corners of a printed page to help ensure plates are lined up correctly, and that designate what will be cropped off at finishing time.

# CHAPTER 6: ASSIGNMENTS

## ◘ Print methods

**1** This assignment involves you documenting different types of printing processes in commercial settings. Research the printers in your area and select a digital, offset lithography, screen print and Risograph printer. Collect as much information as you can about each printing process through primary and secondary research. If possible, visit each printer, ask questions and take photographs of the space. Ask them to show you the equipment and discuss the stages you will need to go through to send a document to print.

**2** Using InDesign, create an A2 information graphic poster for each printing process, documenting all the information you have learned about printers during this process. This version of your information graphic will be printed digitally, so design with this in mind (300dpi and CMYK colour mode). Begin by making sketches and developing your concept. The poster should contain at least two colours and images you've either drawn in Illustrator or edited in Photoshop.

**3** Refer back to Module 1 (see pages 124–127) to make sure you know how to package a file up to print, and how to send it to an external printer.

Pay particular attention to the following:

- Resolution and Colour Mode. The most common problem at the printing stage is bitmapped pictures due to low-resolution imagery. The standard dots-per-inch resolution for printed imagery is 300dpi, which is much higher than you see on a computer screen (a mere 72dpi, which translates to 72 rows of 72 dots). The 300dpi rule goes for photography as well as images and illustrations. Low resolution is also associated with the RGB Colour Mode, the web-based resolution. In Photoshop, check your colour subjects and convert all to CMYK mode before continuing.
- Bleeds. With imagery and colour reaching the end of the paper, an actual section of that colour 'bleeds' into the outer margin of the larger print

sheet. Printers ask for at least 0.3175cm/3mm (⅛ in) around the page. Make sure photographic subjects are sized accordingly, and that you have enough material for the bleed areas. When positioning photo imagery, remember to compensate for the bleed by placing the image to be trimmed in the full space. It may appear slightly off-centre in the electronic file, but when printed and trimmed, it will equalise.

- Fonts. In Illustrator-rendered pieces you can change your type to artwork by selecting the Type > Create Outlines function to retain consistency. You will not need to send a font if the type has been converted. Do not assume that printers have the same fonts as you do. Fonts of the same name come in different versions and from different foundries, and so can have minor characteristic variants. You may also be in breach of your font licence if you send original font files, so outlining is a safe option; just make sure you save an unoutlined version for possible text amends.

**4** When you have completely checked your file, go to File > Package and follow the steps to create a new folder for the work. When you have electronically packaged the file, you'll see that InDesign has collected all of your assets and automatically placed them in titled folders. This process efficiently saves your InDesign file with an IDML (which can be opened in previous versions of the software), a print-ready PDF, a folder with links (images), a folder with typefaces and a set of instructions you can provide the printer. As mentioned above, it is important to check your licensing for typefaces and images before you send them to a printer.

Open each folder and check the contents. If you make a change to the design work after this point, package again or save changes in images to the individual folders that house your assets.

**5** If you are able to, send your posters to be professionally printed on a digital printer, following guidelines set by the printer you contacted.

**6** Additional task
Your poster was sent to print digitally, which is a cost-effective way to produce low-number print runs. Lithography is such a labour-intensive set-up that unless you need a large quantity of prints, it's recommended you use other processes. Screen printing and Risography are similar to lithography in the sense that it takes a lot to expose screens/make the masters and print layers. However, if you have access to these facilities at your school, it's worth experimenting with so you understand the process when approaching a commercial screen printer or Risograph printer.

Using your poster from the previous task as a starting point, and the assignments in Chapter 4, Fundamentals of Colour, follow the step-by-step guide on how to separate images into CMYK layers. You may have to resize/redesign elements of your poster depending on the size of the masters and screens available. Expose each layer to a screen/master and reprint your poster using the screen printing/Risograph process. Start with CMYK, but once you have the screens you are able to experiment with multiple colour ways, spot colours and new colour combinations. If you are able to, send a copy of your poster to the screen printing/Risograph studios you contacted.

## ◘ Print checks

This assignment asks you to research some of the final procedures required before sending artwork to print. Showcase this research as a printed publication, which you can keep as a reference book for further study and design work.

**1** Using information gathered from previous assignments in this chapter, research printed colour, correcting colour proofs and print checks. Make a note of all the stages you should go through before sending a file to print digitally, with offset lithography, with screen printing and with Risograph. Select one form of printing from your research. Create a 16-page publication and a supporting presentation in InDesign, outlining the following information:

- Detail how – and why it is important – to set up a colour comp for proofing. Explore the pros and cons of setting this up, depending on the print media you have chosen to work with.
- Explain how to set up encoded printer's marks or guides and what each mark refers to, along with a demonstration of you trimming, scoring and folding a document. (This could be a physical demo, short film or series of photographs.)
- Talk through how you would use a colour comp at a presentation or meeting with clients. With the traditional printing techniques, consider how digital prints and physical swatches of printer inks and textures can play a supportive role in explaining what you want to achieve with your print. What should you draw attention to? How are you going to 'sell' your idea using the mock-up? Select two details of your project and create large detail images that explain your talking points.

**2** When you are happy with your outcome and supporting presentation, Preflight tools in InDesign, Photoshop and Illustrator will allow you to save in PDF format. Each one offers preset options that allow you to optimise the PDF and customise it according to use.

- Open a file in each program and explore the Adobe Preset options available, then create PDF files in low resolution for electronic approvals. Check them for errors, correct any you find, and try again.
- Email them to yourself as attachments, and make sure they are travelling well electronically.
- Using the same native files in InDesign and Illustrator, create high-resolution files intended for reproduction. Remember to add your bleeds and printer's marks. Save the files and check them on screen before printing them to see how accurate they look.

## Taking stock

When creating a project for print you should be making design decisions right up until the end – including the paper stocks and finishing. The variety of paper types out there is immense: light/heavy; thick/thin; smooth/textured; transparent/opaque; matt/glossy, etc. When colours are added you learn that no two shades of white are alike. The more you observe the differences in paper stocks and samples, the more you will become attuned to selecting what is right for your projects. This assignment not only asks you to observe and make notes about the paper types you find, but also to collate them into a reference book you can refer back to in the future.

**1** Collect samples of as many different types of paper as you can. For example: acetate; scritta paper; blotting; blueprint; carbon; card; cloth; copperplate; craft; crepe; drawing; fine art; gloss-coated; handmade; imitation parchment; napkin; newsprint; offset; parcel; photographic; poster; recycled; rice; synthetic; tissue; tracing; transfer; watercolour; wax; wove; wrapping; or writing paper. Organise them into categories of your choice.

**2** Cut your paper down to 20-cm (8-in) squares. Measure and mark a 3-cm (1-in) column down one of the square edges of each piece of paper. This is where you will bind your paper. Use a ruler and bone folder to crease and tightly fold the column.

**3** Research the various bookbinding techniques available. For example: perfect binding; coil binding; Coptic binding; Japanese stab binding; saddle-stitch bookbinding; screw posts; spiral binding; long-stitch bookbinding; case-bound bookbinding; and otabind bookbinding (also known as layflat bookbinding). Select a binding method for your reference book, considering the materials you have available and the paper you have collected. Some of these methods will not be suitable for single pages, and you may have to attach your paper samples to another page with glue or spray adhesive.

**4** In the corner of each page, make a note of the paper type, weight and texture of each paper sample. Add any other comments which you deem important to record about this paper type, for example, you cannot put it through a laser printer without it melting (acetate is the main culprit of this!).

**5** Once you have made your reference booklet, measure, design and cut an envelope for it to slide into. Remember to leave a little extra space in case you want to add more pages and swatches to your booklet in the future.

**6** Additional task
Repeat the exercise, concentrating now on swatches of print finishes and coatings. These may be harder to locate, but it is worth making a collection for future reference, since some of these finishes can add a hearty price to your printing costs, making it important you know exactly what you are asking for and what you are getting. Options include: die or laser cuts; embossing and debossing; foil stamping/blocking; holographic foils; lamination (gloss/matt/satin); letterpress; pearlescent and iridescent inks; and varnishes and coatings (machine/gloss/matt/silk/UV/aqueous).

## Further reading

Gavin Ambrose and Paul Harris, *Basics Design: Print and Finish*, AVA, 2017

Maryam Fanni, Matilda Flodmark and Sara Kaaman, *The Natural Enemies of Books: A Messy History of Women in Printing and Typography*, Occasional Papers, 2019

Simon Goode and Ira Yonemura, *Making Books: A Guide To Creating Hand-Crafted Books*, Pavilion Books, 2017

John Z. Komurki, Luca Bendandi and Luca Bogoni, *Risomania: The New Spirit of Printing*, Verlag Niggli, 2017

Hedi Kyle and Ulla Warchol, *The Art of the Fold: How to Make Innovative Books and Paper Structures*, Laurence King Publishing, 2018

Peter Lundberg, Robert Ryberg and Kaj Johansson, *A Guide to Graphic Print Production*, Wiley, 2011

Print Club London, *Screen Printing: The Ultimate Studio Guide from Sketchbook to Squeegee*, Thames & Hudson, 2017

Frances Stanfield and Lucy McGeown, *The Printmaking Ideas Book*, Ilex Press, 2019

# Web Design

If you assemble a group of website designers and ask them to provide concrete perspectives that relate to designing for the Web, you will often get the same response: 'Well, it depends'.

For newcomers to the field, this vacuous response elicits more frustration than comprehension. But, at the core, this is the essence of what makes designing for the Web so exciting. Each client brings with them new material, with varying project goals and functionality requirements. While some projects require the active participation of a full development team, most are the collaborative product of a few key members, or perhaps a well-rounded individual. Therefore it is increasingly common for a modern website designer to not only have a working familiarity with the varied steps of a website's development process, but also to be ready to take the lead and make sure that each step is accomplished successfully.

How many different development roles will a website designer be expected to command on a given project? Well, it depends.

Website development processes can vary greatly from individual to individual and from firm to firm. However, to ensure that a project runs smoothly for all parties involved, including the client, it is essential that you develop – and follow – a structured plan, organised into phases and their related steps.

### The planning phase

The planning phase in a website development project is the most crucial, because these initial steps serve to define the process for the entire project.

**Review** Initially, the designer and client should get together to define the client's goals, establish who the target audience is, and discuss required specific features and/or functionality of the site. You should work together to establish the metrics for which the site's success will be determined – such as increase in site traffic, sales, contact and social media reach – with the goal of maximising the return on the client's design investment (RODI).

**Content gathering** The next step is to summarise the information that will be presented on the website. Include the site content (text) as well as defining the visual elements (logos and branding elements, imagery).

**Flowchart** A flowchart is a graphical representation used to display the overall scope of the website. It defines the elements that make up the site's navigational structure (shown as boxes, one per page), as well as the structured flow of traffic through the website (the lines connecting the boxes). It is the crucial foundation for a successful website.

**Software, technology and resources** To determine and identify the programming format in which the site will be developed, anticipate the range of devices on which the site will be viewed, then summarise additional resources that may be required (web font usage, stock photography, etc.), which may add expenses to the project rate.

## The client questionnaire

In most cases, project information is obtained by leading a client through a web-development project questionnaire, of which many can be found online. They are usually grouped by category, such as general questions, functionality questions and design questions. Avoid using technical lingo, which may confuse your client; for example, instead of asking 'Do you require an e-commerce solution?' try 'Do you plan on selling anything on your website?'.

**Training requirements** If instructional documentation, phone support or onsite training will be required in order for your client to maintain their own website, this should be defined in the initial planning phase, as it will add additional time to the project's development.

**Contract** The contract is the end product of the planning phase. Extra care should be taken to make sure that all items discovered and defined in this phase have been factored in to the project's development framework. Successful contracts clearly define the goals, deliverables, roles, timetable, flowchart, copyright and financial information for the project.

## The design phase

The design phase uses the information that was gathered in the planning phase and brings it forwards to define the appearance for the final project. Generally speaking, traditional websites are developed around two to four different layout variations, or templates: one for the initial (home) page, with one to three additional, standardised layouts for the project's interior pages, as dictated by the varying types of information that will need to be displayed throughout the website.

← **Planning** Consider how typography, hierarchy and the navigation of your site can help build the structure you have in mind. Be sure to keep a record of your design decisions to aid working in teams and directly with clients who may need this information for other designed outcomes.

### GLOSSARY

**Content management system (CMS):** A structured framework created by a web designer or developer that allows the client to edit the website without code.

**CSS (Cascading Style Sheets):** The code that controls the appearance of features of the website.

**E-commerce:** Websites created with the goal of selling products online.

**HTML (Hypertext Markup Language):** Elements that form the building blocks of all websites.

**Metrics:** The strategy for measuring the success, or failure, of a project's goals.

**RODI:** Return On Design Investment indicates the success of a project in relation to the project's unique goals.

**Site map:** A recap of the website's navigation structure, intended to direct viewers to a specific page within the website structure.

**Wireframe:** An under-designed representation of the layout structure of a website's main pages.

**404 Error page:** The web page that is displayed as the result of a broken link. If not specified, the web host's default 404 Error page will be displayed.

⊞ **SEE ALSO:**
SCHEDULING, ORGANISING
AND FINALISING, P26

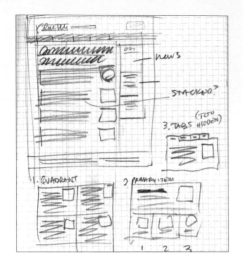
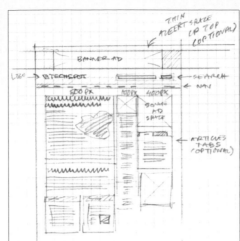
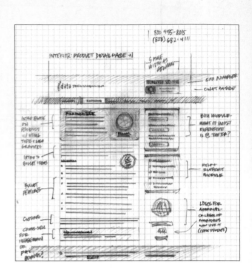

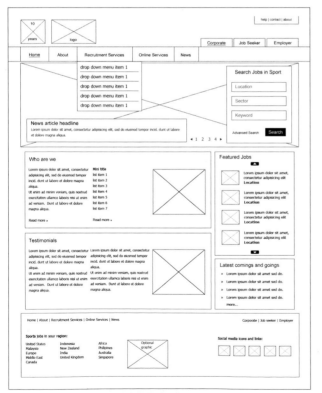

## Wireframe process

As this illustration shows, a wireframe serves as a visual blueprint that represents the framework of a website layout. It is an effective process for efficiently exploring alternative relationships for content arrangement, without focusing on the details related to specific stylisation choices.

## Presentation idea

Present your designs within a mocked-up browser window to convey a sense of realness to your client. Browser templates can be found online, or you can take a screen capture of your preferred browser window, replacing elements with your own designs.

## Client reviews

Holding client reviews at specific points within the design phase will generate important feedback on approaches that might have been overlooked in the initial discussions. Having your client sign off on specific steps within the design phase before moving forwards to the next step will keep the project on track – and justify any additional development expenses should they change their mind and want to proceed in a revised direction.

**Wireframing** This initial step in the design phase defines the visual structure of a web page's layout. Start by creating a series of purposefully under-designed compositions, drawn with lines – similar to an architectural floor plan. Focus on the inclusion of all the required elements, as well as their proportional relationships within the overall composition. Resist defining specific visual choices, as they will be defined in the next step of the design phase.

**The dimensions of a website** The ideal size for a website composition can vary, based on web standards (960 pixels wide), current trends, the target audience/device preferences and even your client's preferred method for viewing online content. Discuss with your client the range of

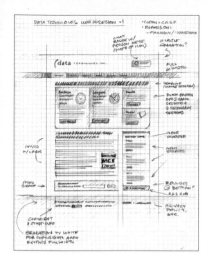 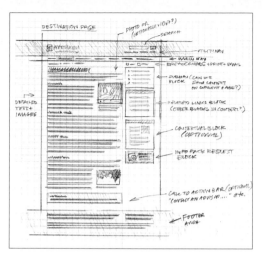 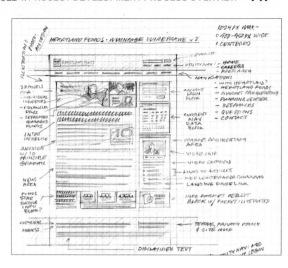

options that are available and what will best suit the purpose of the site. [Client review. Revise as necessary. Client sign-off]

**Design mock-ups** With the desired wireframes selected, the process moves forwards to focus on stylising the elements of your visual composition. Layout compositions are traditionally developed in layered Photoshop documents. Completed files are then exported in (flattened) JPEG format for presentation to the client.

**Final compositional layouts** Once the initial mock-ups have been approved, they can be refined, with a stronger focus on establishing and maintaining consistency, down to the pixel level. In this step – especially if it was not present or readily available in the mock-up step – the actual content should be incorporated into the layouts. It is quite common to discover that adjustments need to be made before moving forwards; for example, allocating more space for longer headlines. [Client review. Revise as necessary. Client sign-off]

**Documentation** Between final approval and the beginning of the production phase, the website designer may be called upon to generate documents that clearly outline the specifications of the project to the programmer, in addition to the layered Photoshop files. This additional documentation can include the following items: wireframes annotated with pixel dimensions; type styling outline,

which defines the type appearance (typefaces, sizes, line spacing, colour use, attributes); and functionality diagrams, defining link behaviours.

## The development phase

The development phase consists of the bulk of the programming work. The specifications defined during the design phase are used as a roadmap for the development of the website.

⬆ **Compositional sketches** Rough sketches not only serve to quickly detail the elements that need to be included in composition, but also the visual relationships among these elements.

## 404 error pages

Misdirects happen. Sometimes they may arise as a result of a linking error or from a removed page. Other times, they can come from a viewer who mistyped the address of a specific web page. While often overlooked as a required element of a website project, a '404 Error' page should be created in order to get your viewers back on track. This page can feature a recap of your site's navigation structure (site map) and also the contact details of your developer.

## Web standards

Web standards are generally regarded standards and technical specifications used in web design, which aim to endorse best practice for designing and developing websites. An early addition was the idea of column grids. After a few iterations, the 960 (pixels)-width system became commonplace, and the 12-column division became something designers were using every day. The next step was to standardise the commonly used elements – forms, navigation, buttons – and to pack them in an easy, reusable way, making a library of visual elements that contain all the code.

**Image prep** Image prep involves cropping/resizing supplied or purchased images for insertion within the layout, then optimising the resulting files in order to generate smaller file sizes that help ensure faster page download times. There is a Save for Web option in Photoshop.

**Coding** Most websites are created using a foundation of HTML and CSS code. HTML (Hypertext Markup Language) is similar to the architectural structure of a building, defining the foundation, wall placement, and so on. The CSS (Cascading Style Sheets) is the code that controls the appearance of features within the building, equivalent to wall colour, furniture placement and inclusion of various decorative elements.

**Additional functionality** As defined in the planning phase, the project may require additional programming. For example, if the website content is controlled by a content management system (CMS), additional code – typically PHP (Hypertext Prepocessor) or ASP (Active Server Pages) code – will need to be inserted within the HTML template structure so that the web page can 'call' content from the website's database (text and images) for display on the page when it is viewed in a web browser. For those uncomfortable with coding in general, you have two options. First is to collaborate with a developer. The second is to modify existing web templates. WordPress, Wix and SquareSpace are all good starting points, but they usually come with limited features and additional costs.

**Content integration** For smaller websites this step will not be time-consuming, because the information will be copied and pasted from a supplied text file and inserted into a web page template. For larger or e-commerce-based websites this step can involve significantly more work; for example, sizing numerous product images or creating inventory listings for inclusion within the e-commerce platform.

← **Interactive web** Website design offers many possibilities due to the flexible nature of coding languages. In this example, formed in response to the climate emergency, the World Weather Network is a constellation of weather stations set up by 28 arts agencies around the world and an invitation to look, listen, learn and act. The site features a series of animations, navigation options and a variety of page styles to reflect the diverse content collected here.

**Test and verify** Using the flowchart as a roadmap, walk through each page of your website to make sure that it functions correctly. It helps to have a fresh pair of eyes to assist you in this step. Test using current browsers (Chrome, Firefox, Safari, IE), platforms (Mac/PC) and devices (desktop, laptop, tablet, smartphone).

**The launch phase**
The purpose of the launch phase is to prepare the site for public viewing.

**Upload to client's web server** Developers usually create a website in a testing, or production, environment, at a different web address from the client's actual web address. Once the website is ready to be launched, the files must be adjusted for the move to the final storage location, the client's web server (or 'host').

**Hosting and domain names** Depending on budget, it is always advisable to buy up as many domain names as you can, joebloggs.co.uk, joebloggs.com, joebloggs.org, etc. 123-Reg offers lengthy packages for reasonable prices and provides a step-by-step guide to linking the domain to your hosting. There are numerous hosting sites available, so shop around to find the best for your money. Be aware that, usually, the cheaper sites do not have the most attentive customer service.

**Code adjustments** If the project requires the inclusion of third-party code, such as Google Analytics (for tracking site statistics), it will be inserted after the site has been uploaded to the client's web server.

**Testing** A final round of usability testing should be conducted. Again, a fresh pair of eyes from individuals not familiar with the project will help point out issues that might have been missed in the project's development. [Client review. Revise as necessary. Client sign-off]

⬇️ ➡️ **Concept to execution** This student's senior thesis project began following the developmental structure of a traditional web design project. Rough sketches were used to define the main navigational structure, as well as desired features and visual imagery. A series of compositional grid systems were explored and the most successful approach was brought forwards to create the final website.

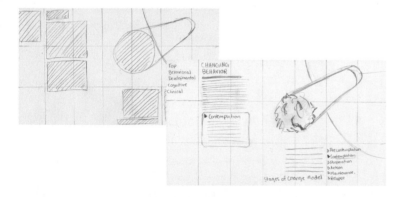

## The post-launch phase

This is the final step in the web project's development, when the designer provides a 'clean' hand-off of the project to the client. It represents the closing of the project development contract, so be prepared to process all last-minute client requests and make sure that all contractual obligations have been met before you define the project as being complete.

Depending on the type of project, the post-launch phase could include the following:

- **Packaging source files** This task involves organising and assembling all files to be returned to the client, such as stock photography images, font purchases, and working Photoshop and Word documents. Include a site map of the final site structure, a summary of the project's technical requirements – including languages used, web fonts and style documentation – and a separate listing of site access passwords, since one site may require different multiple passwords, including passwords to third-party services such as hosting.

- **Documentation and training** If the site is going to be maintained by the client, the developer must compile and document the process for the client, including access to passwords and technical instructions for processing site updates. If personalised training or phone support has been specified as deliverable within the project's development contract, it will take place at this stage.

- **Satisfaction check** Immediately following the initial website launch, most clients will begin receiving feedback from associates, clients and friends. Follow up a few weeks after the launch to make sure that your client continues to be satisfied with your work. A little extra effort here will serve to solidify a positive experience and increase the likelihood of client referrals. Additionally, because you have adopted this step into your project development process, you can incorporate a rough estimate of support into the original project pricing.

| PART 2 | PRACTICE |
| CHAPTER 7 | WEB DESIGN |
| MODULE 2 | **PROJECT STRUCTURES** |

It often falls on the designer to define the appropriate project structure in the beginning, since decisions will cascade into both the design and development processes. Your clients may often cite buzzwords relating to what they want, but it is your role as the designer to listen and decipher what your client actually needs. This module looks at a range of project structures that may define, or be combined to define, your client's project.

### Brochure

This is the most straightforward type of web project. Brochure websites are usually the result of a rapid deployment, meeting the goal of quickly establishing an online presence. First impressions via branding and visual imagery are in the forefront, since the text-based content is typically less developed. Technically, we're referring to static content, HTML and CSS.

### Portfolio

An online portfolio shares many similarities with online brochures, with an enhanced focus on presenting the visual examples. Clicking on an image in an online brochure may take you to a page with product details, whereas clicking on a portfolio image may simply display a more detailed view in the same screen.

### Event/campaign site

You may be asked to develop an event, or campaign, website, which corresponds to a strategic marketing push or to promote an upcoming event such as a concert, lecture or exhibition. These websites typically have a short shelf life, because they are usually attached to a specific date or campaign life cycle. These sites focus on the visual branding, with the addition of actionable items such as submitting RSVPs or purchasing tickets.

### Blog

A weblog is an online journal of posts, or news items, presented in a linear, dated format. Blogs often utilise a content management system (CMS) in order to display the site content dynamically, and by employing the option to allow your site visitors to comment on specific blog posts, you can engage your viewing audience in an evolving conversation.

### Community

Community sites are focused around a need to share information and/or support for a specified interest or topic with their member audience. These sites have the goal of engaging their members to interact with each other by submitting comments, user reviews and aggregated content through social networking and message boards.

### News/reference

A news site is highly driven and based upon information. It is usually controlled by a CMS and can feature an editorial structure for managing content inclusion (contributor, editor, moderator levels). News sites are typically monetised by advertising placement. Banner ads, badges and buttons are designed elements to be included within the layout structure.

### E-commerce

Websites created with the goal of selling products online offer the benefit of being open 24/7, reaching a wider audience than an actual shopfront location. These sites can be created from a range of solutions, from Google/PayPal shopping basket buttons to customised CMS, connected to a merchant gateway (merchant account) featuring a layer of SSL security. E-commerce sites can incorporate many UI display components such as cross-promotional banners, used for 'You May Also Like' and 'Recently Viewed' listings. Popular systems include PayPal, Google Checkout, Magento and Zen Cart.

**GLOSSARY**

**SSL (Secure Sockets Layer):** Provides communication security over the Internet.

**UI (User Interface):** Where interaction between humans and computers occurs.

**SEE ALSO:** PROJECT DEVELOPMENT PROCESS OVERVIEW, P144
WORKING WITH CONTENT MANAGEMENT SYSTEMS, P175

### Popular content management systems (CMS):

**WordPress** An open-source CMS with a reputation for being easy to use. Websites can appear as linear, post-based blogs, or as the administrative back-end for more traditional websites.

**Joomla** Best for medium-sized sites that don't require a lot of complexity. Extensions – free and commercially available – add enhanced functionality to the default system.

**Drupal** Used in larger websites that require more complex features. Enhanced functionality is added by installing modules. Has a steeper learning curve, so most designers on Drupal-based projects team up with a developer.

1

2

3

4

5

6

**1 Dark, not black** Site visitors prefer reading dark main text on a light background because it is easier on the eyes. However, this layout does not feature an abundance of text, so a decision was made to break from the norm.
The sophisticated use of a dark, multicoloured field (instead of black) provides enough visual contrast for the white/pink text to be legible.

**2 Editorial structure** Blog content is intended to be read. This event blog echoes layout styles common to printed publication design, with a visual hierarchy, a simple grid structure, thoughtful typography and a straightforward image layout. These design elements contribute to the overall efficiency of highlighting the important work and discussions being had by the African diaspora.

**3 Communicating visually** When presenting various pieces of information, lean into the fundamentals of web design. In this example, a timeline is portrayed centrally and continues with the scroll of the website for easy navigation.

**4 Creative navigation** There is a range of navigation options in this example. The positioning of a navigation bar at the top of the page, which remains present on each page of the website, can be easily located by the user as they move through the site. On this featured page, thisapproach is varied using a more creative wheel navigation, which becomes part of the design aesthetic.

**5 Bold and effective** A simple provocation, and the input of information is all this website needs to create impact with such an important message. The clear sans-serif typography and bright colour way emphasise the bold approach to understanding migration in a less polarised way.

**6 Galleries** In this example, a series of illustrated cards is presented to the user. In a publication format this is where the presentation ends. In a web format, you are able to click on the cards and hear stories that explore gender and celebrate being trans.

| PART 2 | PRACTICE |
|---|---|
| CHAPTER 7 | WEB DESIGN |
| MODULE 3 | **WEB TOOLS** |

As a web designer you will be relied upon for your production and technical skill sets, in addition to the strategic creativity that you bring to every project. Whether working on your own or in a collaborative environment you will need to keep abreast of software and technological advances; maintain clean and well-organised source files; and possess a working knowledge of current code standards.

As the Internet and the function and use of online media develops, the tools that are used to create them develop too. As the subject area advances it is becoming more complex, usually requiring the need for teams as opposed to a sole worker.

Teams often include a web designer, who will focus on visual elements such as colour theory, typography, composition, etc., and how the page will work. They often know little or no code. A developer will write the code; front-end developers will use CSS, HTML, JavaScript, etc., and back-end developers will use database management, etc. And finally, UX, which stands for user experience. This role is heavily research-led, focusing on user behaviour and motivation, investigating business and users, and verifying the design decisions to make the site functional rather than attractive.

There is no 'correct' way of making a website; in fact you will find web designers and developers that approach it in all manner of ways. However, it is important that you understand the tools that are used in all stages of the process, and how to provide files to each member of the team involved.

**Adobe Illustrator** is a vector-based drawing application for creating graphics that are used in print and/or on the Web. Web designers use this application for the rapid creation of wireframe layouts and flowcharts (exported and shared with the client as PDF files).

Illustrator can also be used for rendering graphics that are incorporated into websites, such as logos or icons, because it's more efficient and intuitive to create complex graphics in Illustrator than it is in Photoshop.

File set-up: RGB colour mode, with 'pixel' as the unit of measurement and 72ppi (screen/web resolution).

Create your artworks in Illustrator at the size they will be used, paying special attention to generating shapes that remain within the pixel-based grid structure. Then copy your artworks from Illustrator and paste into Photoshop as 'Smart Object', which preserves their ability to be edited or updated at a future time.

**Adobe Photoshop** is used by the web designer to visualise the site, but it is the developer who will be responsible for 'slicing up' and coding the web page layout, and for this reason they also need a working familiarity of Photoshop. Industry-wide, this is why most request that the final files, from designer to developer, be supplied in a layered Photoshop (PSD) file.

File set-up: RGB colour mode, with 'pixel' as the unit of measurement, 72ppi (screen/web resolution), and the desired length-width dimensions.

Layered PSD files can often grow to more than 100 layers, with elements present across different views. Even when relabelling and organising your layers into a coherent structure, it can be quite complicated to work with the file. Photoshop's Layer Comp feature lets you take snapshot views depicting which elements are visible/hidden when viewing a specific web page.

⬆ **Adobe Photoshop**
As with the other Adobe applications, the appearance and positioning of the palettes, toolbars and document windows on a website mock-up can be adjusted to suit your individual preferences. The default layout is optimised for working on a laptop, but can be expanded to take advantage of larger monitors.

✱ **Photoshop file etiquette**
This website offers a valuable lesson in organising and labelling your Photoshop files for working in a collaborative environment. www.photoshopetiquette.com

✱ **Adobe TV**
Online video tutorials relating to all Adobe products are an excellent resource for discovering features that have been added to recent software releases. www.tv.adobe.com

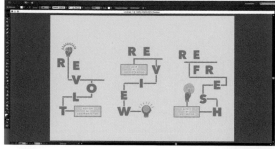

**Illustrator** is an ideal application for drawing and modifying letterforms and vectors. Live, editable text can be converted into vector shapes from original sketches, and further modified to create unique visuals. In this example, the Revolt, Review, Refresh graphics have been drawn systematically with shapes and letterforms.

**Multiple applications**
Vector graphics are good for most platforms, not just websites. For example, the vector images from the Revolt, Review, Refresh graphics have been used to laser cut exhibition graphics, creating a seamless transition for digital to analogue production.

## Generating pixel-perfect artwork

Illustrator will let you render graphics that can break from a pixel-based grid. For example, if you created an icon that was 20 by 20 pixels and, later, manually resized it using the bounding box, the resulting dimensions may become fractions of a pixel (30.565 by 30.565 pixels). While it may look fine in Illustrator, when you place the artwork into Photoshop (or export it for the Web), the artwork will become aliased (or feathered), as opposed to maintaining a crisp edge. Web designers maintain a pixel-based grid in Illustrator by working with the grid turned on (View > 'Show Grid'), based on one-pixel integers (Illustrator > Preferences > Guides & Grid > 'Gridline every: 10px/ subdivisions: 10'); using the dialogue box to define the desired width/length dimensions of rendered shapes; and reviewing the dimensions in the Properties panel to make sure that any resized shapes remain comprised of solid integer values.

## Exporting graphic elements

Until you get a feel for which specific file format you should use, you can take advantage of the 'Save for Web' export feature in the applications described to preview the visual results, while making sure that the file size stays as low as possible. The file sizes of images included in a web page layout will have a direct impact on a web page's loading time. **GIF and PNG** Traditionally used for buttons, logos and simple artwork, GIFs tend to yield smaller file sizes, while PNGs tend to provide better visual results. Both of these file formats support transparency (if needed). GIF also supports animated content (banner ads). **JPEG** Primarily used for optimising photographic images. Usually, the default 80% quality setting generates the best result without loss of image detail. Avoid using a 90% or higher quality setting, since this may actually increase file size.

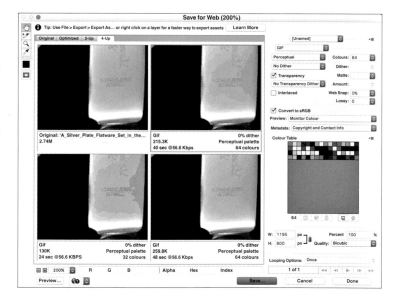

**Visual compression**
Photoshop's 'Save for Web' feature gives you the ability to review different image compression options to see how they will affect your original image. Using their '4 up' display tab (as shown), you can visually compare the compression results and the corresponding file sizes. Your goal is to reduce the file size as much as possible without reducing the visual integrity of your image. Additional features available in this interface include image resizing, as well as image compression to match a specified file size – typically used for creating banner ads.

## Coding

Web pages are usually made up of textual documents, which are annotated in a specific manner indicating to the web browser how they should be displayed – this is known as coding. The most common language used is HTML. Extra stylistic methods such as CSS and JavaScript can be applied along with the backbone of HTML to improve the look and feel of web pages.

**HTML and CSS** To use an architectural reference, the combination of HTML and CSS creates a complete house. The HTML represents the structure of the building, while the CSS is used to define the visual appearance.

A benefit of obtaining a basic comprehension of the programming language HTML is that it provides a means to create the skeleton and structure of text-based information, images and interactions contained in your site. As with any technology, HTML is always on the verge of an upgrade. The newer HTML5 builds on the HTML4.1 code structure, while organising the code differently, based on revised semantics, as opposed to the traditional structure of 'head', 'body', and so on. HTML5 also adds animation that is controlled programmatically – replacing the reliance on additional programs for animation and effects such as sliding elements, colour cycling and 3D extrude effects.

The positive of achieving a level of familiarity with CSS is that the style sheet language (written in HTML) provides flexibility in the presentational look and formatting of the design. CSS code is more versatile (and more complex) than HTML, but CSS cannot live alone without the HTML. It would be like trying to paint a wall that does not exist.

CSS has evolved over the years to not only define the style elements of a specific web page, but to be used as an external library of stylistic definitions for an entire website. This strategy allows developers to make modifications quickly, and have them applied globally.

While 'living' in a separate file, the use of CSS also helps speed up the loading time of a web page, reducing the amount of code that the viewer's browser must download for each page.

Designers should endeavour to learn even the very basics of HTML and CSS, since these coding structures have been with us for quite some time and it is likely that you will come across them in your workload. However, as content management systems (CMS) and templates are becoming prominent due to their ease of use, there are ways around not even looking at code. Adobe Dreamweaver CC, for example, now has CMS built in, which makes site construction more straightforward.

**JavaScript framework** Scripts are another kind of web language, which sits externally to your site, and is referenced in the code, defining how the website behaves and functions in response to certain click requests sent by the user. MooTools, Scriptalicious and jQuery are lead examples of libraries within the JavaScript framework. Animated slideshows, Apple-style touch interactions and display/hide content options are examples of functionality that can be added to a website through scripts.

**Animate CC /ActionScript** Animate CC, previously known as Flash, is a timeline-based application that can be used for animating vector content. It is supported by a robust back-end programming language called ActionScript. For a long time, animation and design in Flash were considered essential skills for web designers and developers, and it is still widely popular. Today, emerging languages/formats such as HTML5, CSS and JavaScript are gaining traction in creating presentations that used to be only feasible in Flash. However, learning to use the updated Animate CC is still an important skill to understand the concepts and practice of timeline-based animation.

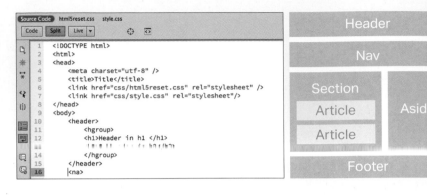

⬉ **Website code**
HTML code is an organised structure of opening and closing tags that tells your browser how to present your site content.

⬈ **Website structure**
This diagram shows the typical organisational structure of an HTML document.

✶ **Code academy**
A highly regarded resource providing free, step-by-step, online courses in Web Fundamentals to introduce novices to coding using HTML and CSS.
www.codecademy.com

⊞ **SEE ALSO:**
FLOWCHARTS AND
WIREFRAMES, P160

**Dreamweaver** Adobe Dreamweaver is the HTML/CSS editor of choice for creating web pages. It remains the industry standard because it generates the cleanest code.

**Adobe Muse** Adobe Muse is a part of Adobe Creative Cloud, and enables designers to build websites without writing a single line of code. The application functionality is extended due to its capacity to use HTML5 scripts via use of Widgets. The Widgets library can be extended with new scripts downloaded from the developer's website (http://resources.muse.adobe.com/collections/widgets). Adobe Muse works seamlessly on all platforms and across all new versions of web browsers. One of its main features is the implementation of Master Pages, responsive design and the use of Scroll Effects.

**InDesign** Adobe InDesign, a vector-based application for creating multi-page documents, can now be used to produce iPad apps. Apps can include audio, video, touch-based interaction, alternate layouts (based on device orientation) and other interactive features.

**Bootstrap and Foundation** Before major developments, browsing the Web on mobile phones or any smart device other than a computer was a challenge. Besides all the different formats of different devices manipulating the look and use of a site, it also introduced content-parity problems as the change in device often meant that information was hidden or skewed. Speed was also an issue, as loading a lot of content drinks your mobile Internet data fast. Ethan Marcotte decided to challenge these issues by proposing to use the same content, but the coding would offer different layouts for the design on each device. He coined the term Responsive Web Design.

HTML and CSS are still used in responsive design, so it is more of a conceptual advancement than a technical one. For a web designer, responsive means mocking up multiple layouts for multiple devices. For the client, it means it works on the phone. For a developer, it is the way in which images are served, download speeds, semantics, mobile/desktop first, and more. The main benefit here is the content parity, meaning that the same website works everywhere.

Bootstrap (available in Dreamweaver CC) and Foundation are both front-end frameworks that handle responsive design tools that allow you to build a site in one format (it is

advisable to always start with the computer screen) which automatically reformats your designs for multiple devices. The downside is that designs often look the same and designers still can't access them without knowing how the code works, so it is usually left to a developer.

**Adobe Dreamweaver**
The Dreamweaver interface can be adjusted to preview the appearance of the web page, a code-only view or a combination of both.

➕ **SEE ALSO:** RESPONSIVE DESIGN AND DISPLAY SIZES, P169

## File-naming conventions

When creating graphics for the Web, all files should be named using criteria that both facilitate proper image indexing by the search engines and correspond with accessibility requirements for special needs visitors. Naming your source files properly will save you from having to rename them each time you export your images.

- Always use lowercase letters.
- Never use spaces.
- Use a hyphen (-) to separate word combinations.
- Use an underscore ( _ ) to separate concepts.
- Do not use full-stops, commas or any other characters.
- Use keywords and/or descriptive phrasing that corresponds with the project's established taxonomy.
- Source files can also be dated (012313) when maintaining version control is a concern.

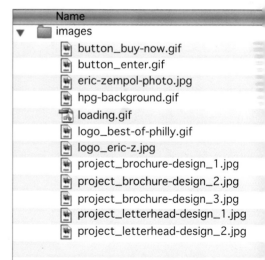

| Name |
|---|
| ▼ 📁 images |
| 📄 button_buy-now.gif |
| 📄 button_enter.gif |
| 📄 eric-zempol-photo.jpg |
| 📄 hpg-background.gif |
| 📄 loading.gif |
| 📄 logo_best-of-philly.gif |
| 📄 logo_eric-z.jpg |
| 📄 project_brochure-design_1.jpg |
| 📄 project_brochure-design_2.jpg |
| 📄 project_brochure-design_3.jpg |
| 📄 project_letterhead-design_1.jpg |
| 📄 project_letterhead-design_2.jpg |

| PART 2 | PRACTICE |
|---|---|
| CHAPTER 7 | WEB DESIGN |
| MODULE 4 | **INITIAL CONSULTATIONS** |

Web designers are usually invited to preliminary client consultations, where they can provide insight into the project's development based on their previous experiences. They assist in defining the technical requirements and content organisation, in addition to visual approaches.

## Meeting tips

- Limit the number of detailed questions you ask. Most clients won't be prepared to focus on specifics at this time.
- Avoid relying on technical jargon.
- Take thorough notes. Nothing communicates the fact that you value your client's time more than pausing to document the points they are discussing.
- Actively listen. Ask your prepared questions and listen to your client's replies. Brainstorm in your own time as part of the proposal process.

These meetings – which are usually limited to an hour-long discussion – can take place in the agency, at the client's location or via conference call. The purpose of this initial discussion is to meet the client and understand their goals for the project. Follow-up meetings may be required to address specific items, but the focus of this step is to clearly define the project requirements for the development proposal.

### Preparation

Before you attend the first meeting, make sure you have a basic understanding of the project. Different project structures (see pages 150–151) will require that you ask different questions.

Prior to the initial consultation, it is common to ask clients to submit six websites for review.

- **Three competitor websites**

  In reviewing these sites, as well as the comments on what the client liked/disliked, a designer can see how high (or low) the bar has been set for defining the anticipated complexity of the project. The designer can also reference technical features, such as banner advertising, e-commerce functionality, social media integration and mailing list opt-ins, which will be discussed in the initial consultation.

- **Three aesthetic reference websites**

  These websites are supplied to efficiently communicate the client's thoughts on the visual styling of their own project. As with the competitor websites, a short dialogue should be supplied that defines what they liked/disliked about the designs. While the goal is not to replicate an existing website, a designer can use this information to derive appropriate cues, such as colour palette, layout structure, typographic styling and use of imagery.

### Consultation topics

**Project goals** Ask questions that guide your client through explaining who they are and defining their current business challenges.

- What is the website supposed to do for your business?
- What sets your company apart from your competition?
- Is clearly defining the benefits and features of your organisation a challenging task?
- Who are the decision-makers on this project?

**Metrics/RODI** Understanding how a client will determine the success of their project and the return on their design investment (RODI) will help you determine the items that will require your focus.

- Increase in sales? Social media following? Site traffic?
- Increase in email newsletter registration?
- How will clients find your website?

**Technical requirements** Use 'plain-speak' to ask questions that define the technical features for the project. From reviewing the competitors' websites, you should have compiled a basic list of items that will be discussed. In addition, you can draw from your own expertise to recommend new features and approaches that may benefit your client.

← **Previous project examples** A useful way to support a project consultation is by talking through the stages of a previous project. This gives your client a clear overview of the way you work and why you make the design decisions you do. It's also helpful to know what will work for your client, and equally what won't. Remember, each client should be treated individually, as every client has different wants and needs.

- How do you currently communicate with clients?
- How often will your website need to be updated? By whom?
- Will you be selling items directly from your website?

**Scope** The size of a website has a direct impact on the project pricing. Guide your client through defining the different sections and subsections of the site. For reference, it can help to review the navigational taxonomy of their competitors' websites. This will serve as the first step for creating the initial flowchart (see pages 144–145).
- Define the sections and subsections of your website.

Additionally, determining your client's level of preparedness will assist you in scheduling the project's development, by clearly defining the client-supplied deliverables.
- For a new site: how much time will you require to generate the dialogue (text) that will be presented throughout your site?
- For a site redesign: how much of your current site dialogue/imagery will remain the same (or be changed) in the revised site?
- Will your website require photography/illustrations? Will you be supplying these items or will you require my assistance?

**Turnaround** You should have an idea of a comfortable development time frame for developing a project at your own pace. If you do not, make an estimate, then triple it, to include time for unforeseen delays, as well as client delays.

A shorter turnaround time requires that you be more aggressive in managing the development of the project.
- Do you require the site to launch by a specific date?
- Is this date flexible or does this date correspond with an event?

**Budget** Don't be afraid to ask this question before you go through the process of crafting a thoughtful proposal. Some clients will be upfront about their budget range. Some will have no idea. Others will prefer that you define your pricing range – so you should give this some thought prior to your initial conversation.

**Closing the meeting**
The meeting closes with a recap of the actionable points. The designer follows up by emailing a list of questions that the client was not able to answer. The designer also explains the next step, which could be a more detailed conversation or submission of the project proposal, which incorporates the points raised in the client consultation.

**Research consultations**
Research consultations with clients and other members of the design team work hand in hand with visual research. Whether it be hand-rendering typography or pinning examples to the wall for an overview, these conversations are vital to get the most out of your design.

**Smashing idea**
SmashingMagazine.com offers many resources that relate to questionnaires and project checklists, specific to varying project structures.

**Plan B**
If the client's budget is unrealistically low, be prepared to offer an alternative solution, such as a DIY service from a web host (or WordPress.com). It's not only polite, but it's good business. Once they grow frustrated by the limitations, they will often return to you.

| PART 2 | PRACTICE |
| --- | --- |
| CHAPTER 7 | WEB DESIGN |
| MODULE 5 | **INFORMATION ARCHITECTURE (IA)** |

The information architecture (IA) of a website is a major component of designing the overall user experience (UX). It is a balance of the intrinsic nature of a website and established user expectations, combined with your client's overall goals. This is the practical and functional expertise that a web designer brings to a website development project and has a strong impact on the perceived success of the endeavour.

### Define the critical pathways

Defining the critical pathways of a website involves understanding the goals for the project and making them clear to the audience. This is achieved by presenting clear calls to action within the page layout, or guiding your viewers through the navigational structure in order to quickly and easily locate the content.

### Navigation

There are no set rules on how to construct the navigation of a site due to the variety in site requirements. Some may need a few main pages and some hundreds. Some may require different navigations for different types of users. However, it is important to avoid presenting too many different navigational options, which may leave your audience confused about which link they should click on next. Instead, use visual cues (such as prominence, positioning and/or scale differences) to visually guide your audience through the site's navigational options. Group similarly themed secondary pages together into subsections and present them using a drop-down (or fly-out) navigational structure.

It is worth considering the use of primary and secondary navigation, especially if the website is large. Primary navigation will point the user in the direction of the content that they came to the site for. Secondary navigation is for any additional information needed through navigation that does not serve the primary goal of the site. This could include 'About us' or 'FAQ', and be in a footer or below the main emphasis of a site.

### Create polite user experiences

A 'polite website' behaves in the way your audience expects. When users click on a hyperlink, they expect a new web page to load in the same browser window. If your navigation element launches a new browser window (popup) or abruptly launches an application like Adobe Acrobat (or your email client), it is considered polite to warn your audience what to expect when they interact with that specific link. Vary the colour of visited hyperlinks to let visitors see where they have already been within your website. Avoid using the underline decoration style for non-hyperlinked items. Let users control their own audio/video experience. Don't force audio/video elements to auto-play as the page initially loads.

### Present digestible content

While it is rarely the role of a web designer, you will often be asked to support clients in crafting dialogue for their websites. Remember, online audiences are on the hunt for information. They approach a web page via the navigation structure, headlines and subheadings, before eventually landing on the desired content.

- Use descriptive keywords in your navigational taxonomy. Avoid generic names like 'products' or 'services'. Select words that more accurately relate to your client's business. For supporting information (Contact, About us), it is considered appropriate to employ the traditional naming conventions.
- Use visual devices like headlines, subheadings, lists and call-out text to guide your viewers through the information.

**↑ Banner ads** Banner ads are used around web-page content to promote and sell products and services. Whether you choose a subtle or vibrant palette, it is important to consider how advertisements sit around other content on the web page. Consider the hierarchy of information and the visibility of the call to action. Web design also offers a platform for animations. Pictured above are stills from a simple animated GIF, showing the range of vibrant visuals in quick succession.

**❶ Reduce the number of clicks**
Try to limit the number of links that your typical viewer would have to click through in order to get to the information you want them to have.

**✱ Usability**
Jakob Nielsen is widely recognised as an authority in web usability. His website presents findings from many usability studies.
www.useit.com

**p5.js** The free JavaScript library for creative coding in action. You can see an input, the remote control, the coding on screen that interprets the input to output, and the output, a computer generator visual.

**Audio visual** These visuals were created using audio reactive code and computer vision. They represent music in different forms through bold colours and dynamic shapes. Many graphic designers are exploring opportunities to 'collaborate' with generative artwork, and how this might then feed into a graphic design practice.

- Be up front in your dialogue. Your first page should contain the most important information that your viewers are hunting for. Stay on point by defining what the product/service is, what it is used for and how it will benefit your client's site visitors.
- Review your site dialogue and infuse it with relevant keywords. Within reason, limit the number of pronouns – he, she, it, they – in favour of including the actual names. This will help your site generate higher organic rankings from the search engines.
- Keep your paragraph text short and concise. Avoid compound sentence structures. Divide long paragraphs into smaller groupings of sentences.
- Use bulleted (unordered) or alphanumeric (ordered) lists to give your audience faster access to the information they are seeking. Additionally, these lists facilitate comprehension between groupings of similarly themed items (bulleted list) or an implied sequential order (lettered/numbered list).

### Establish structure and visual hierarchy

Divide your layout into clearly defined content areas. Create visual relationships by grouping themed items together (for example, a list of recent news items). Vary the scale of your type. The traditional size for paragraph type should be 11–13 points. Headline and subheading type should be presented proportionately larger, in order to make it stand out. Limit the use of bold or italic formatting, only using this to provide occasional emphasis within paragraph text.

Controlled and generous vertical white space within a web page layout is fundamental for segmenting content areas and helping to control visual noise.

### Be inspired

Innovation in web design is driven by the desire to create a better user experience (UX), not just change with the goal of appearing to be different. Review the websites that you visit most often and question everything. Look for patterns and similarities. Adopt (or reject) any trends as you deem appropriate. Considering the development of other creative technologies will also allow you to push your skills in web and interactive design.

### Creative computing

Graphic design is a natural collaborator, and you will find many instances of graphic design being used in combination with other creative disciplines. A prominent example is creative computing. Working with creative programming for web interactions, augmented reality (AR) and virtual reality (VR), or physical computing such as Arduino or Raspberry Pi single board computers to program interactive graphic design experiences, are all exciting and important developments. It is easy to feel overwhelmed by this technology, but there are many free and open-source resources to support an independent enquiry into these areas. p5.Js, for example, is a fantastic, free JavaScript library for creative coding, with a focus on making coding accessible and inclusive for artists, designers, educators and beginners.

**Augmented reality** AR is a technology that superimposes a computer-generated image on a user's view of the real world through a screen, thus providing a composite view. In this example, we can see a script over a view of plants.

| PART 2 | PRACTICE |
|---|---|
| CHAPTER 7 | WEB DESIGN |
| MODULE 6 | **FLOWCHARTS AND WIREFRAMES** |

Flowcharts and wireframes enable both designer and client to visualise the structure of a website and throw light on possible problems. It is recommended that both are tackled before the project begins and are included in the project development contract.

## Flowcharts

In the initial planning phase, flowcharts are created to illustrate the navigational structure of the website, the critical pathways for the site audience, and to define the overall scope of the project. These foundation elements are used in establishing a meeting of the minds between the designer and the client.

Experienced web designers will caution you not to skip this step. Having a visual representation of the website's structure will facilitate discussions relating to detailed considerations that clients may not be able to immediately grasp. Work with your client to establish what pages are needed, write them on cards, and physically decide upon a framework together before you take it onto the computer.

**Navigation structure** By presenting a flowchart with the defined navigational structure, the client can review the specific taxonomy and the presentation order of the links, as well as the distribution of content among primary, secondary and tertiary page structures.

For example, does a primary page ('Our Services') present an overview of the content found on the secondary pages (each of the services)? Or will it serve as the first page for the section (service #1) and provide links to the other, secondary pages?

**Critical pathways** Every website has a purpose and the client's goals for their site should have been defined clearly in the Q+A phase, via the Client Questionnaire (see page 145). In creating a flowchart, the designer's goal is to limit the number of pages that a visitor must view before arriving

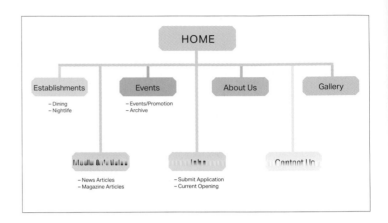

**↑ ↓ Critical pathways** Working with flowcharts and diagrams to help visualise the hierarchy and connections between different pages or areas might seem unnecessarily excessive. However, this is a simple and valuable way of making sure that all aspects of the common-sense organisation of your site have been fulfilled and nothing is accidentally overlooked. Working in this manner helps to explain planned connections to your client and also helps to confirm the minimum number of steps necessary to get from one page or area to another. This is an important factor, since you don't want your client to lose their audience within an overly complex navigation system.

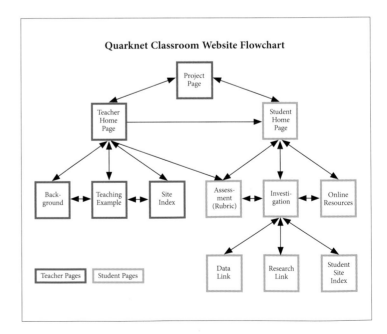

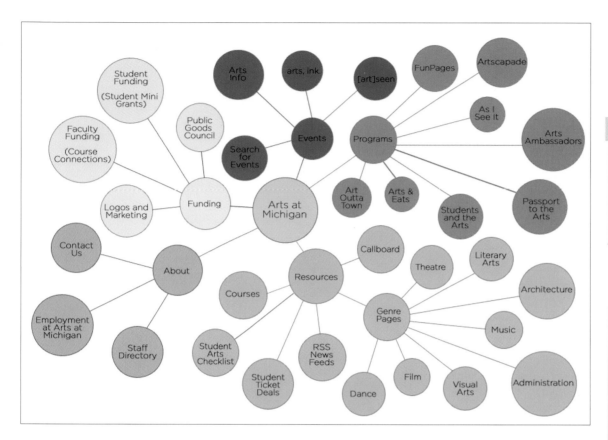

at the desired content or call to action. A generally accepted rule of thumb is three clicks or fewer. However, some calls to action can be incorporated, globally, into the site layout. For example, it would be more efficient to list out the desired contact information on every page, as opposed to isolating it on the 'Contact us' page. Footers, located at the bottom of a website, are particularly good areas to repeat information. Once users have established what is in the footer it will become a point of quick navigation.

**Project scope** In providing a visual representation that defines the size of the project, all parties involved will be able to review the anticipated scope. If the project is amended – as they often are – both parties can refer to the previously approved flowchart to discuss how this may affect project pricing and turnaround.

⬆ **Communicating visually** Flowcharts are an efficient way to communicate the scope and organisation of a web project. This example uses colour to define related sections, and change in scale to identify the critical pathways within the website structure.

➕ **SEE ALSO:** PROJECT DEVELOPMENT PROCESS OVERVIEW, P144

➡ **The grid** A 12-column grid is a common starting point in a website design due to the principles of web standards (see page 147). By aligning elements to a structured grid, the coders will have an easier time bringing your project to fruition.

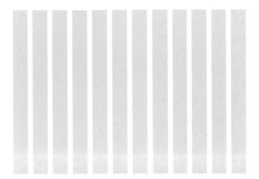

➡ **Establishing visual hierarchy** Define content regions for the elements of your layout. Balance spatial relationships with the goals of presenting content in a hierarchical form.

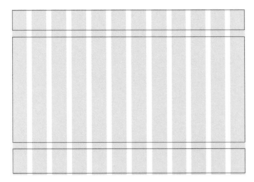

➡ **Incorporate text and navigational elements** Consider the critical pathways through the website. Guide your audience through these pathways by making options clear, using changes of scale and visual prominence.

➤ **Greyscale values** Assigning corresponding greyscale values will help you check that you are presenting your content with the appropriate level of contrast. As colour palettes can be modified as project development continues, you can refer back to your greyscale wireframe to determine the appropriate values that will work with your layout.

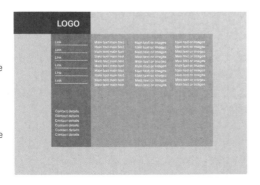

## Wireframes

The wireframe is a purposefully under-designed representation of the layout structure of a website's main pages. Similar to an architectural blueprint, it incorporates all structural elements, as well as defining the visual hierarchy and their proportional relationships within the layout. With a reduced focus on visual style choices, both the designer and the client can have productive discussions that relate to the layout structure without getting stuck on visual distractions such as typefaces or colour choices.

Traditionally, wireframes are created in Adobe Illustrator, because designers are already familiar with it, approaches can be revised quickly, and the artwork that it generates can be imported directly into Photoshop when they are ready to begin the visual design process.

**Start with a grid** Most web designers use the 960 Grid System, a streamlined approach to web development using common dimensions based on a width of 960 pixels, which can be divided into a series of equal columns (8 columns, 12 columns, 16 columns). See Web Standards on page147 for more information.

**Add regions** Insert a series of boxes into your grid that will define the different content areas of your layout, from logo and navigation placement, through the body content, down to the footer area. These boxes should serve to define the proportional relationships between content within your layout.

**Add typography** Define the visual hierarchy between type elements within your layout. Create proportional relationships among your headline and subhead type to guide your viewer through the content. Mix it up and establish a flow. Traditionally, lines (instead of actual words) are used to represent lines of smaller, body copy.

**Add links** Define the interactive elements. Will the main navigation menu feature drop-down menus? Will the layout feature buttons, text-based links or a combination of both? At this stage you are not defining the visual appearance of these links, just their form through annotation.

**Incorporate greyscale values** Your last step in the wireframe process is to assign greyscale values to your content. This step will help you determine the visual strength of your elements without having to focus on the colour palette. This will also help you assign colours, later, based on their relative values.

Don't be afraid to experiment. The purpose of the wireframing process is to quickly discover what isn't working and make adjustments.

**High-definition wireframe (optional)** A hi-def wireframe means adding additional details without getting too specific on the visual elements. It usually refers to inserting actual text to determine ideal type sizes, line lengths and leading.

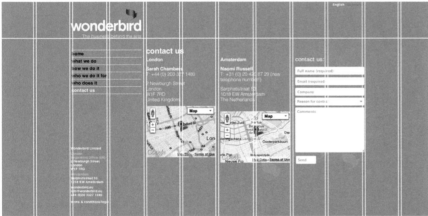

**12-column grid** The design of Wonderbird by Rebecca Foster illustrates well the scope and flexibility of her selected 12-column grid. She consistently uses two columns for left- and right-hand margin spacing throughout. From page to page, as she accommodates different kinds of information and imagery, Rebecca allows detail to extend across varied column widths as appropriate to the information in hand.

## Testing resources

There are several online resources that will help you troubleshoot your work by validating the HTML and CSS code structure, or by checking your website's navigational structure for broken links. The World Wide Web Consortium (W3C) is regarded as the leading mark-up validation service. validator.w3.org/

| PART 2 | PRACTICE |
|---|---|
| CHAPTER 7 | WEB DESIGN |
| MODULE 7 | **COMMON ELEMENTS OF A WEB LAYOUT** |

Above the fold

Below the fold

### All web pages have certain elements in common. These features make up the basic building blocks of a web page.

Before getting down to building and assembling the elements of a web page, let's take a moment to identify the structural zones common to most website layouts. The top area of a website is often referred to as the header. It usually contains a few key elements, such as branding visuals and the main navigation links. Immediately below the header, you have the body area. It is within this area that content will be changing as you navigate through the pages of the website. And at the bottom of the web page, you have the footer area. It typically contains items relating to site ownership and a recap of the main navigational structure, eliminating the need to return to the top of the page to access the links.

**Page title** The descriptive title for the website also identifies the specific page that is being viewed. It is presented at the top of the browser window, or in the browser tab; in the user's bookmark list (if they bookmark the page); and serves as the identifying page title within the search-engine results.

**Favicon** This is a small, branding graphic that appears to the left of the web address. Hosting sites usually require your favicon as an .ico file and 32 x 32 or 16 x 16 pixels. Using a non-standard size will not work in all browsers, and will appear distorted.

**Header** The top area of a web layout. It typically features the company logo in the top-left or centre position due to web standards (see page 147). The upper header area can feature call-out navigation elements such as login/logout for websites that require user registration, or provide access to shopping basket details for e-commerce sites.

**Main navigation/top nav/left nav** Navigation should be kept to a minimum, be easy to identify and easy to use. The main navigation is usually located horizontally across the top area of the screen, under the header. This design pattern (trend) is popular because the abundance of space across the width of the layout usually affords the ability to add additional links to the navigation, as needed, over time. An alternative is to present the main nav, stacked vertically, along the left side of the web layout. However, this design pattern is becoming less popular as designers prefer to position the subnavigation links in this column space. Depending on the type of site, aim for around five to ten navigation buttons.

**Drop-down navigation/fly-out nav** As their names imply, these methods of subnavigation represent ways to visually organise related links, based on the site's organisational structure. Initially, the drop-down menu is revealed (on hover/rollover/tap) to show a series of secondary pages associated with the main navigation link. From those options, related tertiary links are displayed, flying out to the right of the drop-down list. An alternative to the drop-down, which features a full panel of stylised content ranging from subnavigation links to social media feeds, is called a mega menu.

**Breadcrumb navigation** This is a navigational wayfinding element, usually located below the header, presented globally, throughout a website. It helps communicate where the viewer is currently located within the site structure, while providing clickable access to return to a main page. It is most useful in sites that feature a navigational structure that goes at least three levels deep. On websites that feature only a primary or secondary navigation structure, this element would be superfluous.

⬆ **Extending 'below the fold'** As this website example demonstrates, site content often continues past the bottom of the immediate browser window, which is revealed as the visitor scrolls down. Web designers should be sensitive to placing important elements within the top of the website layout, so that they are visible when the page initially loads. Site visitors take visual cues from content being cut off at the bottom of the browser window, as an indicator that they should scroll down. It's called the fold because the same principle applies to newspaper design, as newspapers are often folded in half when held.

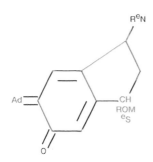

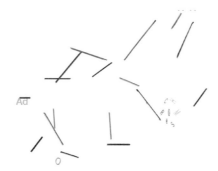

**Feature panel slider** This image slideshow is a visual marketing device that can serve a variety of purposes. Most often it is used to spotlight new products or updated site content, to keep the site looking fresh. Or, it can be used to visually communicate a marketing message, such as product benefits, ease of use statements, and so on.

**Body area** The body area presents a series of content and subcontent that is specific to the type of website being developed and/or the specific page being viewed. Most websites organise content presented within the body using a vertical column structure, ranging from two to four columns.

**Call-out/call-to-action elements** Pull quotes, special notices and/or buttons with calls to action are usually positioned within the body area, above the fold.

**Below the fold** Pulled from newspaper terminology, 'below the fold' refers to content that appears lower on the screen, which viewers do not immediately view when the page loads unless they choose to scroll down. While once it was a firm belief that viewers rarely thought to scroll down a web page, we now know that most do. Usually a visual cue, such as content being cut off, serves as a subtle indicator that the viewer should scroll down.

**Inline text links** Text-based links interspersed through the body copy to facilitate cross-linking among the website's pages, based on topic relevance.

**Anchor link/jump link/top of page link** A navigation element that, when clicked, directs the viewer to an area of a web page. Typically used on pages that present an abundance of dialogue, such as FAQs, or to give the viewer quick access to return to the top of the page.

**Footer** This area identifies the lower section of a web page. Content in this area is presented globally throughout the website and allows the user to navigate certain fundamentals without getting in the way of the design. It can repeat the main navigational elements that are presented at the top of the page, removing the need to scroll to the top in order to continue. Some websites utilise this area to present dynamic content, such as social media feeds, recent news, recent comments and/or special announcements. Corporate websites usually include a series of required, subordinate links to such topics as legal notices, disclosure details, site map, and so on. Additional elements often found in the footer area include address and contact information, dated copyright statement and developer credit-free advertising. Whether you opt for a little or a lot of information, the footer should be designed in keeping with the site, but may have a more minimalistic feel. Make it easy to use.

**Space** Space is essential. It dictates everything, from flow of navigation to readability and willingness to engage. Key spatial relationships, between information and lines of text and general use of open space, all need to be approached with consistency. Space is also important when deciding upon your focal points. An image or piece of text in the centre of white space will appear optically larger and more dominant than one that has been condensed into a smaller space. It is also worth noting that space doesn't always have to be white. Space is the lack of elements rather than the lack of colour or texture.

| PART 2 | PRACTICE |
| --- | --- |
| CHAPTER 7 | WEB DESIGN |
| MODULE 8 | **DESIGNING FOR THE WEB** |

Designing for the web is often a clever mixture of reflecting client goals, understanding user expectations, keeping up with current trends and infusing the project with your own insights and creativity.

↘ **Supporting social media** It is common for websites to have a supporting social media channel that links to and from the site. This allows you to update content and event information quickly without altering a website. Consistency is key. Be sure to follow a design cohesion when creating social media banners and icons, so your user trusts the platform and is more likely to engage with the content in a meaningful way.

→ **Style boards** Presenting varying stylistic design options – independent of a website's structural layout – is a popular strategy for keeping the focus of the discussion on the stylisation possibilities such as colour palette, typefaces, navigation and image appearance.

## Common layout structures

← **Fixed-width layout** Due to the rise of smartphone and tablet use, fixed-width layouts are no longer that common. However, it is important to consider how your site would look on a desktop browser – as if it were fixed width – before moving on to design a responsive alternative.

↓ **Responsive layout** This layout is designed to reposition the elements in response to the width of the browser window. This is particularly important with the Internet being viewed via smartphones.

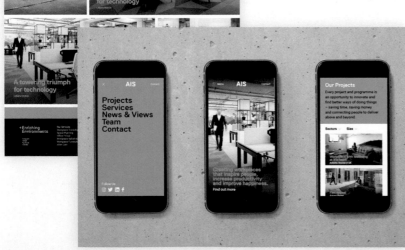

### Client goals

In your initial consultations for the project (see pages 156–157), you will have defined the client's goals and reviewed the expected scope of the website. With the flow-chart to hand (see pages 160–161), these points of information are brought forwards to define the critical pathways of how the visitor moves through the site.

### User expectations

The foundation of web design is rooted in adopting globally accepted sets of behaviours, also known as web standards (see page 147). Novice web designers may feel restrained by following these behaviours, but their acceptance and continuation serve to deliver a consistent user experience as visitors interact with different websites; for example, when the branding element in the header is clicked, the viewer is taken to the home page.

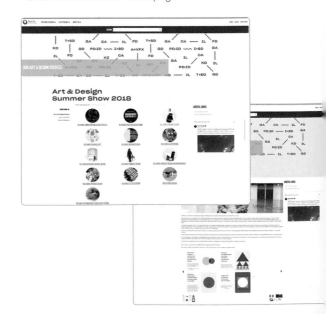

## Web trends

The web is fuelled by innovation. Trends are often rooted in logic: a clever solution that repeatedly springs up across the web because, frankly, it just makes sense. Of course, not all trends should be followed blindly: this is where your own aesthetic judgment as a designer comes into play.

## Flat design

As a result of responsive design, flat design is currently a web trend. Responsive design requires layouts for a variety of formats to be designed, and therefore takes more time than if we were just designing for a computer screen. Due to time constraints with the extra workload, designers naturally began to streamline certain elements, including ditching drop shadows and other dated design trends to prioritise content. Simplifying visual elements, or so-called 'flat design', means that glossy buttons are replaced by vector images and icon fonts that not only load faster, but also look cleaner. The funny thing is, this is the way the Web worked at the very beginning. We have come full circle!

## Layout structures

The most common layout structure is a fixed-horizontal layout, whereas vertical positioning is more fluid, dynamically expanding and contracting to accommodate varying amounts of page content. Alternative options include: proportionate width, such as 80% of the browser window; full-width, 100% of the browser window; flush left, a fixed-width layout aligned to the left side of the browser window; and fixed horizontal and vertical, a 'floating' layout that is popular among online retailers but extremely challenging to maintain in the long term, since content presentation needs may evolve over time, requiring more vertical space.

## Where to start?

The generally accepted starting place for designing a website is to focus on the traditional 'laptop view' at 1024 pixels wide (at screen resolution/72ppi).

Designers usually create a Photoshop document that is 1200 pixels wide by 2500 pixels tall, with an understanding that they're not designing to fill the entire canvas vertically. Some pages will require the insertion of a lot of content, and this height means you don't have to reposition items later on. The more space you dedicate to the elements at the top of a website layout, the more information you will be pushing below the bottom of the browser window, requiring your site visitors to scroll to reveal. A header (with navigation bar) over 200 pixels tall would be considered excessive. Most website designs are compact, using less than half that height.

## Supplying clean files

In an agency environment, most likely you will be supplying your layered Photoshop files to a team of coders. Keep your files organised. Name your layers using a consistent system. Delete unused layers. Organise related content into named folders.

If you find yourself lost and hunting through layers, most likely your developer may also. Use the Notes and Layer Comps features to define complicated items or settings.

❗ **Start with paper**
Work out your concepts on paper before you move ahead to use a computer. Identify all regions where content will be displayed and the amount of visual real estate that specific elements will require.

➕ **SEE ALSO:**

FLOWCHARTS AND WIREFRAMES, P160

## ⬇ ➡ Structuring your information

As digital devices expand and formats change, websites need to be able to expand and change with them. The Adventures in Time & Gender site has a number of different platforms; each has a slightly varied grid structure and navigational elements, but the general design considerations stay the same throughout to provide familiarity for users accessing the site multiple times for different information.

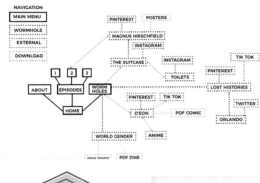

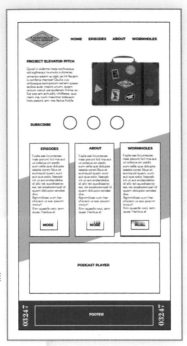

## Grid structures

The compositional grid (see page 162) is a design concept that is pulled forwards from traditional, print-based graphic design. In web design, a vertical grid structure is used to provide visual consistency and make the transition from design to programming phase less complicated.

The 960 Grid System is the leading system, because it can be divided evenly into 12 and 16 columns. The width of website layouts using this system is 960 pixels. The additional space would be used to display the background.

## Web typography

Type presentation online is more fluid than its print-based counterparts. Current technological advances in web design now afford designers the ability to present more thoughtful type solutions, but always check your font is web-friendly before you begin your mock-ups!

The width of paragraph text is controlled by defining a fixed width for the type container, typically reflected in your grid system. If your visitor decides to increase the viewing size in their browser settings – and they will – the content will reflow accordingly.

With the advent of web fonts, designers have access to an ever-increasing library of typeface options that have been optimised for onscreen viewing. Gone are the days of labouring to create pixel-based graphics with typeset words. This is the era of quickly swapping in new typefaces (globally, via the CSS) to text that can be understood and indexed by the search engines.

## Design to evolve

Unlike designing for print – where the project is considered complete when the files are sent to the printer – web design projects will continue to evolve over time. A designer must plan ahead for revisions, including the insertion of additional content, new pages and revised project goals. Failure to do so may require that the site be completely re-engineered at a later date in order to accommodate the requested adjustments.

It is because of this anticipated growth that a web designer should focus on a template-driven approach, distributing content consistently across a series of structured layouts.

It would be unheard of – and quite expensive – to design a 24-page website where each page features a completely different layout structure. The traditional route would be to design a home-page layout and one (or two) interior pages.

⬅ **Consistency** When designing with a variety of different context styles and forms, it's important to embed consistency throughout the design. This assures the user they are still on the right site, and reinforces the design brand, keeping it connected to the content. In this example, the logo and colour scheme is used throughout to achieve this, and allude to the colours of the transgender flag.

The presentation of content and imagery can be adjusted per page, but the overall structure remains consistent with the established template structure – not only for cost implications but also for coherence and design consistency.

## Responsive web design

Responsive web design is the innovation whereby the elements within a layout are modified in response to the device on which the site is being viewed. Primarily, this feature is controlled by the back-end coding of the website, which triggers a media query to apply the appropriate CSS code to reposition the elements accordingly.

Developing a responsive website often stems directly from the client's request. It requires more labour than a traditional project and this can affect the overall project pricing. Responsive website designs will require the artist to create multiple versions of their designs (separate PSDs), which can be reviewed by the client, and eventually submitted to the coding team.

⬆ **Reposition and edit** This is an example of how a browser-based layout has been modified to be viewed on a smartphone and tablet. Many of the core elements are present within the composition, but they have been rearranged to accommodate the smaller viewing screen. Some elements, such as the menu icon, are condensed to reduce visual clutter.

## Type tips

• Audiences prefer dark body text on a light-coloured background, as opposed to light text on a dark background, which tends to 'burn' into your retinas.
• Use solid numeric integers for the type that you specify in your Photoshop document. The typical size for paragraph text is 12 to 13 points, with an open leading of 16 to 18 points.
• The width of a paragraph should be limited to 'an alphabet and a half' (between 20 and 40 characters is ideal).

• While not an absolute, usability experts recommend using a sans-serif typeface, such as Helvetica, for paragraph text and a complementary typeface of your choosing for heads and subhead systems.
• Avoid applying the attributes bold and/or italics to entire paragraphs. Instead, limit these to occasional use in order to highlight specific elements within the paragraph text.
• Avoid using underscore formatting for non-linked text.

## Responsive design and display sizes

At the publication of this book, the current display sizes are:
• Desktop (1600 pixels wide)
• Laptop (1024 pixels wide)
• Tablet (768 pixels wide)
• Smartphone (320 pixels wide)
A traditional (non-responsive) website, when viewed on a smartphone, might be revised to maximise the viewing experience on the smaller screen.
• Reposition/resize the brand mark (logo) and, perhaps, align it to the centre.
• Condense a main navigation bar into a scrollable drop-down menu.
• Remove rollover effects, because there is no cursor to roll over content.
• Space out links to avoid accidental activation.
• Adjust the alignment of subhead titles to be centred within the screen.

• Adjust images to fit in the screen by cropping or proportionately scaling them down (or a combination of both).
• Reposition multi-column content into a single-column view by stacking elements.
• Display content focused on the smartphone user's anticipated needs; for example, a restaurant spotlighting their hours of operation and reservations number on the home screen.
To review how a responsive website could behave, visit the larger websites you view most often from your computer. Resize your browser window, making it narrow. Responsive websites will reposition the elements in order to maximise the screen view. Traditional websites can still be viewed on these devices, but require the viewer to 'pinch-to-zoom' the site in order to get a better view.

## Documenting the details

In a web design project, the list of elements that need to be designed (and specified for the coding team) can grow quite large. Some elements may not be an anticipated factor in the site launch, but will need to be added at a later date. The following list can be used to make sure you have defined the traditional elements of a website.

## Main navigation

Traditionally, the main navigation of a website will appear horizontally across the top. Design for growth and leave space to add an additional navigation link or two.

- Positioning
- Alignment (aligned left, centred, indented)
- Text appearance (typeface, size, colour, spacing, etc.)
- Background appearance
- Active link appearance
- Graphic elements (vertical dividers or a triangle – these are typically used to identify the availability of submenu links)
- Drop-down submenu appearance (text appearance, horizontal rules, background colour, background opacity, graphic element, etc.)
- Fly-out submenu appearance

## Background

A subtle tint is preferred over stark white.

- Solid/pattern/gradient
- Alignment
- Locked into position or scrollable?
- Blend image to solid background colour
- Does the background vary by page?

## Vertical positioning

- How will the layout reposition when the browser is resized?
- How much vertical space should be placed between elements?
- What is the shortest vertical layout size?
- How much space will be consistently above the footer content?

## Footer content

- Appearance of hyperlinks
- Appearance of text (copyright statement)
- Additional elements

## In-line hyperlink states

- Link appearance (typeface, size, colour, underline, etc.)
- Hover link appearance
- Active link/tab appearance
- Visited link appearance

## Navigation button states

A website could feature a wide range of visual buttons, from 'Read More' links to 'Form Submit', to adding items to a shopping basket.

- Default button appearance (height, width, colour, padding, corner radius, typeface, size, type colour, drop shadow)
- Hover button appearance
- On-click button appearance
- Disabled button appearance (typically displayed with incomplete forms)

## Submenus

Submenus are usually stacked on the left of interior pages, for navigating within a subsection.

- Interior page position (right column, left column, horizontally under top navigation)
- Styling (typeface, size, colour, background, graphic elements, etc.)
- Active link appearance
- Fly-out menu appearance (for sub-submenu)

## Text styling

- Body (typeface, colour, size, line spacing, bold/italic, etc.)
- Headings (H1, the largest, to H6, the smallest)
- Paragraph spacing
- Lists (ordered – with numbers/unordered – bulleted)
- Quote appearance
- 'Read More' link appearance
- Excerpt text appearance (and length)
- 'Top of Page' navigation link

## Horizontal rule

- Appearance (weight, colour, etc.)
- Spacing (above/below)

## Image styles

You will notice a trend to display images in a wide format. This is more common than displaying tall-formatted images, as it reduces the amount of vertical space within the layout.

- Display sizes
- Corner radius
- Drop shadow
- Margin
- Caption text appearance (typeface, size, colour, line spacing, etc.)

## Tables

Tables offer a way to pre-format structured content such as charts.

- Border
- First column, first row appearance
- Padding
- Typeface
- Type size

## Banner advertising

- Display sizes
- Number of ads presented within the layout
- Location of ads (header, side column, footer, with content, etc.)

## Forms

A form can be used by visitors for sending a message or submitting a request, such as joining an email list.

- Overall appearance (background, border, padding, spacing, alignment, etc.)
- Types of input fields (text field, multi-line text field, check box, radio button, drop-down menu, etc.)
- Text label appearance
- Required fields
- Submit/reset button text
- Validation/error message (location, text appearance, message)
- Destination of form content (email, database, etc.)

## Animated content

- Buttons/button transition appearance
- Tool tips
- Image slideshow
- Lightboxes (title and caption display, previous/next icon, etc.)

## Social media

- Twitter feed appearance (text styling, link appearance, Twitter logo/emblem, etc.)
- Facebook badge appearance (include 'Like' button, display fans, number of fans, include 'Like' total, show recent post feed)
- Flickr badge appearance (number of images, thumbnail size, etc.)

| PART 2 | PRACTICE |
|---|---|
| CHAPTER 7 | WEB DESIGN |
| MODULE 9 | **MOBILE APPLICATION DESIGN** |

Due to the surge in responsive design, web designers are invited into mobile applications (apps) development to work on projects that are extensions of a client's existing brand. Be it smartphones or tablets, our clients are moving into an exciting new arena and taking us along for the ride.

### App categories
Currently there are three categories of apps that a designer could be assigned to work on. It is crucial to understand the difference among the categories as the development process can be quite varied.

**Native apps** These apps are software developed to run on a specific operating system (Apple OS, Android, Windows Mobile). A designer working on a native app project would be collaborating with, at least, a programmer (of C++) for the project. In order to be approved for inclusion into the marketplace, native apps must first comply with a firm set of development guidelines, as defined by the individual device manufacturer. While that may seem limiting to a designer, the focus is on maintaining a consistent user experience from one app to the next.

**Web apps** A web app lives on the Web. Think of it as a mini web page that has been optimised for viewing on a mobile device. When the app is launched, it subtly loads in the mobile device's browser window – you will know by seeing your browser's bookmark/navigation bar at the bottom of your device screen. Using a JavaScript framework, such as jQuery Mobile, you can incorporate a similar touch-optimised framework that is present in native apps.

### Designing apps
The app development process usually begins before the designer gets involved. The project's producer compiles a project script, or content document, that defines the content that will be displayed on each screen; the

**Buttons** There are many ways in which a navigation button can be designed, but it is important that your user understands it is in fact a button. In this example, the outline clearly indicates the buttons' form, and the use of imagery and invert color upon clicking reenforces this.

**Emoji** An emoji is a pictogram, logogram, ideogram or smiley embedded in text and used in electronic messages and on web pages. The primary function of an emoji is to fill in emotional cues otherwise missing from typed conversation. In this example, the clown emoji indicates fun and playfulness without using any descriptive wording.

**Hierarchy** This mobile application contains a large number of forms, drop-downs and selection tools, so the layout and flow of information has to be considered and tested in depth. The simple, pared-back design allows the pink buttons of navigation to form a hierarchy, prompting the user to engage with the app in a way that will ease the experience.

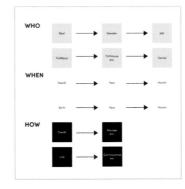

**➡ App icons** Icons are the main branding element for an app project. The rounded corner is applied automatically by the device manufacturer. The glossy highlight is also a default appearance, but this setting can be deactivated programmactically.

### Procreate
An iPad app for digital painting and drawing, this is considered one of the closest digital technologies to painting and drawing in real life. It is a useful resource for mocking up rough visuals and creating professional images to high standards.

### Instagram
A user-generated photo library, great for inspiration and self-promotion if used appropriately. Use hashtags (#) to promote images.

### Pinterest
An extensive catalogue of inspiration and of-the-moment design styles. Be wary you do not use Pinterest to steal ideas.

### Evernote
A handy organisational app that helps you keep track of and prioritise to-do lists. A must-have to help any student to keep on top of things.

---

**⬆ Device GUI** This is an example of Apple's GUI for their iPhone. These elements reflect the structural relationships and common interactions involved with app usage.

navigation and interaction behaviours; specific programming requirements; and lists out required graphics. The more experienced the project's producer is in the field of app development, the more insightful this foundation document will be.

The most efficient method of learning to design apps is to seek out user interaction kits that are available online, and review the range of elements that are typically included. This is also a great way to familiarise yourself with the specific terminology relating to device-specific elements, behaviours and features.

If you are designing a native app, it is strongly recommended that you go to the source and review a user interaction kit that has been produced by the device's manufacturer (Apple, Android, etc.). If you follow their well-documented guidelines, your design decisions should not negatively affect the app approval process.

### Modifying the user interface (UI)
Review the apps that you use most frequently and take note of design patterns for how you interact with the app. For example, where are the 'Cancel' and 'Done' buttons placed? If echoing the positioning of these items would lead to a more intuitive user experience, why break from standard conventions?

When first viewing a sample UI kit, take note of the design specs for major elements (screen size, required screen elements, and so on), then focus on the detailed elements. Use supplied button examples as a reference for

**⬇ App cohesion** This fitness app was developed for users to record and chart their fitness data. There are several elements to the interface, all tied together with cohesive design decisions such as a limited colour palette and flat icon design.

appropriate sizing. Feel free to retain or modify the button colour/appearance as you deem appropriate.

Many UI elements are available to a project's programmer as 'components', preprogrammed for easy, plug-and-play insertion into an app. Modifications to these elements, while possible, may require additional development time. It's best to review what is possible with your programmer before you begin presenting your concepts to the client.

### Supplying art files
As with a website design, you will most likely be working from a layered Photoshop file throughout the design process. This file should be thoughtfully organised and take advantage of Photoshop's Layer Comp viewing feature, offering a preview of each screen, as defined in the project script/content document.

If your app is designed to respond to changes in the device's orientation, you will be specifying the positioning in two separate Photoshop layout files: landscape and portrait.

### App icon design
The icon created for an app is its principal branding element within the consumer marketplace. The concept should be unique and visually represent the utility of the app. As with logo design, you should investigate similar apps to make sure that you are not supplying a graphic that is too similar to an existing one.

You will be supplying the icon artwork, in .PNG file format, to your programmer for inclusion in the app. These files are then converted into an .ico file and included within the app submission. Typically, you will be providing your icon artwork at multiple sizes, from quite small (device view) to large (shop view). You may want to review each icon to make sure that each graphic retains its visual impact at each size.

Citing Apple as a reference, they request five different sizes for use on the device screen, in their Spotlight app, and also in their App Store display. This increases to ten icons if you include a set for their devices with Retina Displays.

Your icon's rounded corner styling is rendered automatically by the device. The glossy 'gel' overlay is also automatically added to your icon, but your programmer can remove that feature, programmatically.

### Templates
As the overlap between apps and websites increases, a number of templates and softwares are being created to make app design more straightforward. As well as Dreamweaver's responsive template Bootstrap and Foundation, many websites let you mock up an app and download a trial to your phone for user testing and to enhance pitches to clients. Search for mobile application mock-ups to see the variety of platforms out there.

## Designing for regular and high-density displays

Apple's high-density Retina Display squeezes double the pixel resolution into their device displays. Creating artwork for both regular and high-density displays will require the designer to deliver two separate Photoshop files, one at the standard size (dimensions vary per mobile device) and another for the high-density display that has the document canvas shown at double the size (note: both files remain 72ppi). If you set up your working Photoshop file correctly, the process of creating the second file is as easy as revising your document's image size and performing 'Save As' to create the second document.

If you are unsure about which size you should design first – big version or small – start by asking yourself if there will be photographic imagery in the presentation. If the answer is yes, then design around the larger size – increasing the scale of placed images within Photoshop will make them blurry/pixellated. Next, you'll want to set up your file using vector shapes, created in Photoshop (or imported as 'Shapes' into Photoshop), and use the layer styling effects to apply colour, bevels and shadows, because vector art will scale without distortion.

And finally, because you will be either reducing by half or doubling your document's dimensions, you want to use even integers in your measurements. Rules, shapes, spacing, point sizes for your text, everything should be divisible by two. This will eliminate the need to revise your second document to achieve a pixel-perfect layout.

| PART 2 | PRACTICE |
|---|---|
| CHAPTER 7 | WEB DESIGN |
| MODULE 10 | **WORKING WITH CONTENT MANAGEMENT SYSTEMS** |

An increasingly popular option for creating an online presence is to use the structured framework of a content management system (CMS), which is a software application that resides on your web hosting account. The CMS serves as an intermediary between the database – where text and images are stored – and the predesigned, dynamic layout structure of the website.

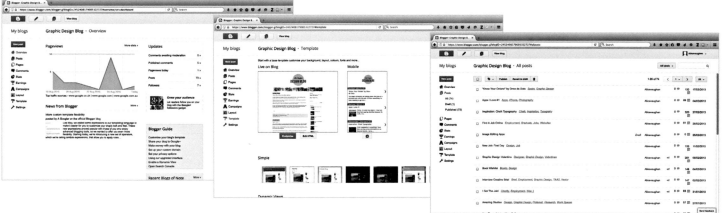

Designers like working with CMS because they spend less time wrestling with programming code, which affords them more time to work on the appearance and overall content organisation of a website.

Clients like working with CMS because it allows them to independently process their own site updates without needing to adjust the programming code or keep paying a designer to do it for them. The website can be edited by logging into the browser-based admin, often referred to as the dashboard. This is a password-protected administration area that allows you – or a designated site administrator – to create new or modify existing content.

Designers often refer to CMS projects as theme integration projects. The project typically encompasses installation of the CMS; selection of a theme; the application of functionality and visual customisations; the integration of the site content; and training and occasional maintenance.

### Platforms

There are many CMS platforms available, ranging from proprietary systems to open-source, free options. WordPress.org, Squarespace.com and Wix.com are all popular open-source options for small to mid-sized websites. Others to consider include Joomla.org, Drupal.org and LightCMS.com.

### CMS installation

CMS applications are typically installed into the clients' web hosting account. Most web hosts usually provide automated installation of the major CMS systems (WordPress, Drupal, Joomla). This set-up process creates the database, where text and images will be stored, and defines the admin/password credentials to access the system's dashboard.

⬆ **Blogger** is a blog-publishing service that provides a number of templates and systems for users to make multiple blogs with time-stamped entries. This student design blog also tracks visits and comments in the User panel, which can be accessed by logging in.

### ← Showcasing

Blogs are fantastic platforms for showcasing a wide variety of images, experiences and viewpoints. This blog cleverly hints at more posts by fading out posts on each side of the one selected.

### ← Blurring the line

As websites and templates become more accessible, the boundary between a website and a blog is blurring. This travel blog is so professional and polished that it could be easily mistaken for a fully functional website.

### ← Trending

Many platforms have a number of features built in, such as a trending posts feature. This allows viewers to jump straight to the most popular content and, in some cases, you, the designer, can choose/manipulate what these trending posts are.

### ← Social media

Blogs are, in theory, a form of social media, so it is a great idea to link them to your other platforms. Instagram is a perfect visual example of how travel on a personal level ties into a blog hobby. However, be wary of your representation, since not everyone wants to see you on a beach on holiday!

### Protect the site

When working with CMS projects, always assign complex passwords to the database and also for the admin access. This will help prevent hacker attacks.

### Selecting themes

A theme is a collection of predesigned web page layouts around a centralised concept, where the arrangement of the pages' structure has been specified by the theme's author. A theme may feature a series of page layouts for different content areas of the website, such as home page; about us page; blog page; contact page; gallery page; portfolio page; full-width layout; and two-column layout. Many commercially available themes are highly customisable, giving the designer the opportunity to make adjustments to ensure the resulting website is unique to the client. For larger projects, a designer might partner with a programmer to create their own theme, from the ground up, based on the project's exact requirements.

### Installing plugins

The functionality of the basic CMS structure can be enhanced by adding plugins, also referred to as widgets or modules. A plugin could be comprised of a contact form, a social media feed, banner ads, weather forecast, live chat, recent post summaries, dated post archive list, keyword-based tag cloud and testimonials, and may automatically add social media 'like' buttons to a web page's layout. Most CMS systems offer a wide range of plugins for free. Additional plugins may be available from commercial entities for a nominal fee.

### Visual customisations

While themes are highly customisable – allowing you to adjust logos, colours, background visuals, etc. – they are limited in some respects and a certain degree of flexibility is required. Most visual customisations can be specified via the theme option settings, and additional stylisations can be controlled by amending the CSS (Cascading Style Sheets) code. Although some CMS do not allow you to adjust the code.

### Integrating site content

Define the navigational structure of the site using the flow-chart as a guide to the established taxonomy, then create the required pages for the website, inserting the specified text and imagery. Crop/resize images as necessary. Define the categories for the news feed or blog posts – these dated entries are usually referred to as posts – and generate a range of initial posts, so as to populate the website with visual examples.

### Training

If your client will be editing their own site, it is reasonable to provide a certain level of training or orientation in working with the dashboard. Often, designers will create a customised user manual that identifies specific elements within the layout and the corresponding instructions on how to update the content, since the process can vary per theme. Many open-source CMS's like WordPress have an online library of user manuals which can be useful to refer clients to for easy things like adding pages.

### Maintenance

CMS and plugins are routinely updated with security patches. You should be regularly processing these updates as you are notified by the system. Comments to blog or news items should always be moderated, to prevent comment-spam from appearing on your live site. Security plugins and/or site monitoring services should be utilised to prevent potential security attacks.

➕ **SEE ALSO:** PROJECT DEVELOPMENT PROCESS OVERVIEW, P144

## Tips on selecting themes

• **The newer the better** Updates to CMS systems usually feature new innovations, in addition to security patches. Themes released (or updated) within the last six months usually take advantage of current innovations.

• **Focus on functionality** Avoid selecting themes that have been created for different intended uses, because they may feature different navigational behaviours. For example, a 'portfolio' theme may be structured so that when you click on a thumbnail, a larger view is presented. Conversely, in a 'corporate' theme, clicking on a thumbnail would launch a new web page.

• **Note the widgetised areas** These spaces are designated locations within the structured layout of a theme. Typically located in the bottom portion of a website, widgets offer the ability to add one to four columns of useful information, ranging from contact details to spotlighted links and social media feeds. The narrow column of a two-column page layout is also typically a widgetised area, expanding in height to correspond with the number of elements you assign to the column widget area. Typically, side column widgets include subnavigation links, search box, archives list, banner ads, etc.

• **Review the customer** reviews, documentation and message board comments, if available.

## GLOSSARY

**Categories:** A taxonomy structure for designating dynamic content (posts) to appear in similar, or different, news feeds within a site. Can be used as search criteria for displaying similarly themed posts.

**CMS:** Content management system. The structured framework of a dynamically driven website.

**Dashboard:** The administrative back-end for a CMS.

**Plugin:** A WordPress term for an element that adds a functional enhancement to the basic CMS structure. Also referred to as widgets and modules.

**Tag cloud:** A keyword-based navigation element where keywords can be selected in order to refine search criteria to display similarly themed posts.

**Widget areas:** Locations within a CMS theme where plugins and widgets can be inserted into the physical layout. Typically, these are located within the side column and lower (footer) area of a web page.

### Theme and plugin resellers

ThemeForest.net
WooCommerce.com
ElegantThemes.com
GraphPaperPress.com
Premium.wpmudev.org
CodeCanyon.net

### WordPress.org versus WordPress.com

**WordPress.org** is the open-source application that you install on your web server. It's yours to edit as you like. You have access to customised themes and plugins. However, you are responsible for processing occasional software and plugin upgrades.

**WordPress.com** is a commercial entity. It's free to start, but many enhancements are available via paid, 'premium upgrade', options. You are required to pay to have sponsored adverts removed, pay to be able to edit the visual styles, and pay to access 'premium themes'. Software updates are processed on your behalf.

### Pages and posts

At the most basic level, a page is considered to be an individual web page within the website's navigational structure. A post is an individual item (for example, a news announcement or blog entry) that is presented in linear, dated format within a page.

| PART 2 | PRACTICE |
|---|---|
| CHAPTER 7 | WEB DESIGN |
| MODULE 11 | **SEARCH ENGINE OPTIMISATION (SEO)** |

As part of any website development project, it is the designer's role to organise and structure the website in a way that helps it to be indexed properly by search engines, such as Google, Bing and Yahoo! The goal is to achieve unpaid, or 'organic', search results.

### Landing page

The search engine will search the landing page for key terms first, so make sure your landing page is full of tags and links to the web's content. This should not only make it more accessible to find, but should bump its position on Google.

### Page title (meta tag)

Meta tags are elements within the HTML code, used by the search engines to properly index your website. Depending on the specific tag, it may or may not be visible when viewing the actual web page. A designer could develop a site without using any meta tags, but it would not perform well in the search engines.

### Keywords (meta tag)

Keywords are the word combinations that web surfers use when they're performing their search queries. An initial step is to define all words and word combinations that a visitor might use to search and locate your site. You can do this on your own (from the dialogue your client supplied), or you can get them involved and ask them to compile their own list.

### Page title

The page title is what appears at the top of your listing in the search results. This is also what appears in a bookmark list and at the top of the browser window/tab. It can be truncated, so arrange the important information first.

Bad: Your Site | Recipes
Great: Chilli: Award-Winning Recipe | Your Site

### Site description (meta tag)

A site description is a sentence of about 20 words that appears within the search results. It should clearly define what information viewers will encounter on your site, using as many keywords as naturally possible.

### Images

Often, viewers discover websites by performing image searches and clicking the link to view the full website. For your images to be properly indexed in the search engines, you should make some adjustments.

- **Retitle your images** Adjust the file name to incorporate keywords or relevant descriptive information. Remember never to use spaces. Use hyphens (-) or underscores (_) to separate words.

  Bad: img00123-23.jpg
  Great: recipe-wins-the-chilli-cookoff.jpg

- **Include ALT tags for the images that you use on the website** Think of this as a caption that you add to each image, which appears in the HTML code. Spaces are fine between words.

- **Do not put important text inside images** The search engines can't read pictures of words.

### Page rank

The more links to a website from other relevant websites, the higher the page appears in search results (SEO). Reciprocal linking – you link to a company's website and they link to yours – such as between a web designer and web developer, can be a good way to do this. Make sure you only include links to reliable sites/businesses/individuals.

**⬆ Search page results**
In the search results, the designated page/site title is displayed first, followed by the complete URL and then the site description.

**↗ Image search results**
A growing number of web viewers rely on image searches to discover websites. Make sure your corresponding artwork is presented so that it can be indexed properly in the search engines. Title the image file's name using relevant keywords, ALT tags and descriptions (or captions).

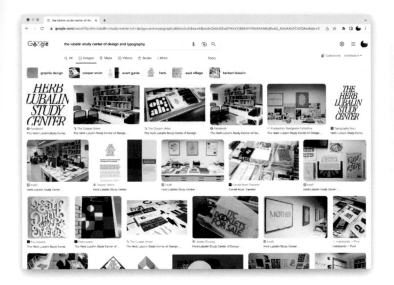

## Putting keywords to work

Create a list of keywords (and keyword combinations) that you think site visitors would be searching for in order to discover your website. Then incorporate these keywords into your site using the following strategies:

- **Use keywords to create descriptive, human-friendly URLs**
  Name your web page documents using the keywords that relate to the information found on that page. Avoid using general terms or insider lingo.
  Bad:  www.yoursite.com/recipe.html
  Great:  www.yoursite.com/award-winning-chilli-recipe.html
- **Use keywords in your headline and subhead text** Within an HTML structure, these elements are usually defined by <h> tags (heading tags). The search engines read the words stylised by these tags and assign them higher priority.
- **Infuse your dialogue to contain the appropriate keywords** Often clients will overlook using keywords within their site dialogue, in favour of using pronouns (he, us, it, they). Where naturally possible, keywords should be used instead. But don't go overboard. The search engines know all the tricks. Strings of random keywords within your dialogue will negatively affect your rankings.
- **Use the keyword meta tag** You can insert a string of chosen keywords into your document's keyword meta tag. However, more weight is assigned to keywords that appear naturally within your site dialogue.

## Practical SEO advice

**For designers** Never promise your client that their new site will receive top ranking in the search engines. A web designer's role is to make sure that a site looks great and is organised so that it can be indexed properly. You have no control over how popular the site will be, nor how high it will rank compared with other sites that may be paying for placement.

To put it in perspective, legitimate SEO/SEM analytics agencies can be hired to increase website rankings. They offer a multi-pronged approach, following the guidelines established by the search engines, and charge up to $20,000 on retainer.

**For your clients** If the designer has followed the advice given above, they will have delivered a website that will be properly indexed. There are also things the client can do to ensure the site ranks highly in the search results.

- Be aware that it can take up to one month for a website to appear in the search engines.
- What keywords are they searching for? Perhaps they are too generic and yielding too many results. Have they tried searching for keyword combinations that feature the city/town where they are located?
- Keep the site updated regularly.
- Promote your website directly to your audience by including your web address on material that you distribute, from business cards to brochures and your email auto-signature.
- Create a presence using social media that drives traffic back to your website. Use status updates to keep your audience informed about new content additions and special offers from your site.
- Have you tried becoming an active participant in online forums and discussion boards? Use your expertise to share tips and advice. Establish yourself as someone people will want to do business with and they will seek you out.
- Have you considered paid placement (sponsored listings) within the search engines? Or sponsored advertising in social media, such as Facebook ads?

| PART 2 | PRACTICE |
|---|---|
| CHAPTER 7 | WEB DESIGN |
| MODULE 12 | **ONLINE PORTFOLIOS** |

Any professional web designer needs a strong and well-conceived online portfolio and the growing list of 'low-tech' options for displaying work online means that even non-web designers have little excuse for not having their work available for review online.

A successful online portfolio is a snapshot of work that reflects your abilities as a graphic designer. As with other design projects, you are designing for your target audience and addressing their needs. In reviewing numerous candidate websites in a single setting, potential employers are seeking a clear listing of skills and work experience, in addition to a complementary stylistic match for the work they produce.

### Elements of an online portfolio

Your online portfolio should be clear, uncluttered and easy to navigate. It should feature fundamental, descriptive information, including your name, field of practice, geographic area, and your current availability. You should also use it to present a summary of your professional biography, organised for easy visual scanning on screen. Include a link to download your CV in PDF format. Finally, invite interested parties to make contact with you by including a clear call to action.

### Prepare your images

Limit the number of visual examples you present in favour of providing a snapshot overview of your experiential range. You can present more examples during the in-person interview phase. Most new designers find it challenging to decide which images to include in their online portfolio. Focus on presenting work that represents a solid foundation of design – typography, composition, colour – in addition to your own aesthetic style. Ideally, your selected examples will complement the scope of work that is being produced by the companies that interest you. If that is not the case, you should work on bolstering your portfolio with new projects.

Portfolio images should be consistent in size and visual presentation. A typical size for a detailed view would be 800 x 600 pixels, at screen resolution (72ppi) and optimised for online viewing. Smaller, thumbnail views can be presented as proportionately reduced artwork or as strategically cropped designs, intended to intrigue your audience into clicking to view in more detail. Website design examples typically feature a browser 'frame' and app designs usually feature the device screen view.

A subcategory navigation structure can be employed to help direct viewers through the project-type examples that relate to the work they are interested in viewing, such as publication design, identity, packaging and advertising.

### Getting started

To set yourself apart from novices or design hobbyists, you'll need your own domain name and a web hosting account. A domain name (for example, www.yoursite.com) is like leasing a car. Web hosting is like renting a parking spot for your leased car. You need both in order to establish your online presence. Both are renewed annually for a nominal fee. With a traditional web hosting account you also get email accounts for your domain, which you should use for professional correspondence.

⬆ **Image as feature** An additional creative element within this site example includes combining typography and images. This clever balance allows for bold statements to be presented throughout the site, and in some instances act as a call to action via a hyperlink to further information.

### GLOSSARY

**Domain name:** The web address for a website. It is renewed annually by the site owner for a nominal fee.

**Web hosting:** A designated online storage space for hosting a website and related email accounts.

➕ **SEE ALSO:**
WORKING WITH CONTENT MANAGEMENT SYSTEMS, P175

## Optional portfolio elements

- Images can be captioned with brief project summaries to spotlight details or your specific involvement within the project (for group work).
- Concept sketches and creative explorations can effectively provide a unique insight into your creative process. Select one project, present it as a case study and use visuals to guide your audience through your process.
- Additional interests that reinforce your design skills (photography, illustration) can be included to demonstrate a broader range of skills and interests, but should be presented with reduced presence, so as not to deter from your focus on seeking employment as a graphic designer.
- Invite site visitors to connect with your professional presence across social media accounts (LinkedIn, Twitter, Facebook Fan Page, Flickr, Pinterest, etc.). But, avoid linking to accounts where you represent yourself informally. Social media links are usually located in the footer, and are particularly good for retaining a relationship with the user after they have left the website.
- Maintain a creative design blog (or Tumblr micro-blog) with shared insights on where you derive inspiration and comments on related design trends.

## Selecting the right domain name

Start by using your own name, as opposed to labouring to conceive a clever business alias. It's easier to associate you with a web address that features your actual name. Use a '.com' domain, because people instinctively type that suffix. Select a name that is easy to remember or difficult to misspell, or consider purchasing multiple names. You can always set your domain names to reroute site visitors to your main web address.

### → First impressions

When a user visits a website, you have a split second to make a first impression and around 15 seconds to persuade them to keep looking. When you design a portfolio, the work is the most important attribute of the site. Make it the first thing you see, and make sure it demands attention. Slug Club has a striking first image, showcasing the product, and bold graphic design to keep the viewer engaged.

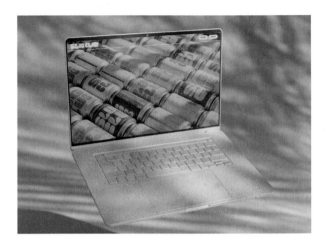

### → ↘ Impactful imagery

The striking imagery continues throughout the Slug Club website. This is important as the landing page in the image above has set the tone of the website. It indicates that this will be a visually striking web experience, which encourages the viewer to stay on the site and explore the multiple pages, images and pieces of information.

Buy your domain name, even if you are not planning on having a website, simply so that no one else can. There are numerous warnings about individuals buying domains and selling them on at increased rates. Buy as many as you can afford—for example, .co.uk, .com, .org, .me, .design, etc. There are so many options available, so it makes sense to own the obvious examples. However, some suffixes are not available in other countries, so it's worth doing some research into what you are buying. And finally, set yourself up a professional email address on the back of your domain, e.g. hello@joebloggs.co.uk.

### Low-tech online portfolios

Popular among non-web designers are the many online resources that provide designers with the ability to upload and share image examples from their portfolio. The utility-driven goal is to have the image examples available on demand, via hyperlink, as opposed to manually attaching images to email correspondence.

Your domain's settings can be adjusted to redirect your site viewers directly from your web address to a user profile. See Working with Content Management Systems (pages 175–177) for more information.

### Traditional online portfolios

If you are seeking positions within the field of web design, the online portfolio serves as a perfect vehicle to demonstrate what you know, from HTML and CSS coding to crafting a memorable user experience. The level of design and coding should be representative of your level of technical expertise.

### Test your work

When you reach the point at which you think you have finished your project, take a break and return with a fresh pair of eyes. Click through all of your links to check that they are functioning properly. Check that your presentation is well-organised and visually consistent, and review your grammar. Conduct a 'beta test' among friends and relatives, and review their feedback. If your parents have a challenging time navigating through your site, a potential employer may experience the same issue. Process all necessary adjustments before sharing your web address with a larger audience.

⬆ **Thumbnails** This mock-up of the Super Gradient portfolio site contains a series of beautifully curated thumbnail images. Thumbnails are a great way to condense and organise information, making your site clean and easy to navigate. In this instance, when clicked, the thumbnails could reveal more information and further in-depth photographs to explain each project.

✱ **Graphic visuals**
A landing page does not have to be photographic or illustrative, the same level of impact can be achieved with bold statements and graphic details, such as the biodesign example below.

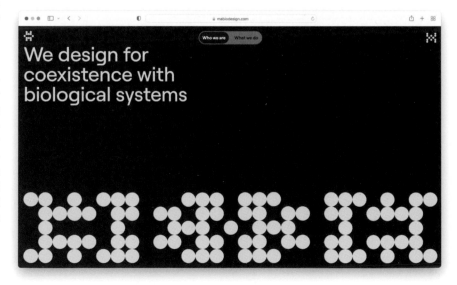

### Social media

Many graphic designers use social media as a means of supporting/linking to their online portfolios, while others replace the online portfolio with the content management system that an existing social media platform provides. Either way, it is advisable to err on the side of caution when linking anything personal to your professional context.

One of the many upsides of social media is that you can update visuals regularly and effortlessly. With followers subscribing to your channels, and the option to be featured and reposted by others, you have a ready-made audience waiting to receive content. The platforms also provide a ready-made creative community. You may find competition there, but you will also find like-minded creatives, collaborators and critical friends to help you develop your graphic design portfolio.

With the connections you'll make and the exposure you will gain, there's no doubt social media can do things that an online portfolio can't, but once a client finds you, a website will always act as your professional anchor, giving you the credibility and authority to make a living doing what you love.

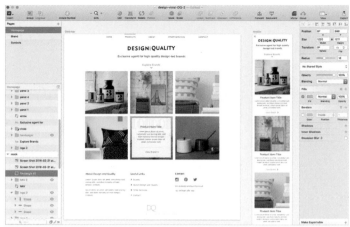

**← ↑ Show off**
If you are presenting yourself as a designer who can code HTML and CSS, your online portfolio is a fantastic opportunity to demonstrate your expertise. In this example the designer is showcasing the website on both a screen and mobile, displaying responsive design skills.

**→ Using grids to break the mould** The Adreno Chromes site presents images set to a grid in an unconventional way. It is important to understand the fundamentals of web design and layout. But once you know the rules, don't be afraid to bend them. There's a lot of competition out there, and you need to stand out from the crowd.

**→ Creative cropping** The images used throughout the site have been creatively cropped. This results in more dynamic images, pulling the viewer in to learn more.

### Email and auto signatures

Regardless of which email system you use regularly (school, Gmail, Yahoo!, etc.), for professional correspondence you should set up and use an email account associated with your own domain name. Where a school email account communicates 'student' and a non-descript Gmail account may say 'hobbyist', your own domain serves as the foundation in creating a professional first impression.

Most email systems provide you with the ability to set up default auto signatures, where you can predefine a standardised closing signature for every email you distribute. Take advantage of this feature, envisioning it as if you are passing along a virtual business card to everyone you correspond with. Typical signature elements include name, desired contact details and links to an online portfolio and social media.

# CHAPTER 7: ASSIGNMENTS

## ◘ First impressions

**1** Make a list of 20 points you'd like a potential employer or client to know about you and your graphic design practice. Share this with a partner.

**2** In conversation with your partner, reduce this list to ten. What's the most important from this list? Where can you streamline or be more efficient with your list of points?

**3** Repeat this exercise with new partners, each time reducing your list to five, three and one.

**4** Fifty-five percent of visitors spend less than 15 seconds on a website. Therefore, you have to be clear and concise, making a good first impression. Using the single point you narrowed down as a point of hierarchy, communicate the three most important points about you and your graphic design practice in a sketch of a landing page for your own website.

**5** Share your sketch with people who do not know your three important points. Can they guess what these points are from your design?

**6** When you are happy with your testing, create a mock-up with colour in Illustrator and repeat the task. Use the results to help make design decisions for your own online portfolio.

## ◘ Counting clicks

**1** In pairs, select two portfolio websites, one you think is successful and another which is not. Count the amount of clicks it takes you to navigate to the following information: Portfolio; About; CV; Contact; Social Media.

**2** In conversation with your partner, reflect on your experience of counting clicks. Was information easy to find? Were things organised well throughout the site? Draw up the navigation of these sites as simple wireframes to help you visualise the experience.

**3** Note the successes of each site on the wireframe. Share with your partner – do you agree?

**4** Annotate where and how you'd improve the navigation on the wireframe. Share this with your partner – did you agree?

**5** In your pair, recreate the wireframes of both sites, implementing your amends. Show this to another group for feedback.

## ◘ Card sorting

Card sorting is commonly used in information architecture and can help web designers answer a variety of questions before the design phase even begins. Card sorting helps designers organise navigation, especially complex navigation, in the most efficient way possible.

**1** In a small group, collaboratively mock up the navigation of a website for your school. For each web page within the site, write a label on a card or a sticky note, such as: About; Subjects; Courses; Students; Contact; Visit; and begin to lay them out flat in order of navigation.

**2** Each time you create a navigation layout, take a photograph. In a group, discuss your choices and offer alternative solutions by physically moving the cards around, each time taking a new photo.

Pay specific attention to how links and sub-links are named and how they are ordered.

**3** Once you have created multiple options for your website, print each photograph of the card-sorting exercise and annotate the positive elements of each layout, and what needs to be improved. It's useful at this stage to work with someone who has not seen your wireframe and ask them how they would move through the site. You can also refer back to the first impressions and counting clicks exercises to evaluate the success of these wireframes.

**4** Once you are happy with your testing, compile your feedback into one solution, and digitally mock up the navigation in Illustrator. Bring the designs back to the group for discussion.

## ◘ Access

**1** Without looking at a website, make a list of what you believe to be accessible web elements and why.

**2** To see some accessible web elements in action, visit the websites of Studio Hyte, a design studio exploring accessibility, aesthetics and technology:

- worldweathernetwork.org
- sunlightdoesntneedapipeline.com
- uninvited.icu
- empathyloading.com

Interact with the accessible options on these sites. Do these options feature in your answers to the first question?

**3** Select a website that has no/few accessibility options for its users and redesign it using what you've found out during the access task. Present your proposal to the class for feedback.

## ◘ Style boards

A style board is a graphical representation of stylistic approaches that you would be proposing to your client. Designed elements are pulled out of the specific web layout so they can remain the focal point of the preliminary design consultations.

This task asks you to create multiple style boards for one contemporary website of your choice:

**1** Start by presenting the styles used in the current website as a PDF for reference. Then, using the same template, create variations that represent the following themes:

- A bold, statement site
- A gentle, minimalist site
- A busy, maximalist site
- An organic site
- A nostalgic site

**2** In the style boards, consider conventional web standards and web accessibility within your design decisions, and identify the following: colour palette (dark, light, mid-tones, accent colours); typography (headline, subhead, body text, text links, quotes, captions, etc.); textures (background patterns, gradients, drop shadows, etc.); buttons (button size, shape, colour, corner radius, drop shadow, etc.); icons (icons as a button element, icons to define content, etc.); and images (cropping, border, padding/spacing, drop shadow, corner radius, etc.).

## Dreamweaver

There are endless tutorials available online that will help you navigate your way around the most up-to-date version of Adobe Dreamweaver. The Adobe site itself has the most comprehensive at https://helpx.adobe.com/uk/dreamweaver/tutorials.html. Use these tutorials to build confidence and learn the correct terminology. When you are ready, complete the tasks below. Remember, you can always return to the tutorials or search for anything you specifically want more practice with.

## Bootstrap

Bootstrap is a framework within Dreamweaver that includes a set of prebuilt components that can save you a lot of time when creating a responsive website. This assignment will take you through how to use Bootstrap, step by step, to create a blank page with responsive settings.

**1** A site in Dreamweaver provides a centralised location for you to save and access the files that make your website work. This is called a root folder. Before you even open Dreamweaver you must save a folder, name it Root and keep all your website content there.

- Open Dreamweaver – if you see a welcome screen, you can close it now.
- Click Site > New Site and name your site.
- Point to the Root folder you will be working on from your computer and click Choose.
- Set workspace to Beginner (top-right drop-down menu).
- Open the Files panel and take a look at the files that make up your website so far (all project

files within your Root folder). If you cannot see updated files, click the refresh icon.

- To create a home page: File > New.
- You are building an HTML page, so select HTML as the document type.
- Select the Bootstrap tab and select Create New to create a bootstrap.css file. Dreamweaver will create this file based on some of the settings you select next.
- Since you are starting with a blank page, make sure you uncheck the prebuilt layout option.
- Next, expand the customise settings – these settings define the default layout that will be created once the HTML file is saved.
- It's really helpful to design with a grid when making a website. Columns will help you organise and align components on the page. The column default is 12. Gutter refers to the space between each column and should be left at the 30px default.
- The screen sizes here refer to the different widths for small, medium and large screens. When you create your website, Dreamweaver makes it easy for you to switch between each of these screen sizes and customise the design for each one. (I would advise you to keep the default settings at this stage.)
- Click Create.

**2** Save your new page: File > Save. Make sure you are saving to your Root folder. Name the file index.html and then click Save.

Notice the Files panel shows more files and folders. It now includes the index.html file you created as well as folders that Dreamweaver automatically created. You won't be editing any of these default files, and it's important to leave them intact to ensure your pages work correctly.

## Titles and containers

**1** Building on the previous assignment, this task will help you to add the title that will display in the tab of the web browser and set your page apart in future search results, as well as add the container that will wrap the contents and make the design fit the width of the page.

- Click the Split View button in the document toolbar to see your live design and have access to the code simultaneously. By default,

the code sits below Live View, but you can move the code to sit vertically on the left. To do this, go to View > Split Vertically, then View > Uncheck Live View on Left, so the live view will appear on the right.

- To add a title to the page, click anywhere in Live View, then find the Properties panel below. Add your title to Document Title and it will appear between the title tags in the HTML.
- An asterisk (*) will appear on the file tab (index. html*). This indicates that there are unsaved changes. Save your file, using File > Save or Command + S on your keyboard.
- Select Preview in Browser (the small globe icon in the lower right). Select the browser you prefer. At this point the only content on the page is the title you just added; can you see it in the tab of the browser?
- Next, you need to add an element called a container to hold all of your page's content. Select the Insert panel and go to the Bootstrap Components category. Bootstrap components are page elements that already have responsive behaviour built in.
- There are two options for empty containers you can use to hold your page's content. The first is a container element and it allows you to define a fixed width for your web page. The container fluid component, however, allows the design to stretch the entire width of the page no matter what the screen size.
- Click anywhere in Live View and look for the word 'body' in the heads-up display – you want to make sure you are about to add this element to the right area of the code, right after the body tag in the code window.
- Now click to add the Container Fluid element on the right-hand panel. Two things have happened. You will have a blue border in Live View, with a display that indicates the container you just added. It is an element called a div, and it's identified by a class name, which is container fluid. In Code View, you can see the same thing written out in HTML: you have a div with a class name of container fluid <div class"container-fluid"></div>.

## CHAPTER 7: ASSIGNMENTS CONTINUED

**2** Make a note of all the terminology and abbreviations that are being used in these exercises. Make sure you understand what everything means, and what its purpose is.

For example:
- A div is an empty container (HTML element). On its own it doesn't do much; however, you can tell this div to behave in certain ways using CSS, which is where this class name comes in.
- CSS is another web design language that tells HTML elements what to do and how to look. In order for the CSS to work correctly, however, it needs to know what element it will be styling, and that's why HTML elements are sometimes identified with class names. So, when you add these Bootstrap components, they come with class names, and some of their behaviour is predefined in the bootstrap.css document that was generated when you created the page.
- The difference between a regular container and a container fluid: they are both empty containers but they resize differently according to the rules they were given in the Bootstrap CSS.

So far you have created a page, and set it up so that you can add content. At the moment, there is nothing to see, since all the containers are empty.

### ◘ Structure and content

In this assignment, you will build the overall structure of the page by adding the HTML components to provide the framework for the page. Add placeholders for the main menu navigation, a slideshow, the main body of content, a thumbnail image and a footer.

**1** Without navigation, websites appear unstructured and disorganised, and offer little support for the user to navigate around the information. This task will help you set up a Navbar (Navigation Bar), while explaining how good navigation can positively impact users' experience of the site. The first section you will add to the page is the main menu. Again, you can use a Bootstrap component for this.

- Make sure the container fluid div is still selected – if not, click on the div node in the DOM panel; it will highlight in both Code View and Live View. The DOM is a really useful panel that allows you to see the entire structure of your web page in a visual and hierarchical way.
- In the Insert panel, under Bootstrap Components, find the Navbar component – it has a drop-down menu of various menu styles you can use. Click on Basic Navbar.
- Select the Nest option when prompted. This will place the Navbar inside the container selected. In this example, the Navbar is a child element that lives inside the container, which is its parent element.
- As you can see from the DOM panel, the Navbar is nested inside the container fluid.
- You can now see the Navbar in the Live View. Dreamweaver also adds the necessary code in the Code View.
- To expand Live View, click the Live button, above the editing area. This will expand Live View and allow you to see more of what is going on. You can see that the Navbar has some content that appears by default – Brand/Links/Search, etc.
- You can use the live menu scrubber to simulate how the Navbar will look across different screen sizes. (Pull the right-hand bar across Live View.) Notice as the display size gets smaller, the menu collapses to a hamburger icon, which is a common interface for mobile device browsing.
- Click the Split button to go back to Split View, so you can add your next bit of content.

**2** A Carousel is a slideshow for images and text used on websites. Dreamweaver offers this template, so it's important to understand its use. However, you should consider other ways of designing layouts for your images. After this task, take a look at contemporary examples and judge for yourself whether the Carousel is the right option for your site.

- Because you've been doing some clicking around, you'll want to make sure you are about to add the next component in the right place. In the DOM, find the node that says div >

class="container-fluid", then select its child element, which is the node that says nav > class="navbar navbar-default". If you don't see the child element, you might have to click on the div node to open up the stack.
- Now you want to add a Carousel element after the Navbar. In the Insert panel, select the Carousel element and select After when prompted. This adds the Carousel element after the Navbar element you have selected.
- Click Save. Dreamweaver presents a dialogue alerting you that the Carousel placeholder image is being added to the images folder in your site set-up/Root folder. Click OK.
- In Live View you can interact with the slideshow (Carousel) and preview it at different sizes.

**3** Next you are going to add some heading and paragraph text in the main body of the web page. To do this, you first need to set up a container to add the text to. It's good practice to organise your sections in containers, as this will make it easier to style and restyle this section later.

- First, make sure you are in the right place in the code. Click div > id = "carousel1" class="carousel slide".
- In the Insert panel select the HTML category from the drop-down.
- Scroll down until you see the Article element. Select Article and select to place it after the Carousel when prompted.
- Now click the Heading: H1 button from the Insert panel. Choose to nest it inside the article when prompted.
- Finally, select the paragraph from the Insert panel. Choose to place it after the Heading: H1 when prompted.

**4** A thumbnail is a small image representation of a larger image. These are important attributes in a website because they make it easier and faster for a user to look at or manage a group of larger images, and they don't interfere with loading speeds as high-resolution, larger files would.

- Click the Article node in the DOM panel so you can add a thumbnail after the text you've just created.

- In the Insert panel, select Bootstrap Components from the drop-down.
- Find and click the Thumbnails component.
- Choose to place it after the article when prompted.
- Click Save. Dreamweaver presents a dialogue alerting you that the thumbnail placeholder image is being added to the images folder in your site set-up/Root folder. Click OK.
- In the DOM panel you can see that the thumbnail is built in an interesting way. First, Dreamweaver creates a row panel (div> class="row"), which spans the width of the page. Inside that row is a column (div> class=col-md-4"). This column contains the text and image that make up the thumbnail.

**5** Conventionally, the footer is an area at the bottom of a web page that contains data which is common to other pages and therefore needs to be consistent throughout the site. It forms part of the package of web standards, typically containing contact details, copyrights, references and other important tidbits of information.

- Select the node with the class of row from the DOM panel. In the Insert panel, go back to the HTML category and select Footer.
- Choose to place the footer after the thumbnail row when prompted.
- Save the page and choose to preview it in the browser. It doesn't look like much yet, but you have your structure in place. The page is not styled at this point, but it will be easier to change that now you have your foundation.

**6** You have now made a basic template, which can be amended how you see fit. With a bit of research, you now need to change the placeholder content that Dreamweaver adds when you use the predefined components from the Insert panel. Add your own labels to the menu navigation, and change the structure to match your final design. Replace the caption text for the slideshow and thumbnail sections to match the images. Finally, add text to the main heading and paragraph in the body of the page and replace the footer content with some copyright information.

- Apply some style and layout to the text. Use the CSS Designer to add colour and reposition the text in different sections of the page.
- Change the menu to give it a more modern look and blend it with the rest of the page design. Override the default styling of the menu to change the background colour, border and positioning of the menu within the page to get the look you want to achieve.
- Finish the page by giving it a more polished look and change the default style of the images so they look effective on any device.
- Apply CSS to the slideshow images to make them stretch the width of the page/modify the thumbnail images to fit the width of their container.

## ◘ Content management systems

A content management system (CMS) is software that helps users create, manage and modify content on a website without the need for specialised technical knowledge – a tool that helps you build a website without needing to write or understand code.

Explore the trial versions of CMS such as Cargo, Squarespace and WordPress. All have free options or student discounts. These are great tools to design your own portfolios if you are not interested in web design. They are equally good tools to design and leave with clients so they can amend the sites without your input.

## ◘ Alternative coding platforms

If, on the other hand, you love coding, there are a variety of alternative coding platforms not included in the Adobe package. A good place for a beginner to start is with p5js.org, a JavaScript library for creative coding, with a focus on making coding accessible and inclusive for artists, designers, educators and beginners. p5.js is free and open-source, includes an in-browser editor and a library of code to explore and use in your own projects. thecodingtrain.com has a range of step-by-step tutorials to get you started (also available via YouTube).

## ◘ Online portfolio

Using all the information you have gained from this chapter, create an online portfolio of your work. You can use code or CMS, but your site must answer the following questions:

- What is the purpose of your online portfolio? What is your call to action?
- What information is fundamental to the user, and which information could be removed?
- How will your user navigate your information? What web standards should you be implementing?
- Have you considered accessibility in your design decisions?
- What information should be consistent across all pages? For example, your name?
- Should your site be responsive? If so, how does this affect your design?

Once you have the first draft of your site, share it with your class for feedback and amendments. Complete this cycle until you are happy with your online portfolio.

## ◘ Further reading

Jim Maivald, *Adobe Dreamweaver CC Classroom in a Book*, Adobe Press, 2018

Jeanine Meyer, *Programming 101: Learn to Code with the Processing Language Using a Visual Approach*, Apress, 2022

Muazu Muhammad, *Website Design With HTML And CSS*, Wiley, 2011

Charles Petzold, *Code: The Hidden Language of Computer Hardware and Software*, Microsoft Press, 2022

Megan Sapnar Ankerson, *Dot-Com Design: The Rise of a Usable, Social, Commercial Web*, NYU Press, 2018

# 8 Expert Paths

By now you should have a good idea of which career path excites you, and will be interested in discovering what it might be like to work in a specific design field. Although expert knowledge in any one of the highlighted disciplines in this chapter will serve you well in the marketplace, remember that design is a collaborative field, and that it is becoming increasingly interdisciplinary. In fact, many of the skill sets in each path should be part of your repertoire. Build your expertise in the area that excites you the most, but find out enough about all of them to collaborate intelligently. Be aware that any job in the creativity industry will be quite fluid, and as a result you will be expected to work with tools that do not even exist yet.

In this unit, each branch of a discipline is highlighted with the skills needed, the ups and downs you might encounter on the job, and some examples of the best in the business. It will provide you with resources and options to help you develop a career path that best suits your skills and aptitudes.

## TYPOGRAPHY

Type designers and typographers are considered specialists who design, style and/or set type for print and digital platforms. The role varies, but it's important to acknowledge that type designers and typographers not only create and arrange type to make written language legible, but also consider how design concepts and aesthetics can alter the way we interpret messages. As a result, a career in typography has a huge impact on the fundamentals of visual communication.

### Examples of work

As a typographer you will be working with the arrangement of type to 'set' text, including selecting typefaces and adjusting point sizes, line lengths, leading, tracking and kerning. The term typography is also applied to the style, arrangement and appearance of the letters, numbers and symbols created by the process.

As a type designer you will design and create new letterforms and adapt others for projects. Type design is considered a craft since it requires an insightful understanding of the various typographic histories and an acute attention to detail to render all elements of a comprehensive typeface.

Many typographers do not design typefaces, and some type designers do not consider themselves typographers. But this line is constantly challenged and blurred by contemporary designers working with typography – great examples being the wave of experimental typography being produced across all scripts, and the use of type as image in a huge array of design projects.

## Skills required

- A firm, creative understanding, as well as a love of typography and communication design and its many histories.
- An element of patience and rigour since most typographic projects require focusing on the details.
- Due to ongoing and rapid changes in computer technology and desktop publishing software, you will need continual training to stay on top of advancements in graphic design applications.

## Pros . . .

- Everybody needs typography in some capacity, so there is a wealth of career and freelance opportunities available to someone with a strong skill set.
- Due to digital advances, the craft is accessible to anyone with the interest to pursue it. Nevertheless, it may take a very long time for the serious artist to master.
- It is very rewarding to create a tool that aids another designer's creativity.
- A large part of type design supports access to information; you can make language clear or communicate the tone of a message quickly with these tools.

## . . . and cons

- The attention to detail and need for focus when working on type-based projects can be draining, isolating and time-consuming if your heart's not in it.
- Typefaces are purchased via a licence, and often people illegally share and use typefaces without proper payment or accreditation to do so.
- It is frustrating to see a typeface you have created used inappropriately or manipulated beyond your control.
- The type design field has been dominated by white, European men, which has resulted in a limited view of the possibilities of type-based projects. This is being challenged every day, with many exciting (historic and contemporary) examples of type design being brought into the spotlight.

## ⭐ Best in the business

**Aries Moross:** With work spanning the fields of artistic direction, moving imagery, typography and illustration, Moross explores a more colourful and playful approach to typography. https://www.ariesmoross.com/

**Boris Meister:** Independent graphic designer creating editorial and identity design across print and digital. https://borismeister.ch/#top

**edition.studio:** Studio and type foundry founded by Victoire Coyon and Adrien Menard. https://edition.studio/type-foundry

**Eye Magazine:** Printed magazine about graphic design and visual culture. https://www.eyemagazine.com/

**Naïma Ben Ayed:** Latin and Arabic type design and visual communication. https://naimabenayedbureau.com/

**Nodo Type Foundry:** Created by Ariel Di Lisio and Aldo Arillo, this foundry specialises in developing retail fonts and custom type services. https://nodotypefoundry.com/

**Studio Kat Rahmani:** Studio specialising in communication design and consultancy within the fields of typography, type design, visual identity and editorial design. http://katrahmani.com/

**Studio Pianpian and Max Harvey:** Interdisciplinary design studio creating books, signage systems and web design in the cultural sector. https://www.infoandupdates.com/

**Sulki and Min:** Founded by Choi Sulki and Choi Sung Min, this studio creates graphic identities, promotional materials, publications and websites for many cultural institutions and individuals. https://www.sulki-min.com/wp/index-random/

**Type Together:** Type foundry created by Veronika Burian and José Scaglione creating text typography for intensive digital and print editorial use. https://www.type-together.com/

**Vocal Type Co:** Type foundry founded by Tré Seals to challenge the singular perspective of design dominating the industry. https://www.vocaltype.co/

## Career options

An understanding and application of typography is fundamental to most career paths within graphic design, but if you are particularly passionate you may find a career as the following:

- Art worker
- Digital/interactive designer
- Letterpress specialist and/or technician
- Publishing/editorial designer
- Sign painter
- Type designer

## ➕ See also:

**A Written Form of Stuttering** http://stotts.nl/#home

**Badass Libre Fonts By Womxn:** https://www.design-research.be/by-womxn/

**Decolonizing Typography Resources:** https://futuress.org/stories/decolonizing-typography-resources/

**International Society of Typographic Designers:** https://www.istd.org.uk/

**Khatt Foundation, Center for Arabic Typography:** https://www.khtt.net/

**People of Craft:** https://peopleofcraft.com/

**The People's Graphic Design Archive:** https://peoplesgdarchive.org/

**What is Queer Typography?** https://soulellis.com/writing/tdc2021/

**What the Font?** https://www.myfonts.com/pages/whatthefont/

## PRINT AND EDITORIAL DESIGN

Print and editorial design encompass a huge breadth of disciplines, and are considered two of the more traditional routes for a graphic designer to pursue. Modern print and editorial design originate from movable type, first created by Bi Sheng (990–1051), who used baked clay. The Yuan-dynasty official Wang Zhen is credited with the introduction of movable wooden type, a more durable option, around 1297. Cast-metal movable type began to be used in Korea in the early 13th century, and the first font is believed to have been cast there in the 1230s. In the 15th century the Gutenberg printing press manually set text in movable metal type. Each page was set in relation to margins, gutters and borders, and printed in multiple copies – a huge leap from handwritten manuscripts. With evolutions in print-production methods and the influence of early 20th-century art and dominant design schools, such as the Bauhaus, the designer began to gain control over print and the page.

### Examples of work

Print and editorial designers now work in an unprecedented range of media and technologies. Many new forms of print and editorial design have been generated over time, and aesthetic considerations are wide-ranging.

Print and editorial designers make up a large section of the graphic design workforce. Aside from the obvious – creating printed materials such as publications, posters, magazines, zines, etc. – the role can involve art direction, illustration, and print and production skills. Being responsible for the layout and visual aesthetics of print and editorial, you will be expected to have a solid understanding of typography, layout, pacing, hierarchy and legibility.

An editorial designer will decide how images and text sit together in print and on screen. As we move deeper into a technology-orientated world, more and more editorial design, for magazines, newspapers and journals, for example, is being created digitally. This means that editorial design increasingly demands the attention of many different graphic designers with varied specialities.

### Skills required

- As a print or editorial designer you should be up to date with contemporary trends, have skills in publishing and page assembly programs such as InDesign, and be able to work to strict deadlines.
- A basic understanding of print for production and good social skills will enable you to liaise with your printer.
- A good communicator, both in the sense of composition and visual language, but also when working with clients and large teams with multiple voices and contributions.

### Pros . . .

- It is a wonderful feeling to receive a beautiful, physical outcome back from the printer – and even better to see it in a shop or library!
- Unless you specialise in creating print and books about design, you get to learn about a whole breadth of new subjects that you may not come across in day-to-day life.
- Print and editorial design allows a lot of scope to be really experimental and creative.

### . . . and cons

- The designer tends to be the last step before production, meaning that if someone misses their deadline it cuts into your time.
- Designing a publication is a huge task. It takes a lot of time and energy, and it is very unlikely that you will spot all the tiny mistakes before going to print. And if someone does, be prepared for endless back-and-forths with amends and adjustments.
- You will often find yourself designing print books for screen and digital editorial pieces for print. Both require different design approaches, and therefore represent a big increase in workload.

### ✪ Best in the business

**London Centre for Book Arts:** Based in what was once the heart of London's print industry, LCBA is an artist-run, open-access studio offering education programmes for the community and affordable access to resources for artists and designers. Founded by Simon Goode and Ira Yonemura.
https://londonbookarts.org/

**Victionary:** Founded by Victor Cheung as a passion project that focused on producing design publications, this has since expanded to include collections, art prints, travel guides, children's books and games under two additional brands.
https://victionary.com/

**Visual Editions:** Co-founded by Anna Gerber and Britt Iversen, Visual Editions is a creative agency that uses narrative and storytelling principles through printed editorial as well as interactive and digital platforms.
https://www.visual-editions.com/

## Career options

Print and editorial design are some of the most common career paths within graphic design, so it is worth considering the following careers:
- Art director or creative director
- Art worker
- Digital/interactive designer
- Print designer
- Printmaker
- Publication designer

### ➕ See also:

St Brides Foundation https://www.sbf.org.uk/
Center for Book Arts https://centerforbookarts.org/

# INFORMATION DESIGN

The role of an information designer consists of discovering and converting information, data and commentary into a visual format. The responsibility of the graphic designer in this context is heightened, partly because it is your responsibility to make complex information more accessible and easier to understand and navigate, without losing its complexity. But also, as with many graphic design roles, you have the power to manipulate and persuade thought and opinion.

## Examples of work

Information design traditionally involves producing graphs or charts, diagrams, infographics and illustrations to deliver often complex information in a way that is both easy to understand and visually appealing. As the discipline develops, and as our obsession and preoccupation with data grows, more and more experimental ways of translating data are being generated.

Graphical representation of data is useful for identifying and illustrating trends and patterns, and for converting spreadsheets and reports into easily digestible visuals. An information designer will have both the creativity to envisage how information might be presented in a visual format, and the mathematical and logic skills to understand and process that data themselves, along with the graphics, art and technology capabilities to produce the final visualisation.

## Skills required

- An analytical, logistical and mathematical approach to design problems is fundamental to being an information designer, both in terms of handling the data, but also transitioning it into something meaningful.
- Perspective. You will be handling information that you could easily misinterpret with bias. An understanding that views of information may be different to your own is paramount in this discipline.
- An understanding of systems and messages. Your visual communication needs to be coherent and confident.

## Pros . . .

- There is potential within this discipline to do some good and bring about meaningful change to opinions and behaviours.
- Information design is constantly expanding into new territories – no longer does your representation have to sit on a piece of paper. In installations, interactive websites and exhibitions, your representation can live anywhere.
- Really suited to the curious because every project will unearth something you didn't know previously.

## . . . and cons

- A lot of rigour and brain power sits behind this analytical approach to design, which is not for everyone.
- The details can make or break a project about information, so perfectionism could push you over the edge.

## ✪ Best in the business

**Giorgia Lupi:** An advocate of Data Humanism, Lupi is a renowned information designer and partner at Pentagram. http://giorgialupi.com/

**Mimi Onuoha:** Onuoha's multimedia practice uses print, code, installation and video to explore the social relationships and power dynamics behind data collection. https://mimionuoha.com/

**RNDR:** An interactive design studio creating design visualisations, interactive installations, generative identities, prints and programs to visualise information. https://rndr.studio/

**Stefanie Posavec:** A designer working in book design, information design, data visualisation and commissioned artworks that use data. http://www.stefanieposavec.com/

## Career options

- 3D visualisation artist
- Data journalist
- Data visualisation designer
- Interactive designer
- Wayfinding systems designer

### ➕ See also:

**Data Feminism:** https://data-feminism.mitpress.mit.edu/
**Sandra Rendgen's Blog:** https://sandrarendgen.wordpress.com/

## STRATEGY AND IDENTITY

Strategy, identity and branding are all about ideas. A graphic designer working in these areas should have strengths in developing innovative and convincing concepts, and stamina for this high-energy, fast-paced industry. Multidisciplinary in nature, when working in this area you are expected to have an array of other supporting skills, which may span copywriting, art direction and production for illustration, animation, photography or film.

### Examples of work

Generally involved in most parts of the process, a graphic designer working in strategy, identity and branding will be informed by research and analytics, collaborating with the production, planning, account and client to carry a project through to completion.

A strategy, identity and brand developer should be detail-orientated and flexible, and have well-developed design and problem-solving skills that employ communication, clarity and simplicity. Organisations spend a lot of money to keep their strategy, identity and branding current and innovative as this is the bridge between the company and the user/customer. Large companies employ in-house designers who develop and update their logos, but many turn to external graphic design firms and individuals who specialise in this field for an outside perspective to develop their brand.

### Skills required

- A fundamental interest in brand research and marketing psychology.
- A creative understanding and love of visual semiotics, symbolism, illustration, colour theory and brand design.
- Knowledge of innovative marketing materials, campaign approaches and copywriting skills.
- Great communication skills. Listening carefully to a client at the beginning and throughout the branding process is central to the design process.

### Pros . . .

- Opportunities for visual creativity and clever communication, especially for those designers interested in identity, marketing and sales.
- Opportunities to engage interest in marketing, strategy, psychology and business.
- It is always gratifying to see a brand or campaign you helped develop launch, expand and succeed.

### . . . and cons

- Many have created their 'perfect logo' only to have it modified beyond recognition, or trashed inadvertently by a visually uneducated client. Such is the life of a designer.
- Some advertising organisations and roles can make for notoriously unhealthy, high-stress environments.

### ✪ Best in the business

**A Practice for Everyday Life:** Art direction, identities, publications, exhibitions, type design, signage, packaging and digital for cultural institutions and events. https://apracticeforeverydaylife.com/

**Anagrama:** Branding and design services for clients around the world. https://www.anagrama.com/

**Fable:** A strategy-centric consultancy creating brand identities, custom typography and campaigns. https://fable.design/

**Landor & Fitch:** A global brand consulting firm and design giant operating offices in 25 cities worldwide. https://landorandfitch.com/

**Litmus:** Branding and digital marketing agency focusing on branding, social media marketing and web development. https://www.litmusbranding.com/

**Pentagram:** The world's largest independently owned design studio owned and run equally by 25 partners – all of whom are leaders in the design industry. https://www.pentagram.com/

**Studio Dumbar:** Working across strategy, visual identity and motion design for clients all around the globe. https://studiodumbar.com/

**Wolff Olins:** Brand consultancy agency, transforming businesses, people and the way they impact the world through brand, strategy and change. https://www.wolffolins.com/

### Career options

Work in identity, branding and advertising is fast-paced and demanding, but the progression and flexibility within this industry could really pay off financially with any of the following career paths:

- Account manager
- Art director
- Creative director
- Designer
- Digital designer
- Strategist
- Brand development

### ➕ See also:

D&AD: https://www.dandad.org/
Hiii Brand: http://www.hiiibrand.com/

# PACKAGING AND 3D DESIGN

Packaging and 3D design can span fabric printing or design for packaging and materials. Working primarily on visuals that will translate onto – or become – physical surfaces and objects, the role requires a good knowledge of production techniques and requirements, from screen printing to manufacturing processes. With great demand for these skill sets in many industries, a packaging designer might work in-house for a brand, or go freelance across a wide range of different projects.

## Examples of work

From product packaging, materials and environmental sustainability, packaging and 3D design are vital to the future of graphic design. A 3D designer will work on a range of projects in the studio. Examples of this could be expressing a brand's personality in a physical form, which could be anything from translating designs onto a surface to designing an innovative piece of cardboard engineering.

Packaging and 3D designers will regularly find themselves immersed in research tasks, collective brainstorming, concept sketching, exploring materials, physical prototyping and concept testing. To create impactful and eye-catching pieces, these projects require a good level of concentration from start to finish.

## Skills required

- An understanding of how to apply ergonomics, human-centric design and the 3D form to branding and graphic design more generally. You need to be a strong, creative thinker, have curiosity, be inventive and also able to problem-solve in a way that is relevant to both brands and consumers.
- You will need a strong ability to communicate your ideas, whether that is through sketching, writing, verbal or other means. A lot of this work relies on communicating to clients and teams. Expect to be involved in client presentations, briefings, a presentation of development, etc.
- Rigour and a comprehensive understanding of materials, construction, crafting and making (both by hand and CAD). Ongoing prototyping is inevitable.

## Pros . . .

- There is something satisfying about realising your ideas and concepts through shape, form and materials.
- You get to work closely with manufacturers, who translate designs into production samples. This can be an excellent and interesting learning experience.
- The joys of solving a problem. Packaging and 3D design are about challenging things and doing them in unexpected ways, so when you've got that idea, nothing feels better.

## . . . and cons

- The industry is fast-paced and high-pressured to deliver creative ideas and outputs in a very tight time frame.
- Clients and colleagues often forget that 3D design development and manufacture take a little longer than 2D. You often do not get enough time to complete tasks to the high standard you would want to.
- Environmental concerns and sustainability options make this industry difficult, but rewarding if you can get it right!

## ✪ Best in the business

**Bloom:** An innovative branding agency working across identity and packaging design.
https://www.bloom-london.com/
- **Burgopak:** This agency is a structural packaging design company that has some unusual patented packaging products that are created from a cardboard engineered sliding mechanism.
https://burgopak.com/
**Design Bridge:** An international agency specialising in creative, out-of-the-box packaging solutions.
https://www.designbridge.com/
**Elmwood:** A global design consultancy working across multiple formats, including packaging and 3D.
https://www.elmwood.com/
**Helen Friel:** A paper engineer and author with experience in art directing and creating paper artwork for editorial and advertising clients. She also illustrates interactive and immersive books for both children and adults, including the first pop-up book to be sent into space.
https://www.helenfriel.com/
- **Pearlfisher:** An international design company with a focus on sustainability, Pearlfisher builds and creates desirable brands and packaging, from powerful identities to multisensory worlds.
https://www.pearlfisher.com/

## Career options

- Art director
- Packaging designer
- Paper engineer
- Print designer
- Product designer

## ➕ See also:

**World Packing Design:** https://www.packagingoftheworld.com/

# IMAGE MAKING

Image makers, including illustrators, photographers and graphic artists, are commissioned by clients to communicate ideas in advertisements, books, magazines and newspapers, through to apps, for TV and film, in both print and digital media. While these pathways are driven by a complete desire to create, experiment and develop concepts and aesthetics, the turnaround times for complex, detailed pieces of work can be quite pressured.

It is common for these disciplines to happen in isolation, since much of the work depends on the skill set of an individual. Therefore, most graphic artists, illustrators and photographers work freelance and are based in home studios or in collaborative workspaces. As the scale and time frame of commissions will vary, excellent communication and time-management skills are essential in order to meet deadlines and keep track of finances.

## Examples of work

As an image maker it is important to develop a confident, personal style while showing your flexibility in approach and method. Some image makers may lean towards more traditional ways of working, such as pencils and paints, combined with image-making software like Procreate, Illustrator or Photoshop. There is no right or wrong way to create an image – naturally, everyone will develop their own unique process, which is one of the real beauties of image making.

Likewise, a photographer will be working with the camera and making the majority of the design decisions on site. However, it is more than taking a picture. Technical planning and post-production are vital to any photographer. The majority of time can be spread across planning, budgeting, researching, test shooting, sourcing a team, liaising with a client and, finally, editing. This discipline involves a great deal of preplanning and focus to get the job done.

With one approach varying greatly from the next, different forms of image making might be defined by the equipment used to the context – for a particular industry, event or point of interest.

## Skills required

- Time management, organisation and concentration are required when working in any area in isolation.
- A comprehensive understanding of traditional and digital means to create imagery and perform post-production. Illustrator and Photoshop are considered the industry standards, but there are a multitude of other options out there.
- Responsive and communicative personality. Working offsite means there is pressure to include your client in the development of your work and to respond to questions promptly.

## Pros . . .

- Opportunities to immerse yourself in creative thinking and storytelling.
- Option to decide on your own working environment, whether that be at home, in a co-working space or a rented space – it's completely up to you.
- To see your images in use across a wide scope of contexts, being interacted with by a multitude of audiences.

## . . . and cons

- Often results in isolated working, which can be a struggle for many.

- Turnaround times, especially for editorial commissions, are fast, often with little notice. Expect to miss out on jobs for not picking up emails quickly or having your laptop with you at all times in case amends need to be made on the train!

## ✪ Best in the business

**Hattie Newman:** Through creating sets and images that live across multiple formats, Newman's sketches and ideas quickly outgrow their pages and leap to life. http://hattienewman.co.uk/

**Jono Sandilands:** An experimental graphic artist, Sandilands makes work at the intersection of design, printmaking and screen-based-technology. https://www.jonosandilands.com/

**Victoria Ling:** Working with photography and animation, Ling's aesthetic is clean and minimalist, with a keen attention to detail, texture and colour. http://www.victorialing.com/

**Will Mower:** A graphic artist, designer and illustrator, Mower designs simple toolkits with striking results across printmaking, ceramics and interactive works. https://willmower.com/

## Career options

A career in image making is really limitless. You will often find that image makers are in other roles, using image making as a supportive addition to their professional creativity. For more specialist image-making careers, consider:

- Artworker
- Graphic Artist
- Illustrator
- Image researcher
- Printmaker
- Print technician
- Photographer

# MOVING IMAGE AND ANIMATION

The field of motion graphics has transcended its early beginnings in film and TV opening titles, and is now vital to the new media environment, interactive applications, post-production, advertising, animation and digital environments for the Web and broadcast.

## Examples of work

Motion graphics designers and animators overlap various disciplines, including illustration, visual effects and typography. These projects tend to happen collaboratively within large teams, with each team member taking responsibility for a smaller, specialised part of the project.

The emphasis in the motion graphics industry is on the pace of communication – how quickly you can appeal to either a specialised demographic or a wide audience and communicate the product, proposal or information as clearly as possible? Or how can you slow your audience right down and help them experience a message in a completely new way? From corporations to production houses, web, digital and interactive media, the music industry, television and film, this industry is adapting quickly to new technologies while revisiting traditional analogue methods of motion graphics all the time.

## Skills required

- A good eye and fluency in design programs (such as Animate, After Effects, Maya, Illustrator, Photoshop, FinalCut) go hand in hand with a current working knowledge of software, hardware and industry developments.
- Good appreciation of pace, rhythm and storyboarding and an interest in storytelling and narratives are a must for sequential image making.
- An ability to work comfortably with complexity and layering, both literal and metaphorical, is essential for creating meaningful and coherent animation.

## Pros . . .

- If your work really communicates the concepts in innovative ways, it will be sought after.
- Motion graphics designers are multidisciplinary and know how to collaborate. They are also masters of word and image and of many facets of design, being versed in all the core skills.
- Motion graphics is growing and expanding with new technologies, meaning there are always new experiences to be had. The use of motion in VR, AR and other interactive mediums is an exciting field in which this discipline naturally belongs.

## . . . and cons

- Much of the initial concept work will be time-consuming. Clients may not know exactly what they want, and you will probably have to develop many versions to actually pull it out of their heads.
- Turnaround speed can be fast. Be realistic on what you can achieve in the time available to avoid missing your deadline.
- Motion graphics and animation can be labour-intensive, and you can find yourself stuck in front of a screen for hours on end. It really is a labour of love!

## ✪ Best in the business

**Amanda Godreau:** Multidisciplinary artist creating motion advertisements, narrative shorts and motion titles.
https://www.amandagodreau.com/

**Erik Winkowski:** Winkowski treats video like collage, cutting up, drawing over and remixing scenes from everyday life in playful, unexpected ways.
https://www.erikwinkowski.com/

**Monique Wray:** Illustrator, animator, and director utilising character design and bright colours to convey narratives.
https://www.madebysmall.tv/

**Plastic Horse:** Animation studio using bold shapes and bright colours to tell stories.
https://plastichorse.co.uk/

**Tristesse:** Design studio using motion graphics in unique ways, such as motion within static posters.
https://www.tristesse.ch/

**Universal Everything:** An international media art and design creative collective, unique immersive experiences with motion design.
https://www.universaleverything.com/

## Career options

Moving image is a creative and rewarding pathway for your career. Although competitive, one of the benefits is the multitude of options and specialisms you can focus on within this industry:

- Animator
- Character designer
- Foley designer
- Filmmaker
- Motion graphics designer
- Sound designer
- Storyboard artist
- VFX designer

## UX/UI

In the early days of the Web, the original designers who took the first stabs at web and digital development were print-based graphic designers. Now, over a few short years, there is an entire industry focusing solely on web design and development, online communications, interactive design, user experience (UX) and user interface (UI) design.

### Examples of work

Companies and organisations hire hundreds of UX/UI designers annually to help them create and perfect their online/digital presence and identity. For the more interactive designer with a liking for heavier coding, design studios and advertising agencies have teams of web developers, coders, programmers and information architects to handle the online needs of their clients. Creations will include interactive interfaces, e-commerce installations, content management systems and social networking platforms. No matter where your intrinsic skills lie, the field of UX/UI has quickly become a rich tapestry of varying disciplines and skills in which any designer can match their talents and interests.

The current population of UX/UI professionals is made up of those passionate about emerging media. Countless personal hours are spent learning and mastering the latest programming and web languages. Days are spent in a trial-and-error limbo as designers research and modify bits of coding to get the interface to react just as the client expects it to. During months of work, from initial thumbnails to final launch, developers and designers work together to create accessible sites, platforms and projects that can be easily accessed and instantly understood by people all over the world. Millions of cups of coffee or tea are poured as these self-starters stay up into the small hours learning digital languages that are never uttered nor seen, but are experienced instead. All of this happens because there are always those who have the abilities and interests to see the possibilities in the expanding world of the Web and digital media.

### Skills required

- A profound understanding of typography, composition, layout, balance, colour theory, and imagery creation and manipulation.
- A growing familiarity with the use of web and programming languages – and an eagerness to learn more.
- Understanding of the concepts of user interaction and client goals, and their relationship to the interface.
- Eye for detail, to the pixel level for the visual, and the ability to write clean code.

### Pros . . .

- The excitement of being at the forefront of a constantly evolving technology and cross-platform and multi-device designs.
- Near-immediate edits and updates to a body of work with little fuss, as compared to print design.
- More opportunities for freelance and home-based work situations for UX/UI designers.

### . . . and cons

- Projects can be long and complex, and require a lot of focus. Projects are always ongoing, requiring regular upkeep.
- Technology updates are time-consuming and sometimes expensive, but you must stay current with revised standards in the industry.

### ⊗ Best in the business

**Jazmin Morris:** Creative technologist, educator and founder of TechYard. https://www.arts.ac.uk/creative-computing-institute/public-programme/tech-yard

**Kenneth Lim:** Interaction designer and coder working with text and language. https://limzykenneth.com/

**Mahalia Henry-Richards:** Artist and designer working with spatial design, user experience and interface design. https://www.mm-hr.com/

**Mindy Seu:** Designer, technologist and founder of Cyberfeminism Index. https://mindyseu.com/

**Studio Hyte:** Design studio working between graphic design, interaction and emergent communication. http://studiohyte.com/D/index.html

### Career options

Careers in UX/UI design are extensive and all require further training on top of graphic design principles. If you're cut out for the commitment to this exciting, ever-changing and growing industry, the following careers could be right for you:

- App designer
- Creative coder
- Developer
- Digital designer
- Digital product designer
- Games designer
- Interactive designer
- Social media specialist
- VFX producer
- Web designer/developer

### ⊕ See also:

**Web Design as Architecture:** http://www--arc.com/

**p5.js Community Statement:** https://p5js.org/community/

# ENVIRONMENTAL DESIGN

Environmental graphic designers work with architects and interior designers to create distinctive design works that visually define the built environment. These projects can include exhibition design for museums, galleries and public art installations; wayfinding and architectural signage; pictogram design; mapping; complete branding and identity systems; and themed environments. Their work is in demand by the retail and entertainment industries, property developers and city planners, and is a critical factor in public facilities and transportation where clear signage and efficient crowd circulation are essential.

### Examples of work

Environmental graphic designers are among the most collaborative in the design disciplines, partnering with experts in many areas to research, and then deliver, functional design in an informative and entertaining way. They combine their skills with those of digital media experts to create sophisticated interactive communications and also work with product designers and industrial designers on fabrications, with landscape architects and with clients in hospitals, schools and businesses.

Large architecture firms may have environmental graphic design departments in-house for signage, wayfinding, identity and supporting print materials. Others consult graphic design firms that offer environmental design services for big projects that require complicated information visualisation. Both types of firms may work with freelancers on a portion of, or a complete, project. As with any graphic design project, in the first stage of development – the programming phase – the environmental graphic designer determines the client's objectives and researches the potential needs of the building/space, users or audience. This enables the client and designer to determine the amount and location of signs and other fabrications for estimating. Then, the designer begins the conceptual design process with a combination of sketches and 3D models or digital illustrations rendered in 2D or 3D. When the design is refined enough for estimates, the environmental graphic designer supervises the bidding process for fabrication of the architectural elements, works with the design team to select the fabricators, and is often on site for the actual installation of elements.

### Skills required

- Strong drawing skills and design skills in composition, form, colour, scale and texture.
- Ability to visualise three-dimensional space.
- Familiarity with the codes and regulations for signage, and an understanding of symbolism and multilingual needs.
- Understanding of human factors, including visual and lighting requirements, colour perception and behavioural psychology.

### Pros . . .

- Your design work could become a permanent installation.
- Opportunities for a very hands-on research experience.
- You can see the effect your work has in public spaces on a large array of people.
- You work with architects, structural engineers, industrial designers and fabricators.
- You get to work in 3D.

### . . . and cons

- The process is long and complicated.
- Mistakes can be expensive and time-consuming.
- Your deadlines are affected by the entire team and can make scheduling complex.

### ✪ Best in the business

**Daily tous les jours:** Combines technology, storytelling, performance and placemaking to create unique, experiential environments. https://www.dailytouslesjours.com/en

**Martin McGrath Studio:** Design practice focused on exhibition design and the creative direction for physical and digital environments in museums, galleries and cultural institutions. https://martinmcgrath.com/

**The Decorators:** Multidisciplinary design collective creating spatial design projects that aim to reconnect the physical elements of a place with its social dimension. https://www.the-decorators.net/

**The Liminal Space:** Studio synthesising complex topics and translating them into tangible objects and experiences that people can relate to and interact with. https://www.the-liminal-space.com/

### Career options

Working as an environmental designer means that no two projects will be the same. If you enjoy the responses of people and society, look at the following career options:

- Exhibition designer
- Production designer
- Set designer
- Service design
- Interaction design

# Glossary

**AAs ('author's alterations'):** Edits made to the content of a file by the client. Usually handled before sent to press. If edits are made while the job is at the printer, AAs can prove very costly.

**Abstraction:** An aesthetic concept describing something that is drawn from the real, but has been 'distilled' to its barest minimum form, colour or tone, often removed from its original context.

**Ad server:** A web-based system for inserting advertising content dynamically into a web page.

**Additive colour:** System used on monitors and televisions, based on RGB (red, green, blue). When combined, these form white light.

**Adobe Acrobat:** The family of Adobe programs that create and manage PDFs.

**Advancing and receding colour:** Colours in the red spectrum appear to advance to the human eye, whereas those in the blue spectrum appear to recede.

**Alignment:** The setting of text relative to a column or page.

**Analogous:** Similar, comparable, alike; for example, two colours that are near to each other, such as grass green and leaf green, are analogous.

**Anchor link:** A navigational link that directs the user to a specific section of a web page.

**Anchor point:** In a design program, a point on or at the end of a curve or line that can be 'grabbed' by the cursor and moved around the canvas, either to change the curve shape or to move the curve.

**Artboard:** In Illustrator, the virtual 'ground' into which images are placed.

**Associations:** Connections between colours and emotions, culture, experience and memory.

**Asymmetry:** A composition where elements are juxtaposed and do not mirror the other forms on the page.

**Audience:** In its broadest sense, the consumers, voyeurs and occasionally participants of design work.

**Banding:** Series of lighter or darker bands running across an area of solid colour.

**Baseline:** The line on which the lowercase letters sit, and below which the descenders fall.

**Baseline grid:** Locks text onto consistent horizontal points.

**Bleed:** The overhang of content beyond the page tramline, so when trimmed this content runs straight to the edge.

**Book jacket:** Packaging that advertises both product and publisher.

**Brainstorming:** A visual aid to thinking laterally and exploring a problem, usually by stating the problem in the centre of a page and radiating outward spokes for components of the problem. Each component can then be considered separately with its own spokes, so that each point, thought or comment is recorded.

**Calibration:** Colour settings that should be set to show colour on screen as it will be in print.

**Canvas:** The virtual 'ground' that images are placed onto in Photoshop.

**Categories:** A taxonomy structure for designating dynamic content (posts) to appear in similar or different news feeds within a website. Can be used as a search criteria for displaying similarly themed posts.

**Centred:** Text that is aligned in the middle: symmetrical, with an even gap at the end of each line.

**Clip:** The name for a sequence of images or length of developed film or video.

**CMS (content management system):** The structured framework of a dynamically driven website.

**CMYK:** Cyan, magenta, yellow, key (black): the four colours that make up the full-colour printing process.

**CMYK break:** The computed percentages of C, M, Y and K ink that make up a colour.

**Coated:** A hard, waxy surface, either gloss or matt, and not porous (ink sits on the surface).

**Coated one side:** A paper that is coated on one side and matt on the other.

**Colorimeter:** Hardware that attaches to or hangs in front of your screen, allowing you to calibrate and profile your monitor.

**Colour modes:** The expression of colour in numerical values that enable us to mix them efficiently: CMYK, LAB, RGB.

**Column:** Vertical block of text.

**Complementary colour:** Colours that lie opposite each other on the colour wheel.

**Composition:** The arrangement of elements or parts of a design (text, images) on the page.

**Comps:** Comprehensive sketch, a close approximation of the printed product.

**Concertina folds:** Folds in alternate directions.

**Connotations:** A colour's broader associations, for example: green – jealousy, naivety, nature.

**Consistency:** The considered selection of design elements that have similar attributes.

**Contextualisation:** The process of placing something within the interrelated systems of meaning that make up the world.

**Contrast:** Obvious differences in elements in a composition; size, form, colour and weight.

**Critical pathways:** Defining the desired route of a website's audience, as it relates to taking an action (purchasing, contacting, registering, etc.).

**Crop mark:** Vertical and horizontal lines at the corners of an image or page to indicate to a vendor where to trim off the bleed area.

**Customer profile/profiling:** The process of creating a series of parameters or set of information that defines the desires, trends or interests of a demographic so that designs can be pitched or marketed to them.

**Dashboard:** The administrative back-end for a content management system (CMS).

**Data:** Facts or pieces of information of any kind.

**Denotations:** What the colour means, or is; for example, a red rose is a green stem with red petals.

**Depth of field:** The zone of sharpness in an image from the nearest point to the furthest point that appears to be sharp.

**Diagram:** Drawing or plan that explains the parts of something, or how something works.

**Didactic:** A pragmatic and unambiguous method of giving clear information.

**Die cut:** A die that cuts predetermined shapes in different materials.

**Digital presses:** Automate direct image transfer from digital file to paper without printing plates.

**Digital printing:** Method of printing that uses a plateless computer-controlled press.

**Domain name:** The web address for a website. It is renewed annually by the site owner for a nominal fee.

**Dot gain:** A printed dot that becomes bigger than intended due to spreading, causing a darkening of screened images, mid-tones and textures. This varies with different paper stocks.

**Downsampling:** A form of compression that lowers the resolution of images by eliminating unnecessary pixel data.

**DPI (dots per inch):** Term to describe the resolution (sharpness) of an image.

**Drop-down (menu):** A navigational element that is revealed when a visitor clicks a main navigational link to reveal related links (subsections) that are displayed below.

**Dummy:** A prototype or mock-up of a final designed project, finished to a stage that it resembles the real thing for final proofing and client approval.

**Duotone:** A method of printing an image using only two colours, usually black and a spot colour.

**Earmark:** Identifying or distinguishing marks or characteristics of a typeface.

**Element:** One small part of a composition, such as a point or line, an image, a letter or a word.

**Email client:** An application used to review and compose emails.

**Embedding:** A PDF removes the need for multiple requisite files by including fonts and compressed imagery in one file.

**EPS (Encapsulated PostScript):** Graphics file format used to transfer PostScript documents that contain an image, within another PostScript document.

**Export:** To save a file in a format of your choice, such as a PDF, that is supported by other programs and can be viewed or printed without the use of your design software.

**F stop/focal length and aperture:** Size of aperture or 'iris' inside a camera, which controls the amount of light that hits the film or pixel sensor; the range on a general camera is f4 (large aperture) to f22 (small aperture).

**Favicon:** A small branded element that appears in the web browser's URL field, bookmark list or favourites list.

**Filter:** Plates of glass or plastic attached to the front of the lens in order to accentuate different qualities. For example, a polarising filter cuts down light glare; a colour filter enhances different colours.

**Flexography:** Method of printing that uses rubber relief plates.

**Fly-out (menu):** A navigational element that is revealed by extending out to the side of a main navigational element.

**Focal point:** The point where you want to draw the reader's or viewer's eye, which can be achieved with hierarchy and design solutions that make certain elements stand out.

**Font:** One size, weight and width of a typeface: Garamond Roman 12pt is a font.

**Footer:** The lower section of a web page layout, usually featuring navigation and copyright information.

**Four-colour process:** A standard, usually digital, printing technique that creates all its colours by combining cyan, magenta, yellow and black (CMYK).

**FPO:** For position only; the use of a temporary placeholder or low-resolution image in place of the high-quality counterpart during the design process.

**Frames:** A frame is a single graphic in a collection of graphic images that when built up make a moving image. The speed of an animation is measured by the amount of frames per second.

**French folds:** Sheets of paper are folded in half, so that they are double thickness. The two folds are at right angles to each other, and then bound on the edge.

**Gamut:** The complete range of colours available within one system of reproduction, e.g., CMYK gamut or RGB gamut.

**Gang-run printing:** Printing many different jobs on one large sheet.

**Gatefold:** A way of folding paper so that the outer quarters of a page are folded to meet in the centre. The result works like symmetrical doors that open onto an inner page.

**Gestalt psychology:** A theory that suggests that the mind perceives and organises holistically and finds patterns in that which appears to be unconnected.

**GIF (Graphics Interchange Format):** A GIF is a compressed file format consisting of a number of frames that make up a (usually) short animation.

**Gravure:** Method of printing that uses plates with recessed cells of varying depths.

**Grid:** Series of horizontal and vertical lines on a page, used as a visual guide for lining up words and images.

**Ground:** The page, surface or area in which the design will be placed.

**GSM:** Grams per square metre, or g/m2.

**Gutter:** The gap between two text blocks or pages on either side of the book fold or binding.

**Handle:** An anchor point in a design program connected to the main vector path by tangential lines that can be manipulated to change the shape of the curve.

**Header:** The top section of a web page layout, usually featuring branding and the main navigational structure.

**Hierarchy:** The different 'weight' or importance given to type or image.

**High-resolution image:** An image with an extreme level of sharpness achieved by a higher amount of dots per inch.

**HTML5:** The fifth version of the HTML standard markup language used for structuring and presenting content on the Internet.

**Hyperlink (navigational link):** A clickable navigational element that allows site visitors to navigate through the website.

**Hyphenation:** The point at which a word is broken at the end of a line in continuous text, and a hyphen is inserted.

**Identity:** A unified, identifiable look for a product or organisation.

**Image map:** An HTML document that contains clickable hyperlinks.

**Information Architecture (IA):** A balance of the intrinsic nature of a website and established user expectations, combined with your client's overall goals.

**Inline text link (navigational link):** Hyperlink within the body of a web page layout.

**The Interactive Advertising Bureau (IAB):** An organisation that documents and works to define the standards for online advertising.

**ISO (International Organisation for Standardisation):** Sets a standard range for virtual film speeds in digital cameras.

**JPEG (Joint Photographic Electronic Group):** File format used to compress digital images.

**Justified:** Lines or paragraphs of type aligned to both margins simultaneously, creating different spacing in between words.

**Juxtaposition:** The process of putting two or more unrelated or opposite elements or objects together to create different effects.

**Kerning:** Adjustments to the spaces between two letters (used extensively for capitals).

**Keyframe:** Either the frame of an animation at a key stage, or a frame in a clip where a transition is due to start.

**Laid:** A paper that has lines on its surface from its means of production. Often used for stationery.

**Lateral thinking:** A form of research where the emphasis is on indirect, creative forms of inquiry and thinking.

**Law of closure:** The mind creates a solid object on the page from suggestions of shapes and the placement and proximity of elements.

**Layer Comps (Photoshop):** A feature that allows the user to record which items are viewable in a complex, multi-layer document.

**Layout:** Placement of words and images on a grid or document to organise information.

**Layout roughs:** Loose concept sketches for page design that organise space without showing detail.

**Leading:** Measured from baseline to baseline, the horizontal space between lines of type. Related to the historical use of strips of lead in letterpress.

**Letterpress:** A type of block printing using inked wooden or metal movable type and pressing it onto paper to create an impression.

**Letterspacing (tracking):** The space between letters, which can be adjusted.

**Ligatures:** Two or more letterforms joined to create a single character.

**Linear reasoning:** A form of thinking that implies strategic thought process, one in which step-by-step logic is employed.

**Linen:** Similar to laid, but finer lined.

**Linguistic:** Of, or relating to, language.

**Lists (unordered/ordered):** An unordered list is a bulleted list of similar concepts. An ordered list is grouped in order, by using an alphanumeric sequence.

**Lossy:** A compression format that removes or 'loses' certain areas to achieve a smaller file size. Reopening the file causes the program to 'guess' at the missing data, possibly creating a lower-quality version.

**Low-resolution image:** A low-quality image with a low level of sharpness achieved by a lower amount of dots per inch. Used mainly for digital outcomes.

**LPI:** When printing halftones, such as in one-colour newspapers and reproductions, the lines per inch is the number of lines that compose the resolution of a halftone screen.

**Margin:** The usually blank space to the top, bottom and sides of a page between the trim and the live printing area. Headers, footers and page numbers are traditionally placed within this area.

**Market research:** The process of collecting and collating data from questionnaires, interviews and comments from the public regarding a concern, a problem or a possible solution.

**Matt:** A dull, non-shiny quality of paper, used for newspapers, for example.

**Measure:** The length of a line of text on a page, based in inches, centimetres, points or picas.

**Metaphor:** Word or image that sets up associations; for example, a 'piece of cake' is a metaphor for easy.

**META tags:** Elements within the HTML code, used by the search engines to properly index websites.

**Metrics:** The strategy for measuring the success – or failure – of a project's goals.

**Monetised:** Earned revenue from online marketing activities, such as banner ad placement.

**Navigation (breadcrumb):** A path-based navigation that identifies the user's location within the structure of a website.

**Navigation (drop-down):** A navigational element that is revealed when a visitor clicks a main navigational link to reveal related links (subsections) that are displayed below.

**Navigation (fly-out):** A navigational element that is revealed by extending out to the side of a main navigational element.

**Negative space:** The white or coloured area around an element, e.g. a margin of a page.

**Offset lithography:** The digitally produced printing plate is treated chemically so that the image will accept ink and reject water.

**Onomatopoeia:** In typography, the use of type to suggest the sounds of a spoken language, such as adding a large 'o' to the word 'open'.

**Opacity:** The transparency of a colour or tonal value measured in percent. The ability to edit the opacity of design elements means the designer can make images that can overlap and can be seen through.

**Optical adjustment:** Making adjustments to letterspacing by eye, not mechanically.

**Organic results:** Search engine results based on the natural appearance of keywords within a site dialogue.

**Ornaments:** Typed characters that embellish the page. Also known as flowers.

**Orphan:** The last line of a text paragraph appearing at the top of the next page.

**Overprint:** To print additional content or another colour over a previously printed image.

**Page plan/flatplan:** A document with a series of numbered thumbnails set out in an ordered grid that represents each page in a book.

**Panel:** Device used to highlight information. Also known as a sidebar.

**Pantone Matching System (PMS):** An international system to ensure reliable colour selection, specification and control.

**Paper grain:** The direction of wood fibres that make up a piece of paper.

**Patch:** The space on a bookshop's shelf occupied by spines of books from the same series.

**Path:** A drawn line in a design program, mathematically determined; also called a vector.

**PDF:** The Portable Document Format is a universal file format that can be viewed in a large amount of programs and browsers. Its reduced file size makes it useful for sending in emails and online.

**PEs:** 'Printer's errors' are mistakes and omissions found at the proofing stage by the designer or client that did not, for whatever reason, make it from the supplied file to the press. The cost of these errors is usually absorbed by the vendor as a matter of customer service.

**Perfect binding:** Method similar to paperback binding, where loose sheets are encased in a heavier paper cover, then glued to the book spine. Edges are trimmed to be flush with each other.

**Photomontage:** The assemblage of various fragments of photographs.

**Pixel:** Pixel images are made of small dots that are individually assigned a colour and that build up to make the bigger picture.

**Placeholder:** A temporary or low-resolution image in place of the high-quality counterpart during the design process.

**Plates:** Separate printing plates for separate colours that overprint to create colour images in four-colour offset printing.

**Plugin:** A WordPress term for an element that adds a functional enhancement to the basic CMS structure. Also referred to as widgets and modules.

**PNG:** A Portable Network Graphics format is used for lossless compression. The PNG format displays images without jagged edges while keeping file sizes rather small, making them popular on the Web. PNG files are generally larger than GIF files.

**Poetic:** A style that is less clear, but more artistic, more open to interpretation.

**Point:** A dot on a page, such as a period (.).

**Point size/pica:** The relative size of a font. There are 72 points in an inch.

**Positive space:** A form, image or word printed or formed on the page.

**PPI:** Pixels per inch or pixel density is interchangeable with DPI, but usually refers to the resolution of an unprinted image displayed on screen or captured by a scanner or digital camera.

**Primary colour:** Red, yellow or blue.

**Primary research:** Gathering material that does not pre-exist, such as photographing, drawing, making prototypes, interviewing people.

**Proof or prepress proof:** A complete mock-up using inks, overlays and other cheaper finishes to provide an idea of what the finished product should look like post-production.

**Proximity:** The relationship of one object to another.

**Quality control strip:** Usually incorporated in printed sheets outside the grid to monitor the quality of plate-making, inking and registration. Checking black sections helps point out colour casting.

**Quantitative:** Related to quantities of things, or measurements (numerical).

**Ragging:** When text is aligned left some words at the end of the lines might jut out further than the rest and cause uneven-looking paragraphs.

**Ranged (or ragged) left/ranged (or ragged) right:** Text that is aligned to a column or margin, either left or right.

**Raster:** Assemblages of pixels on a 2D grid system that can be viewed on computer screens or print media.

**Ream:** Standard quantity of paper; 500 sheets.

**Recto:** The right-hand page in a book.

**Registration marks:** Hairline marks at the corners of a printed page to help ensure plates are lined up correctly and designate what will be cropped off.

**Relief:** A printing process that uses a raised surface, such as letterpress.

**Repetition:** The repeated use of select design elements within the same composition.

**Repetition with variation:** The alteration of select aspects of a repeated element.

**Representation:** Something that looks like, resembles or stands in for something else. In drawing, this is also known as figurative, since it deliberately attempts to mimic the thing drawn.

**Resolution:** The clarity of a digital image. A low-resolution image (30dpi, for example) will have clearly visible pixels; a high-resolution image (300dpi, for example) will not.

**Responsive web design:** The content of a website layout is coded to reposition itself in response to the specific devices on which the website is being viewed.

**RGB (red, green, blue):** The colour system used to project colour on a computer screen. By combining these three colours a large percentage of the visible colour spectrum can be represented digitally.

**Rhetoric:** A style of arguing, persuading or engaging in dialogue. For a designer, it is a way of engaging the targeted audience.

**RODI:** Return on design investment indicates the success of a project in relation to the project's unique goals.

**Rollover folds:** A way of folding a page so that successive folds turn in on themselves and the page is folded into a roll.

**Rotations:** The number of times that an animated GIF file will play, from the first frame to the last.

**Roughs:** Loose sketches for concept and compositional development that do not include fine detail.

**Saddle stitching:** Binding method where sheets of paper are folded in the centre, stitched together along the fold, then glued into the cover spine.

**Sans serif:** Without serif. Typefaces such as Univers, Helvetica, Aksidenz Grotesque and Futura are characterised by their lack of serifs. Predominantly associated with the 19th/20th centuries.

**Satin:** A form of paper between matt and gloss.

**Schematic:** Simplified diagram or plan related to a larger scheme or structure.

**Screen printing:** Method of printing that uses stencils.

**Screen resolution:** The resolution of a file that will be viewed on a screen is 72 pixels per inch (PPI). When designing for high-density displays, the document's dimensions should be doubled, not the resolution.

**Secondary colour:** A mix of any two primaries: orange, green or violet.

**Secondary research:** Gathering material that already exists, such as design work, colour samples, written texts, newspaper/magazine articles.

**Semantics:** The study of meaning in language and elsewhere.

**Semiotics:** A system that links objects, words and images to meanings through signs and signifiers.

**Serif:** Structural details at the ends of some strokes in old-style capital and lowercase letters.

**Shift-scheduling:** Allowing presses to run all day and night.

**Simultaneous contrast:** The human eye tends to differentiate between two neighbouring colours by emphasising their differences rather than their similarities – background colours affect foreground colours (the image).

**SLR:** Single lens reflex cameras use a viewfinder and mirrors so that the photographer's sightline goes through the main lens and results in a what-you-see-is-what-you-get image.

**Spot colour:** Any flat colour, like Pantone or Toyo colours, printed as a solid and not made up of CMYK.

**Statistical:** Related to the collection, classification and organisation of (often numerical) information.

**Stock:** A generic form or type of paper, such as tracing paper or matt coated.

**Storyboard:** A document similar to a flatplan, but with a sequence of thumbnails that specifically lays out the narrative for a comic strip or film.

**Stress/axis:** The angle of the curved stroke weight change in a typeface. Seen clearly in letters such as 'o'.

**Style board:** A presentation of proposed website stylisations for review by a client, independent of the overall website structure.

**Subtractive colour:** System used in printing, based on CMYK colours.

**SVG:** Scalable Vector Graphics are vector image formats that provide support for interactivity and animation.

**SWF:** ShockWave Flash, the file extension format for displaying animated vector files on the Web.

**Symbolism:** A way of representing an object or word through an image, sound or another word; for example, a crossed knife and fork on a road sign means a café is ahead.

**Symmetry:** A composition where elements are balanced or mirrored on a page.

**Syntax:** The study of the rules for the formation of grammatically correct sentences.

**Tag cloud:** A keyword-based navigation element on a website, where keywords can be selected in order to refine search criteria to display similarly themed posts.

**Taxonomy:** A way to group related content in a structural format.

**Theme:** A collection of predesigned web page layouts, designed around a centralised concept, where the arrangement of the page's structure has been specified by the theme's author.

**Thumbnail:** Small, rough visual representation of a bigger picture or final outcome.

**TIFF:** A Tagged Image File Format is a graphic file format used for storing images.

**Timeline:** The linear timeline in Animate and After Effects in which keyframes can be fixed in order to designate animated milestones in a production.

**Tool tips:** A message that displays when a user hovers with a mouse over a linked element.

**Type anatomy:** The language used to describe the various parts of letterforms.

**Typeface:** The set of visual attributes (design or style) of a particular group of letters: Garamond is a typeface.

**Typographic rules:** Printed lines that direct the reader's eye.

**Uniform Resource Locator (URL):** The address of a website.

**User interface (UI):** The space where humans interact with machines. It is a part of the larger user experience (UX) of a website or application.

**User experience (UX):** The experience a user has with a website.

**Varnish:** A liquid sprayed or spread onto paper to give it a hard-wearing surface so that printed ink stays intact.

**Vector graphics:** Shapes and lines built by algorithms, which will not reduce in quality when expanded or reduced in size.

**Verso:** The left-hand page in a book.

**Vibration:** Complementary colours of equal lightness and high saturation tend to make each other appear more brilliant, and cause the illusion of motion along the edges where they meet.

**WebGL:** Web Graphics Library uses JavaScript to render interactive graphics within any compatible web browser without the use of plugins.

**Web hosting:** A designated online storage space for hosting a website and related email accounts.

**Weight:** Colours differ in perceived weight'. It is generally assumed that blue-greens look lighter, whereas reds appear stronger, and therefore heavier.

**White space:** The open space surrounding a positive image that defines shape and directs hierarchy.

**Wove/smooth:** A smooth, uncoated paper that is very porous (ink sits under the surface).

**x-height:** The height of a lowercase 'x' in any typeface.

**Zone Information Protocol (ZIP):** A means of compressing files into a smaller size, so they can be transferred digitally with ease.

# Bibliography

Josef Albers, Nicholas Fox Weber, *Interaction of Color: New Complete Edition*, Yale University Press, 2013

Nick Asbury, Greg Quinton, Beryl McAlhone, David Stuart, *A Smile in the Mind - Revised and Expanded Edition: Witty Thinking in Graphic Design*, Phaidon Press, 2016

Edward Barrett, Frank Bentley, *Building Mobile Experiences*, The MIT Press, 2012

Sofie Beier, *Type Tricks: Your Personal Guide to Type Design*, BIS Publishers, 2017

John Berger, *Ways of Seeing*, Penguin Modern Classics, 2008

Russell Bestley, Ian Noble, *Visual Research: An Introduction to Research Methods in Graphic Design*, Bloomsbury Visual Arts, 2018

Katy Börner, *Atlas of Knowledge: Anyone Can Map*, The MIT Press, 2015

Amaranth Borsuk, *The Book*, The MIT Press, 2018

Cath Caldwell, Yolanda Zappaterra, *Editorial Design: Digital and Print*, Laurence King Publishing, 2014

Rob Carter, Ben Day, Sandra Maxa, Philip B. Meggs, Mark Sanders, *Typographic Design: Form and Communication*, John Wiley & Sons, 7th edition, 2018

Daniel Chandler, *Semiotics: The Basics*, Routledge, 3rd edition, 2017

Karen Cheng, *Designing Type*, Laurence King Publishing, 2019

Jennifer Cole Phillips, Ellen Lupton, *Graphic Design: The New Basics*, Princeton Architectural Press, 2nd edition, 2015

Stephen Coles, Erik Spiekermann, *The Geometry of Type: The Anatomy of 100 Essential Typefaces*, Thames & Hudson, 2016

David Crow, *Visible Signs: An Introduction to Semiotics in the Visual Arts*, AVA Publishing, 3rd edition, 2015

Johanna Drucker, Emily McVarish, *Graphic Design History: A Critical Guide*, Pearson, 2nd edition, 2012

Stephen J. Eskilson, *Graphic Design: A New History*, Laurence King Publishing, 2019

*Eye: The International Review of Graphic Design* (magazine)

Alan Fletcher, *The Art of Looking Sideways*, Phaidon Press, 2001

E. M. Ginger, Erik Spiekermann, *Stop Stealing Sheep and Find Out How Type Works*, Verlag Niggli, 2019

Steven Heller, Veronique Vienne, *100 Ideas That Changed Graphic Design*, Laurence King Publishing, 2012

Steven Heller, *Merz to Emigré and Beyond: Avant-Garde Magazine Design of the Twentieth Century*, Phaidon Press, 2014

Steven Heller, *Teaching Graphic Design History*, Allworth, 2019

Jost Hochuli, Robin Kinross, *Designing Books: Practice and Theory*, Hyphen Press, 2008

Keith Houston, *The Book: A Cover-to-Cover Exploration of the Most Powerful Object of Our Time*, W. W. Norton & Company, 2016

Theo Inglis, *Mid-Century Modern Graphic Design*, Batsford Ltd, 2019

Ellen Lupton, *Design is Storytelling*, Cooper Hewitt, 2017

Ellen Lupton, J. Abbott Miller, *The ABC's of Triangle, Square, Circle: The Bauhaus and Design Theory*, Princeton Architectural Press, 2019

Ellen Lupton, *Thinking with Type: A Critical Guide for Designers, Writers, Editors, and Students*, Princeton Architectural Press, 2nd edition, 2010

Ellen Lupton, *Type on Screen: A Critical Guide for Designers, Writers, Developers, & Students: New Typographic Systems*, Princeton Architectural Press, 2014

Colleen Macklin, John Sharp, *Iterate: Ten Lessons in Design and Failure*, The MIT Press, 2019

Per Mollerup, *Marks of Excellence: The History and Taxonomy of Trademarks*, Phaidon Press, 2013

Jens Muller, *The History of Graphic Design: Volume 1 (1890-1959)*, Taschen, 2017

Jens Muller, *The History of Graphic Design: Volume 2 (1960-Today)*, Taschen, 2018

Joseph Müller-Brockmann, *Grid Systems in Graphic Design: A Handbook for Graphic Artists, Typographers, and Exhibition Designers*, Niggli Verlag, 2008

Janet H. Murray, *Inventing the Medium: Principles of Interaction Design as a Cultural Practice*, The MIT Press, 2012

Ken Visocky O'Grady, Jenn Visocky O'Grady, *A Designer's Research Manual*, Rockport Publishers, 2nd edition, 2017

Alan Pipes, *Drawing for Designers: Drawing Skills, Concept Sketches, Computer Systems, Illustration, Tools and Materials, Presentations, Production Techniques*, Laurence King Publishing, 2007

Alan Pipes, *Production for Graphic Designers*, Laurence King, 5th edition, 2009

Norman Potter, *What is a Designer: Things, Places, Messages*, Hyphen Press, 4th edition, 2008

Paul Rand, *Design, Form, and Chaos*, Yale University Press, 2017

Alice Rawsthorn, *Design as an Attitude*, JRP Ringier, 2018

Sandra Rendgen, *History of Information Graphics*, Taschen, 2019

Sandra Rendgen, *Information Graphics*, Taschen, 2012

Timothy Samara, *Making and Breaking the Grid, Revised Edition: A Graphic Design Layout Workshop*, Rockport Publishers, 2017

Adrian Shaughnessy, *How to be a Graphic Designer, Without Losing Your Soul*, Laurence King Publishing, 2nd edition, 2010

Wang Shaoqiang, *Portfolio Design and Self-Promotion: My Graphic DNA*, Promopress, 2nd edition, 2018

Catharine Slade-Brooking, *Creating a Brand Identity: A Guide for Designers*, Laurence King Publishing, 2016

Kassia St Clair, *The Secret Lives of Colour*, John Murray, 2018

Beth Tondreau, *Layout Essentials: 100 Design Principles for Using Grids*, Rockport Publishers, 2011

Bradbury Thompson, *The Art of Graphic Design*, Yale University Press, 2018

Victionary, *DESIGN(H)ERS: A Celebration of Women in Design Today*, Victionary, 2019

## Online resources

http://www.aiga.org/
Website, membership, blog and programmes of events for graphic designers.

http://www.coroflot.com/
Online platform for graphic design jobs.

http://www.designobserver.com/
Online magazine dedicated to design and designers.

http://www.eyemagazine.com/
Online blog exploring concepts and critique in visual communication.

http://www.eyeondesign.aiga.org/
Online editorial platform showcasing and discussing new work from the world's most exciting designers.

https://futuress.org/
A learning community and publishing platform to democratise design education and amplify marginalised voices.

http://www.istd.org.uk/
Promoting the typography and graphic design of specialists and students through annual competitions.

http://www.kerningthegap.com/
Collective of like-minded people promoting women in design.

https://www.librarystack.org/
An online archive and lending library for new digital projects across visual art, design, architecture, film and theory.

https://monoskop.org/
The Wikipedia of art and studies.

https://peoplesgdarchive.org/
A crowd-sourced virtual archive of inclusive graphic design history.

http://www.spd.org/
Online platform of jobs, competitions, events and resources for publication designers.

http://www.thedieline.com/
Online platform dedicated to package design.

http://www.theotherbox.org/
Celebrating people from under-represented backgrounds in the creative industries.

http://www.thersa.org/
Dedicated to enriching society through ideas and action.

https://lectureinprogress.com/
Career advice and opportunities.

https://peopleofcraft.com/
Showcase of creatives of colour.

https://the-dots.com/
Online networking platform for creatives, hosting news, projects and job opportunities.

https://weareshesays.com/
Focused on the engagement, education and advancement of women in the creative industries.

https://www.itsnicethat.com/
Creative stories, practitioners, publications and events.

https://www.myfonts.com/WhatTheFont/
Online application to identify fonts.

https://www.tdc.org/
Promoting typography via competitions, events and membership.

# Index

# Acknowledgments

Adank, Thomas © A Practice for Everyday Life: p20l

Adank, Thomas Courtesy La Biennale di Venezia and A Practice for Everyday Life: pp129tl, cl

Aloof, http://aloof.com: pp48t, 79

Ashmore, Lucy, www.moreorless.work: pp14-15, 24t, 50tr/tc, 156

Base Design: pp6c, 59r

Bell, Sarah: pp101br, 102, 103tr/br

Bessermachen DesignStudio, design and packaging; Stiig Helgens Binggeli, Brandhouse, for archetypes and the idea, www.brandhouse.com: p130t

Brandient, www.brandient.com: p117

Bridgeman Images: p39b

Cassels, Alfred: pp101bc, 113

Chipp, Kidd, Knopf Publishing: p85tc

© Christie's Images/Corbis: pp2r, 35

Coffey, Marcy Zuczek, www.wfgd.net: p34c

Deep, www.deep.co.uk: pp42bc, 46tr, 70b, 81t, c, 119, 151tc, 164, 166bl, 172tr

Design & Practice: pp8, 76b, 92tr, 129bl, 158t

Dillon, Hannah, Drexel University, www.hannahdillon.com: p33

Duranti, Alice, communicationobsession.com: p25t

Edwards, Victoria: p83t

Eland, Suzie, www.typeassembly.com: pp63tr, 84, 85bl

Elboreini, Engy: pp59l, 114t, c

Émigré, http://emigre.com: pp39t, 69

Flynn, Megan, Drexel University: p83cl

Foster, Rebecca, www.rebeccafosterdesign.co.uk: pp163t/c/b

© Frost* Collective, www.frostcollective.com.au: pp128t

Germano, Frank, Man on Fire Design: p37tr

GINGERMONKEY, www.gingermonkeydesign.com: pp16t, 62

Goldberg, Carin, www.caringoldberg.com: pp53bl/br

Gordon, Laura, www.laura-g.co.uk: pp55, 151c

Grand Union Design, email: studio@grandu.co.uk: pp50tl, 51t

Grundy, Peter, http://grundini.com/, pp85tl, 97bl

Gundelsberger, Caitlin, www.caitlin-g.com, Drexel University: pp32t

Haring Jr., Don: p19

Hart, Jennifer, Drexel University, www.jenniferhartdesign.com: p97cl

Hojong, Song, Instagram: songhj_: p182t

Hsiung, Leo: p71r

Huff, Priscilla, www.priscillahuff.com: pp149t/cl/bl

Jackson, Connor: pp42bl, 139bl

Karnes, Eric, erickarnes.com: p25bl/br

Kubota, Maya Puspita www.mayakubota.com: p18

Kusumahadi, Chiquita: pp63b, 71b

Langdon, John, www.johnlangdon.net: pp36br

Leyler, Phil, www.dribbble.com/heduaral p173br

Lewandowski, Catherine, Drexel University, www.c-lewandowski.com: p34tc

Lor, Roberta, https://robertalor.webflow.io: pp169b

Luo, Shuna, www.shunaluo.com: pp17bl/bc/br, 29

Materials, Valeria: p159tr

Matter Strategic Design, www.matter.to: pp131t/tcl/tcr/131b

Matthiersen, Kia, www.kai-matthiesen.com: pp83tr, 133bl

McCune, Sascha, Drexel University, www.sasha-em.com: p82tl

Morton, Katie, Drexel University: pp45tr/cr/br

Mortula, Luciano, Shutterstock.com: p97br

Mousegraphics, www.mousegraphics.eu: pp34tl, 133br, 135t

Neumeister, http://neumeister.se: pp56tl

Nowakowski, Nicole: pp69b, 151bl

Palmer Brewster, Toby, tobypalmerbrewster@gmail.com: pp13bl/bc/br, 101br, 103tl/cr/bl, 105, 132

Panayi, Andreas: pp42br, 58b, 80c, cr

Park. Ed, Courtesy La Biennale di Venezia and A Practice for Everyday Life: pp77t, 129tl

Patel, Chandni, www.chandnipatel.co.uk: pp13tl/tc/tr

Penmore, Rebecca, www.formlines.co.uk: p176

Pestana, Joana, joanapestana.com: p137tl

Pitch Black Graphic Design: p80b

Polimekanos, www.polimekanos.com: pp46cr/bcr

Pople, James, www.behance.net/jpopledesign: pp47tr/cr/br, pp96tl/tr

Pughe, Jade: pp151tl, 159tl

Ray, Fever: p63c

Rey, Rocio: p15t

Rice Creative, Images shot by Arnaud De Harven, http://rice-creative.com: pp21tr

Scher, Paula, Pentagram Design, www.pentagram.com: pp3cr, 69tr, 70t, 73, 82b

SeanPavonePhoto, Shutterstock.com: p97t

Selvedge Magazine, 14 Milton Park, Highgate, London, N6 5QA; www.selvedge.org: pp49tr/cr/br, 140

Shine, Nyki, http://nykiforever.wix.com/portfolio: pp48bl/bc

SMACK | Creative Digital Studio, www.SMACKagency.com: pp3cl, 49tl/cl

Soppelsa, Moreno, Shutterstock.com: pp138tr, 139tl

Students from the Graduate Diploma at Chelsea UAL: pp18-27

Studio Bureau: pp3l, 3r, 95b

Studio Hyte, https://studiohyte.com, 58t, 148, 165r

Summer Studio, www.summerstudio.co.uk: pp100br, 137tr

Sverre Jarild taken for Design and Architecture Norway (DOGA) at the Innovation for all – European Business Workshops in Inclusive Design: p157

The Collected Works: p2l, 112

The Working Assembly, theworkingassembly.com: pp7r, 52, 54, 57cr/br, 78

Thomas, Bugg: pp6r, 10tr, 68, 159br, 165tr, tc, 180, 182b, 183bl

Vasily, Smirnov, iStockphoto.com: p134bl

Vaughan, Alice: p175

Warnham, Hayley, www.hayleywarnham.com: pp22b

Wiederspahn, Ashley: pp129tr, cr

Willey, Matt: pp2bc, 7l, 8c, 9c, 23b, 42t, 44b, 81b

Image courtesy of Works That Work Magazine: pp56tr, 46b, 47b, 135br

Yang, Lynn: p72

Zed: p168

Zhou, Ji www.zzzoezhouuu.com: pp11, 28

All step-by-step and other images are the copyright of Quarto Publishing plc. While every effort has been made to credit contributors, Quarto would like to apologise should there have been any omissions or errors – and would be pleased to make the appropriate correction for future editions of the book.

With thanks to Zak Peric for his contribution to the article on Animate and After Effects, on pages 118–119, and for the assignment on pages 122–123

With special thanks to Eric Zempol (1970–2014) for his work on the Fifth edition of this book.